INSIDE
the
HORNET'S
HEAD

INSIDE
the
HORNET'S
HEAD

AN ANTHOLOGY OF JEWISH AMERICAN WRITING

Edited by
JEROME CHARYN

THUNDER'S MOUTH PRESS
NEW YORK

INSIDE THE HORNET'S HEAD
An Anthology of Jewish American Writing

Published by
Thunder's Mouth Press
An Imprint of Avalon Publishing Group Inc.
245 West 17th St., 11th Floor
New York, NY 10011

AVALON
publishing group incorporated

Collection copyright © 2005 by Jerome Charyn
Pages 303–306 serve as an extension of this copyright page

Library of Congress Cataloging-in-Publication Data is available.

ISBN 1-56025-740-7
ISBN 13: 978-1-56025-740-0

9 8 7 6 5 4 3 2 1

Book design by Jamie McNeely
Printed in the United States
Distributed by Publishers Group West

To Saul Bellow, Stanley Elkin, and Leonard Michaels:

in memoriam

CONTENTS

INTRODUCTION

JEROME CHARYN

1.

I did not stumble upon *Augie March* lightly. I gave it as a gift to the most beautiful girl in my high school class, Valerie K. Hadn't it won awards? And wasn't it about a Jewish bumpkin like myself? (So I'd heard secondhand.) I meant the book to bring me closer to Valerie, but it never did. And then, a year or two later, I actually read it and was overwhelmed by its bounty. It was a book that never stopped to breathe, and I was breathless in its wake. Leslie Fiedler calls it "unlike anything else in English except *Moby-Dick*." It had the same largeness of imagination . . . and a wondrous eagle called Caligula instead of a white whale.

But it was much more than that. It was a model and a manifest for a boy from the Bronx, a kind of open-sesame into the art of writing. I'd been nowhere, had seen nothing outside my own little ghetto: all I had was a crazy babble of tongues, an exalted gangster talk, a mingling of Yiddish, Russian, and all the books I'd ever read—whole scenes ripped from *Anna Karenina*, whose heroine would have been much better served in the Bronx, where we loved tall, aristocratic women with husbands that were beneath their dignity—all the dialogue from every film I'd ever seen, which included the entire repertoire of MGM and the other majors, and the rough but chivalrous language of the street, where we were all knights in pegged pants. And when Augie says that "we are meant to be carried away by the complex and hear the simple like the far horn of Roland when he and Oliver are being wiped out by the Saracens," I knew what the hell he was talking about.

Augie's adventures have little to do with the magical places he visits—the mountains of Mexico or the plains of Paris. They are only desiderata, icons, throwaways, bits and pieces of décor in a landscape that shifts right under our feet and sends us scrambling on to the next page and the next. Augie, says Leslie Fiedler, is "a footloose Jewish boy [who] becomes Huck Finn," with his own Mississippi—a river of words. If the Mississippi gives Huck a godlike strength, nurtures him, soothes him, allows him to shove beyond the perimeter of his own lies, then it is language that soothes Saul Bellow and carries Augie March from adventure to adventure, so that he is never used up, no matter how much narrative is crammed into a single sentence. The book is a constant rush of dialogue and detail, of shenanigans and magic tricks, or as Bellow himself writes in "Where Do We Go From Here: The Future of Fiction," the modern hero is "an oddly dispersed, ragged, mingled, broken, amorphous creature whose outlines are everywhere, whose being is bathed in mind as the tissues are bathed in blood, and who is impossible to circumscribe in any scheme of time." He's a "cubistic" character, an "uncertain, eternal, mortal someone who shuts and opens like a concertina and makes a strange music."

To read *The Adventures of Augie March* is to live inside a hornet's head—to hear and feel an endless clatter . . . whose sting is a source of terror and delight. We cannot recover from *Augie March*. Its sting remains with us for life. And we have to ask why. Part of the answer is in Bellow's bona fides. Born in Quebec in 1915 (and died in Brookline, Massachusetts, on April 5, 2005), Bellow grew up in Chicago's South Side ghetto during the reign of America's most notorious beer baron, Al Capone—and almost all of Bellow's male characters in *Augie March* have some kind of gangster mentality. They strut, they wear swell clothes, and they bully us with their words, which Fiedler reminds us, land "like kisses or blows." And they capture the *tumult* of the city. Like George Gershwin, who had his share of little wars on Manhattan's Lower East Side, another cradle of gangsters (and Capone's original turf), he was raised "in the heart of noise." As one of Gershwin's own colleagues said: "He hears the noise and finds music in it." And *Augie March* might be considered Bellow's own "Rhapsody in Blue," but with a much more hysterical and alarming beat.

"I am an American, Chicago born," Bellow's narrator insists at the very beginning of the novel, "and go at things as I have taught myself, free-style, and will make the record in my own way." We're not caught within some ghetto tale, a lightning rise from rags to riches, a celebration of America's ability to spit out righteous little citizens—noble, healthy, and clean. Augie is a monster of the New World, more American than America itself. And we have to examine this within the context of the Jewish American writer. It's not the success of *Augie March* that's startling—a Book-of-the-Month

Club selection and winner of the National Book Award for fiction (it was published in 1953). But suddenly, with one blow, like a fist coming out of nowhere, Saul Bellow made "[h]is appearance as the first Jewish American novelist to stand at the center of American literature," as Fiedler says. It's hard to grasp this fifty years after the fact. But Jewish American writers had always lived in a terrible kind of ghetto, as if they were quaint little children, talented ventriloquists who were miming the American idiom for their Yankee readers, and if they were good, they might be rewarded with a few leftovers and shown off as the most current Jewish clown . . . until another clown was discovered and took this clown's place. They were entertainers, dimwits, who couldn't really enter the canon of American literature, like Hemingway, Faulkner, Fitzgerald, or Edith Wharton and Eudora Welty, when women began to be noticed as writers, rather than quaint knitters of patchquilt prose. Henry James, America's first "experimental" writer, who understood the music and the hieroglyphics of modern fiction, couldn't even fathom the *idea* of a Jewish American writer. When he visited the Lower East Side in 1907, he was repelled by what he saw and heard in "the flaring streets. . . . There is no swarming like that of Israel when once Israel has got its start," he writes in *The American Scene*. He discovered "a Jewry that had burst all bounds." He worried over "the Hebrew conquest of New York." And East Side cafés were nothing but "torture-rooms of the living idiom."

James's words were echoed in every English department of every prominent university in the United States, where Jews couldn't possibly teach English literature, because they couldn't enter into the spirit of Milton, or Chaucer, or Shakespeare, no matter how hard they mimed. Lionel Trilling, the son of a Bronx tailor, and America's most eloquent literary critic, was the first American Jew to receive tenure in the English department of an Ivy League school (Columbia), and it didn't happen until 1945! The tailor's boy had already published books on Matthew Arnold and E. M. Forster, essays on Sherwood Anderson, Kipling, and F. Scott Fitzgerald, and would soon publish essays on Henry James and *Huckleberry Finn*. And he might never have taught at Columbia if he hadn't had such a melodious name—Lionel Trilling. Also, by 1945 America—and much of the world—had begun to change. The first images of GIs liberating the ghostly remains of Hitler's concentration camps had brought attention to the Jews, and a kind of niggling sympathy that *almost* humanized them. It was the Jewish freedom fighters and terrorists of the Haganah and the Irgun that finally altered the psychological and symbolic landscape, as Jews were seen as warriors rather than victims, and as "winners" once the state of Israel was voted into existence in 1948. America was now ready for Bellow's "atomic bomb." The country seemed to need an urban myth, as "relentless urbanization [had made] rural myths and images no longer central to our experience," according to Fiedler.

Bellow had literally concocted a new America in *Augie March*, with language as American as the Mississippi, and with rhythms that seemed to incorporate Faulkner, Dreiser, and Anderson, as if Bellow were a country boy and a city boy at the same time, rural *and* urban, and as if his concertina could include every strand of music out of America's past . . . except for one, that of Ernest Hemingway. In his best stories, Hemingway was a minimalist who believed, with Flaubert, that each particular sentence was an island unto itself, that the white space between sentences could contain an entire planet, and that the real thunder of a text derived from the reader's own imagination. The reader connected these islands inside his head. He (or she) was as much the creator as "Hem." But Bellow's own daring was to narrow that space between sentences, almost eliminate it, as if he returned to the picaresque of Fielding and Cervantes, but with a modern twist—the hero is as schizoid and haunted as the twentieth century. And Augie is always around, exhausting the reader with his parodies and puns, his constant riffs, thrusting the reader right inside the hornet's head, where he experienced *Augie March* like an abundance of battlefields . . .

2.

And so America had a king, at least that part of America that could read a book. Just as Dostoyevsky had said that all Russian writers of fiction had come out from under Gogol's overcoat (Gogol had written a bizarre, surreal story about a stolen overcoat that assumes a life of its own), so American writers at mid-century, Jews and gentiles, had come out from under the wings of Caligula, Bellow's eagle who "crackled his feathers or hissed as if snow was sliding." Suddenly the novel had burst out of its narrative skin and had become an assault on language itself, a great whooping war cry. And other warriors and adventurers, demonic jokesters, including Nabokov, Pynchon, John Hawkes, and John Barth, would soon gain acceptance and recognition in good part because of Bellow. I doubt that Günter Grass's *The Tin Drum* and Gabriel García Márquez's *One Hundred Years of Solitude* would have found many followers in the U.S. if there had been no *Augie March* to initiate readers into the notion that a novel could be a jungle of words . . . or a much wilder thing. Even Faulkner, the wildest of American novelists after

Melville, was grounded in his imagined South, his "postage stamp" of Yoknapatawpha County, and Bellow was grounded in nothing at all. Like Caligula, his language could soar and then rocket down into some abyss. No one was safe, neither Augie March nor the reader.

But Bellow's book would give a particular nudge to Jewish American writers, make them visible for the first time, not as ventriloquists, but as human beings with a singular vision and voice that could reach across America. Bellow himself would help Isaac Bashevis Singer (an immigrant who'd arrived in America as an adult and wrote exclusively in Yiddish) with a superb and stunning translation of "Gimpel the Fool." And the fire that Bellow breathed into the story, his own magical rhythm, came from Bellow's largeness of spirit, the almost Talmudic need of one master to recognize another. Singer's concerns are less elliptical than Bellow's, but in "Gimpel," at least, we can find a prototype of Augie March—the dreamer who weaves stories out of the air. Yet Augie's world is comic, and Singer's comedy spills into nightmare.

Bellow would also solidify the reputation of a younger writer, Philip Roth, in *Commentary*, a magazine that was one of the first to value this new, farcical American voice that could often be so mocking of Jews themselves. In the late forties (*Commentary* was founded in 1945), the fifties, and the early sixties, the magazine didn't follow any pattern of "political correctness." Under Elliot Cohen, Theodore Solotaroff, and Norman Podhoretz (at first), the magazine seemed eager to experiment and to discover and sustain new writers. Singer, Roth, and Bernard Malamud were all published with a certain regularity and rhythm within its pages.

Malamud and Roth would both win the National Book

Award in the 1950s, after *Augie March*, and with books of stories rather than novels, a difficult feat, since publishers *hated* books of stories—stories weren't supposed to sell. The three of them—Bellow, Malamud, and Roth—were soon called the Hart Schaffner & Marx of American fiction (Hart Schaffner & Marx being an upscale Jewish clothier that dressed successful Jewish gangsters, singers, actors—the whole hoi polloi). Bellow would remain the spiritual father of this little club, with Singer as a kind of kissing cousin from an older world.

But there were more immediate cousins, like Stanley Elkin, Herbert Gold, Grace Paley, Cynthia Ozick, Tillie Olsen, Leonard Michaels, and Leonard Cohen, who had the same sense of danger in their prose, a crazy concertina with its own variety of registers that could play on and on without the need to end. Elkin seems the closest to Bellow in his insistence upon the mingling of high and low styles, rhetoric and tough-guy talk, and his first novel, *Boswell* (1964), is like a mirror world of *Augie March*, homage in the form of parody. Elkin, Paley, Ozick, and Roth all have a particular thing in common with Bellow—the invention of an idiolect that has exploded traditional English, flooded it with rhythms that had never been there before, given it an elasticity and an electrical pull. It's hardly an accident. Elkin's language, like Bellow's, is a lethal weapon, a dive-bomber readying to attack the American heartland, to take revenge on a white Protestant culture that had excluded all minorities for so long (not just African Americans and Jews), but the attack is always masked; it comes with a kiss, with a jibe and a bit of buffoonery. One can find the same sabotage in the films of Woody Allen, like *Annie Hall* (1977), where Allen's alter ego, Albie Singer, attacks *all* of America outside of New York City;

Annie Hall still managed to win an Academy Award for best picture of the year . . .

But Bellow's attack is buried in the nucleus of his book; Augie's an orphan of sorts who never knew his dad. It's as if that monster, Augie March, gave birth to himself. "Look at me, going everywhere! Why, I am a sort of Columbus of those near-at-hand. . . . I may well be a flop at this line of endeavor. Columbus too thought he was a flop, probably, when they sent him back in chains. Which didn't prove there was no America."

And that's how the novel ends, with Augie the self-creator bumping along on his little lifeboat of words.

3.

Perhaps the most lasting and powerful legacy of *Augie March* is that it inspired an archaeological dig—it helped bring back forgotten masterpieces such as Henry Roth's *Call It Sleep*. First published in 1934, the novel slept in its own sarcophagus until all the brouhaha began to broil around the Jewish musketeers of Hart Schaffner & Marx. The book was republished in 1962 by a small press; I happened to grab hold of a copy and instantly fell into the dream of its "Mississippi," a marriage of James Joyce and ghetto English and Yiddish of the Lower East Side. I was a little priest of literature at the time and brought *Call It Sleep* to my editor, Robert G., who was about to publish my own first novel.

"Bob," I said, "it's a fucking masterpiece. Read it. You gotta publish it in a bigger edition. I'll be the editor. We'll make a million."

I was a wild child, *his* wild child, and we would have lunch twice a week at Barbetta's, a north Italian restaurant on West Forty-sixth Street favored by Mafia chieftains and rich, melancholy men with melancholy mistresses and wives. I'm not quite sure what else Bob did other than take me to lunch. He'd come out of Cornell, had scribbled a novel of his own, and was a senior editor at a publishing house whose prodigy I'd become. They were banking on me as the next Saul Bellow, which just proves how much magic Bellow had in 1964 and how "innocent" Bob was, since every major publishing house was banking on another Bellow or two. The king had just come out with *Herzog*, which was a much bigger bombshell than *Augie March*. Moses Herzog was like a relative of Joyce's Leopold Bloom, but I didn't have the same affection for him as I'd had for Augie March. Herzog, we're told, likes to make love in the missionary position, and I couldn't imagine Augie, with all his slurpings, ever saying that. No matter. *Herzog* was number one on the best-seller list.

I was drinking white wine with Bob. I knew nothing about white wine. The novel I'd written was about an aging Yiddish actor on Second Avenue. I hadn't seen too many Yiddish actors, but I'd tramped the Lower East Side as a kid and had discovered pictures of the great stars, like Maurice Schwartz and Molly Picon, in the lobby of a decrepit theater next to the Williamsburg Bridge. Still, the book seemed authentic enough to Bob. Bashevis Singer had sent him a letter declaring that his protégé and wild child had a mysterious understanding of cafeteria culture. Bob liked to keep the letter in his wallet and wave it to me during lunch.

"That's our meal ticket," he'd say, showing off in front of the waiters, who adored him, because Bob was as loyal to Barbetta's as the Mafia chiefs. There weren't many other editors around, since most publishers, like Viking and Holt, were on the East Side, but a couple of young editors happened to be in the restaurant. And Bob would gloat with that letter in his hand.

"Fellas, meet Jerome. He doesn't write. He paints—like Chagall, swear to God."

The first chapter of my novel had just been published in *Commentary*, and these young editors pretended to have seen it. "Your kid's a comer," they said. "Roth and Malamud had better make a little room . . . Book-of-the-Month Club, Bob. Or at least a Pulitzer."

They were con artists and flatterers, and when they returned to their table, I brought up *Call It Sleep*. But Bob wouldn't bite at whatever little bait I had.

"It's old-fashioned," he said. "I couldn't even finish the book."

A month or two later a pocket edition of *Call It Sleep* appeared, and was reviewed on the front page of the *New York Times Book Review*, which rarely ever happened to a reprinted book. The reviewer was Irving Howe, another member of the Jewish "gangster" critics, with Alfred Kazin and Leslie Fiedler, who'd risen out of the ghetto to reinterpret all of American literature. Howe celebrated *Call It Sleep*, and it would go on to sell more than a million copies and bring Henry Roth, who'd become a chicken farmer and slaughterer in Maine, back from the dead. Roth might have remained a chicken slaughterer if *Augie March* hadn't exploded upon the landscape and redefined the parameters of American literature; but one writer Augie wasn't able to rescue was Anzia Yezierska, who flourished in the 1920s as a kind of ghetto princess, received much more acclaim than Henry Roth . . . and a Hollywood contract, and then fell into complete silence until 1950 when she published a novel-cum-memoir, *Red Ribbon on a White Horse*, about her own unraveling as a writer. Like Saul Bellow, she'd worked in the WPA Writers Project during the Depression (a Kafkaesque federal relief agency that paid writers to produce by the "pound"). But Bellow went from writers' relief to the Merchant Marines in the middle of World War II (like Augie March), to a teaching job at Bard College, a Guggenheim Fellowship in 1948, and to a stint in Europe, where he wrote much of *Augie March*, just as Augie claims to be writing his own memoirs while he sits in Paris.

The fact is that Yezierska fell into fashion . . . and fell out. And she never belonged to that same wild school as Bellow and Paley and Elkin and Gold and Philip Roth. How could she? She wasn't born into English, hadn't learned it as some brat in the streets of Chicago or the Bronx. Her prose would never have the elasticity of *Augie March*; there was a much different kind of hornet inside her head, the music of lament . . .

No one really knows when she was born. It was *around* 1880. There were no birth certificates in her Polish shtetl. She arrived in America in 1901, according to Irving Howe, who documents her story with a great deal of tenderness in *The World of Our Fathers* (a monumental study of the migration to America of East European Jews). I would never have tumbled onto her without Irving Howe. The name stuck in my head, *Anzia Yezierska*, like a tiny, poetic lexicon that was as strange and oddly familiar as the Old World itself. I couldn't call her Yezierska. She was *Anzia* from the start, like a lost child. Howe made her five years younger ("born in 1885"), but that was the mask Anzia wished to wear—the "maiden" who'd gone out to Hollywood rather than the forty-year-old. She'd been a servant girl, a charwoman, a sewing machine operator in a sweatshop . . . and a frustrated professor of cooking. She'd studied English at night school like so many greenhorns. But Anzia was different. She started to sew with words. She wanted to become a writer in this borrowed, twisted Yankee tongue. And like Virginia Woolf, she desperately desired a room of her own. "My earliest dream of becoming a writer flashed before me," she declares in one of the last stories she ever published. "My obsession that I must have a room with a door I could shut. To achieve this I left home. And so I cut myself off not only from my family, but from friends, from people. The door that I felt I must shut to become a writer had shut out compassion, feeling for pain and sorrow, love and joy of friends and neighbors. Father, Mother, sisters, brothers became alien to me, and I became alien to myself."

Her story, in Howe's hands, has more than a hint of Jewish pathos and melodrama—a miraculous rise out of the ghetto, a journey to Hollywood, "Yiddish accent and all," a drying up of her talent, a descent into "loneliness and poverty," with a few books published "but little noticed: all in her fervent signature, pitiful in their transparency." Then her autobiographical novel at sixty-five (she was closer to seventy), with a title chosen from an old Jewish proverb, says Irving Howe: "Poverty becomes a wise man like a red ribbon on a white horse." And Howe insists that "[i]n some groping, half-acknowledged way she had returned to the world of her fathers—a final reconciliation, of sorts."

Her own father was a Talmudic scholar who totally rejected her career as a writer. "A woman alone, not a wife and not a mother, has no existence."

And Howe wouldn't permit Anzia one little ironic touch. She did indeed wear her poverty "like a red ribbon on a white horse." But the "old Jewish proverb" was her own, invented by Anzia as a bit of deviltry. What Howe couldn't quite comprehend was that Anzia was a "hunger artist," like Kafka. "She is destined to eat herself alive forever," according to

Vivian Gornick, who wrote the introduction to Anzia's collected stories in 1991, when a new generation of writers and readers began to resurrect her.

There was so much confusion around such simple facts. Suddenly this isolated priestess of art had a daughter, two husbands, a college degree, a short but not quite love affair and fling with America's foremost "Puritan," philosopher John Dewey, a different name—Hattie Mayer—and twenty lost years between Hester Street and Hollywood. *Red Ribbon on a White Horse* is dedicated to her daughter, Louise Levitas, who is never once mentioned in the book. In fact, Anzia tells us in the final chapter: "I too had children. My children were the people I wrote about. I gave my children, born of loneliness, as much of my life as my married sisters did in bringing their children into the world."

Anzia was hiding, like any hunger artist, but it's thanks to this invisible daughter—abandoned by her mother at four—that we have some image of what Anzia *might* have been about. Her birth is still unclear. She was the youngest of seven children, born in the Polish-Russian village of Plotsk (often called Plinsk in her own writing). Her family arrived at Castle Garden, an artificial stone island off the Battery, used as a processing station for immigrants *before* Ellis Island. Levitas believes the Yezierskas arrived around 1890 and were immediately Americanized into the "Mayers." And Anzia, who was ten at the time, became "Hattie Mayer." Ten isn't fifteen or twenty, and she might have seized English if she'd labored in the classroom like a little bandit, but her father, a total tyrant in his religious zeal, didn't allow her much schooling, and she had to help support him and the rest of the family. Thus began the saga of Hattie Mayer as a servant girl and seamstress. But in 1899 she would opt for that room of her own, while still supporting her family, and moved into a monklike cell at the Clara de Hirsch Home for working girls. She conned the wealthy patrons at the home into giving her a scholarship to study "domestic science" at Columbia University Teachers College, so that she could return to the ghetto as a cooking teacher with a college degree. But she had to invent a high school diploma for herself, since she'd never been near any high school.

"Domestic science" didn't do her much good. The Board of Education considered her sloppy and unkempt and wouldn't give her a permanent teacher's license. She had to drift from school to school as a substitute teacher. Somewhere in her twenties she decided to write, and the nom de plume she settled on was Anzia Yezierska—her very own name. The truth is that Anzia had no name; she was an invented creature, a forlorn child of the New World, without a language of her own.

In December 1917, *after* she'd abandoned her child and her second husband and was living like a monk, utterly devoted to the craft of writing in this invented English of hers, she ran to John Dewey, the doyen of education at Columbia. "[B]urning-eyed and red-haired," she cornered him in his office, hoping he would intervene in her fight with the Board of Ed, and poor John "never knew what hit him," Vivian Gornick reminds us. A New England "pragmatist," he was susceptible to gypsies like her. Married, with children of his own, he took Anzia under his wing, permitted her to audit his seminar in philosophy, found her work as a translator on one of his projects, and gave the little gypsy her first typewriter. He would also take walks with her through the Lower East Side. Dewey was reticent. But Anzia clutched at him with her eyes, wouldn't let him retreat. They began to exchange letters on the sly. Anzia lived within the dream of John Dewey as some godlike creature. He worried about his "evasion of life. . . . I must begin humbly like a child to learn the meaning of life from you." She remained the hunger artist in spite of loving him and criticized his stilted, academic prose, his "clear head and cold heart." But his letters were warm and passionate. "In your letters . . . you are St. Francis, loving the poor."

The Puritan was obsessed with her, as much as his own nature would allow. "You are translucent," he wrote while he was on a lecture tour. He began writing poems to Anzia that he hid inside his desk. He talked about his "unillumined duties" and "thoughts which travel th' untracked wild / Of untamed desire."

Finally, he acted on his desire. He arrived at Anzia's tenement, took her to dinner, and then strolled with her in a neighborhood park. He kissed her, fumbled with her breast, and Anzia's body stiffened against his touch. "His overwhelming nearness, the tense body closing in on me was pushing us apart instead of fusing us," she would write in *Red Ribbon*, trying to recapture the moment. "A dark river of distrust rose between us. I had not dreamed that God could become flesh."

The spell was broken for John. He withdrew from Anzia, asked her for his letters back. She insisted on keeping them. Dewey disappeared on a lecture tour that lasted three years. Her own sentimental education was already over. The hunger artist in Anzia now consumed her. She wrote stories that were rejected everywhere. "The stories had become her whole existence," writes Louise Levitas. Then magazines began to buy them and soon swallowed her up as the "Sweatshop Cinderella," even though she hadn't worked in a sweatshop for years. It was the start of the Jazz Age, and readers loved the notion of an immigrant working girl who could deliver the ghetto to them in good English. Samuel Goldwyn bought the film rights to Anzia's first collection of stories, *Hungry Hearts*, for ten thousand dollars (a fortune in 1920), and beckoned her to Hollywood to work on the script. And Anzia had her revenge. The Board of Education that had shunned her as slovenly invited Anzia to lecture on her book . . .

Red Ribbon starts with Anzia as a starving writer on Hester Street who receives a telegram that invites her to pack her bags . . . and she's on her way to Hollywood. "I felt like a beggar who drowned in a barrel of cream." But Hollywood couldn't satisfy her own hungry heart. It was nothing but a "fish market in evening clothes." And Anzia left without having written one line. But she'd been picked up by influential journalists and her portrait appeared in all the Sunday supplements. She went to Europe, met with Joseph Conrad and Gertrude Stein, and on the trip back she decided to travel steerage like the ordinary immigrant that she had once been. But Anzia couldn't revisit her own past. She was horrified by the stench and the filth, and after one night she was transferred to second class . . .

Still, the Jewish Cinderella couldn't last. She kept repeating her own immigrant tales. "I can never learn to plot and plan. It's always a mystery to me how I ever work out a beginning or an end of a story."

By the end of the decade she'd stopped being a mystery to her readers. Anzia was no longer read. The Depression didn't have much use for ghetto princesses. And she would never regain those lost readers during her lifetime. But she labored continually, often spending two or three years on a single story. "I went on writing and rewriting, possessed by the need to get at something unutterable, that could only be said in the white spaces between the words." ("The Fat of the Land")

These white spaces were her own lost language—the Yiddish, Russian, and Polish of her childhood, *before* America. This is why she was so brutally shut out. Anzia wrote like an amnesiac, with missing musical chords. And the white spaces in her stories unsettle us, because they have all the sadness of the *unsaid*. One of her most discerning critics, William Lyon Phelps, claimed that Anzia "has, in one sense of the word, no literary style. . . . In the works of Tolstoy, the style is like plate glass, so perfectly does the plain, simple word fit the thought, but in Anzia Yezierska's tales there is nothing. One does not seem to read, one is too completely inside."

And Anzia is like the dybbuk of Saul Bellow and all the stylish writers that clustered around him in the sixties; she's that troubled "ancestor" who didn't dare mix the high and the low, who was like some eternal veteran of a night-school war in which she had to spend herself to embrace the Yankees and offer them a glimpse into her private and public ghetto. She was too brittle to "evolve," to wear the mask of style after style. Anzia loved to wear masks, to fabulate and confound her own history, but as a writer she had no mask—she was pure emotion in a language that didn't really fit. It leaves us with the guileless charm of unadornment . . . and permanent grief. She didn't go back into any orthodoxy, as Irving Howe suggests. She persisted as a hunger artist to the very end, and her style of no style moves us more than that of most other writers.

Before there could be a king like Bellow there had to be a ghetto princess like Anzia, the golem that gave birth to Saul

Bellow and his flowering in the fifties. He would seize Yiddish *and* Henry James and everything else around him. He had no desire to explain himself to Americans, as Anzia did. He *was* America the way Anzia could never be, certain of himself, ready to fight any establishment catch-as-catch-can. And Jewish American literature exists in the shifting tonalities, the shrinking white spaces, that finally wed Anzia to Saul Bellow and Philip Roth and Woody Allen . . .

Note: One can only lament that Leonard Cohen has stopped writing novels and that Woody Allen is much more obsessed with film than with narrative fiction: both were once genuine hunger artists.

I've included Allen Ginsberg, because at least in *Kaddish* he too had lived inside the hornet's head.

GRANDMA LAUSCH

from *The Adventures of Augie March*

SAUL BELLOW

I am an American, Chicago born—Chicago, that somber city—and go at things as I have taught myself, free-style, and will make the record in my own way: first to knock, first admitted; sometimes an innocent knock, sometimes a not so innocent. But a man's character is his fate, says Heraclitus, and in the end there isn't any way to disguise the nature of the knocks by acoustical work on the door or gloving the knuckles.

Everybody knows there is no fineness or accuracy of suppression; if you hold down one thing you hold down the adjoining.

My own parents were not much to me, though I cared for my mother. She was simple-minded, and what I learned from her was not what she taught, but on the order of object lessons. She didn't have much to teach, poor woman. My brothers and I loved her. I speak for them both; for the elder it is safe enough; for the younger one, Georgie, I have to answer—he was born an idiot—but I'm in no need to guess, for he had a song he sang as he ran dragfooted with his stiff idiot's trot, up and down along the curl-wired fence in the backyard:

Georgie Mahchy, Augie, Simey
Winnie Mahchy, evwy, evwy love Mama.

He was right about everyone save Winnie, Grandma Lausch's poodle, a pursy old overfed dog. Mama was Winnie's servant, as she was Grandma Lausch's. Loud-breathing and wind-breaking, she lay near the old lady's stool on a cushion embroidered with a Berber aiming a rifle at a lion. She was personally Grandma's, belonged to her suite; the rest of us were the governed, and especially Mama. Mama passed the dog's dish to Grandma, and Winnie received her food at the old lady's feet from the old lady's hands. These hands and feet were small; she wore a shriveled sort of lisle on her legs and her slippers were gray—ah, the gray of that felt, the gray despotic to souls—with pink ribbons. Mama, however, had large feet, and around the house she wore men's shoes, usu-ally without strings, and a dusting or mobcap like some-body's fanciful cotton effigy of the form of the brain. She was meek and long, round-eyed like Georgie—gentle green round eyes and a gentle freshness of color in her long face. Her hands were work-reddened, she had very few of her teeth left—to heed the knocks as they come—and she and Simon wore the same ravelly coat-sweaters. Besides having round eyes, Mama had circular glasses that I went with her to the free dispensary on Harrison Street to get. Coached by Grandma Lausch, I went to do the lying. Now I know it wasn't so necessary to lie, but then everyone thought so, and

Grandma Lausch especially, who was one of those Machi-avellis of small street and neighborhood that my young years were full of. So Grandma, who had it all ready before we left the house and must have put in hours plotting it out in thought and phrase, lying small in her chilly small room under the featherbed, gave it to me at breakfast. The idea was that Mama wasn't keen enough to do it right. That maybe one didn't need to be keen didn't occur to us; it was a contest. The dispensary would want to know why the Char-ities didn't pay for the glasses. So you must say nothing about the Charities, but that sometimes money from my father came and sometimes it didn't, and that Mama took boarders. This was, in a delicate and choosy way, by ignoring and omitting certain large facts, true. It was true enough for *them,* and at the age of nine I could appreciate this perfectly. Better than my brother Simon, who was too blunt for this kind of maneuver and, anyway, from books, had gotten hold of some English schoolboy notions of honor. *Tom Brown's Schooldays* for many years had an influence we were not in a position to afford.

Simon was a blond boy with big cheekbones and wide gray eyes and had the arms of a cricketer—I go by the illustrations; we never played anything but softball. Opposed to his British style was his patriotic anger at George III. The mayor was at that time ordering the schoolboard to get history books that dealt more harshly with the king, and Simon was very hot at Cornwallis. I admired this patriotic flash, his terrific per-sonal wrath at the general, and his satisfaction over his sur-render at Yorktown, which would often come over him at lunch while we ate our bologna sandwiches. Grandma had a piece of boiled chicken at noon, and sometimes there was the gizzard for bristleheaded little Georgie, who loved it and blew at the ridgy thing more to cherish than to cool it. But this martial true-blood pride of Simon's disqualified him for the crafty task to be done at the dispensary; he was too disdainful to lie and might denounce everybody instead. I could be counted on to do the job, because I enjoyed it. I loved a piece of strategy. I had enthusiasms too; I had Simon's, though there was never much meat in Cornwallis for me, and I had Grandma Lausch's as well. As for the truth of these statements I was instructed to make—well, it was a fact that we had a boarder. Grandma Lausch was our boarder, not a relation at all. She was supported by two sons, one from Cincinnati and one from Racine, Wisconsin. The daughters-in-law did not want her, and she, the widow of a powerful Odessa businessman—a divinity over us, bald, whiskery, with a fat nose, greatly armored in a cutaway, a double-breasted vest, powerfully buttoned (his blue photo, enlarged and retouched by Mr. Lulov, hung in the parlor, doubled back between the portico columns of the full-length mirror, the dome of the stove beginning where his trunk ended)—she preferred to live with us, because for so many years she was used to direct a house, to command, to govern, to manage, scheme, devise, and intrigue in all her languages. She boasted French and German besides Russian, Polish, and Yiddish; and who but Mr. Lulov, the retouch artist from Division Street, could have tested her claim to French? And he was a serene bogus too, that triple-backboned gallant tea-drinker. Except that he had been a hackie in Paris, once, and if he told the truth about that might have known French among other things, like playing tunes on his teeth with a pencil or singing and keeping time with a handful of coins that he rattled by jigging his thumb along the table, and how to play chess.

Grandma Lausch played like Timur, whether chess or

klabyasch, with palatal catty harshness and sharp gold in her eyes. Klabyasch she played with Mr. Kreindl, a neighbor of ours who had taught her the game. A powerful stub-handed man with a large belly, he swatted the table with those hard hands of his, flinging down his cards and shouting *"Shtoch! Yasch! Menél! Klabyasch!"* Grandma looked sardonically at him. She often said, after he left, "If you've got a Hungarian friend you don't need an enemy." But there was nothing of the enemy about Mr. Kreindl. He merely, sometimes, sounded menacing because of his drill-sergeant's bark. He was an old-time Austro-Hungarian conscript, and there was something soldierly about him: a neck that had strained with pushing artillery wheels, a campaigner's red in the face, a powerful bite in his jaw and gold-crowned teeth, green cockeyes and soft short hair, altogether Napoleonic. His feet slanted out on the ideal of Frederick the Great, but he was about a foot under the required height for guardsmen. He had a masterly look of independence. He and his wife—a woman quiet and modest to the neighbors and violently quarrelsome at home—and his son, a dental student, lived in what was called the English basement at the front of the house. The son, Kotzie, worked evenings in the corner drugstore and went to school in the neighborhood of County Hospital, and it was he who told Grandma about the free dispensary. Or rather, the old woman sent for him to find out what one could get from those state and county places. She was always sending for people, the butcher, the grocer, the fruit peddler, and received them in the kitchen to explain that the Marches had to have discounts. Mama usually had to stand by. The old woman would tell them, "You see how it is—do I have to say more? There's no man in the house and children to bring up." This was her most frequent argument. When Lubin, the caseworker, came around and sat in the kitchen, familiar, bald-headed, in his gold glasses, his weight comfortable, his mouth patient, she shot it at him: "How do you expect children to be brought up?" While he listened, trying to remain comfortable but gradually becoming like a man determined not to let a grasshopper escape from his hand. "Well, my dear, Mrs. March could raise your rent," he said. She must often have answered—for there were times when she sent us all out to be alone with him— "Do you know what things would be like without me? You ought to be grateful for the way I hold them together." I'm sure she even said, "And when I die, Mr. Lubin, you'll see what you've got on your hands." I'm one hundred per cent sure of it. To us nothing was ever said that might weaken her rule by suggesting it would ever end. Besides, it would have shocked us to hear it, and she, in her miraculous knowledge of us, able to be extremely close to our thoughts—she was one sovereign who knew exactly the proportions of love, respect, and fear of power in her subjects—understood how we would have been shocked. But to Lubin, for reasons of policy and also because she had to express feelings she certainly had, she must have said it. He had a harassed patience with her of "deliver me from such clients," though he tried to appear master of the situation. He held his derby between his thighs (his suits, always too scanty in the pants, exposed white socks and bulldog shoes, crinkled, black, and bulging with toes), and he looked into the hat as though debating whether it was wise to release his grasshopper on the lining for a while.

"I pay as much as I can afford," she would say.

She took her cigarette case out from under her shawl, she cut a Murad in half with her sewing scissors and picked up the holder. This was still at a time when women did not smoke. Save the intelligentsia—the term she applied to herself. With the holder in her dark little gums between which all her guile, malice, and command issued, she had her best inspirations of strategy. She was as wrinkled as an old paper bag, an autocrat, hard-shelled and jesuitical, a pouncy old hawk of a Bolshevik, her small ribboned gray feet immobile on the shoekit and stool Simon had made in the manual-training class, dingy old wool Winnie whose bad smell filled the flat on the cushion beside her. If wit and discontent don't necessarily go together, it wasn't from the old woman that I learned it. She was impossible to satisfy. Kreindl, for example, on whom we could depend, Kreindl who carried up the coal when Mama was sick and who instructed Kotzie to make up our prescriptions for nothing, she called "that trashy Hungarian," or "Hungarian pig." She called Kotzie "the baked apple"; she called Mrs. Kreindl "the secret goose," Lubin "the shoemaker's son," the dentist "the butcher," the butcher "the timid swindler." She detested the dentist, who had several times unsuccessfully tried to fit her with false teeth. She accused him of burning her gums when taking the impressions. But then she tried to pull his hands away from her mouth. I saw that happen: the stolid, square-framed Dr. Wernick, whose compact forearms could have held off a bear, painfully careful with her, determined, concerned at her choked screams, and enduring her scratches. To see her struggle like that was no easy thing for me, and Dr. Wernick was sorry to see me there too, I know, but either Simon or I had to squire her wherever she went. Here particularly she needed a witness to Wernick's cruelty and clumsiness as well as a shoulder to lean on when she went weakly home. Already at ten I was only a little shorter than she and big enough to hold her small weight.

"You saw how he put his paws over my face so I couldn't

breathe?" she said. "God made him to be a butcher. Why did he become a dentist? His hands are too heavy. The touch is everything to a dentist. If his hands aren't right he shouldn't be let practice. But his wife worked hard to send him through school and make a dentist of him. And I must go to him and be burned because of it."

The rest of us had to go to the dispensary—which was like the dream of a multitude of dentists' chairs, hundreds of them in a space as enormous as an armory, and green bowls with designs of glass grapes, drills lifted zigzag as insects' legs, and gas flames on the porcelain swivel trays—a thundery gloom in Harrison Street of limestone county buildings and cumbersome red streetcars with metal grillwork on their windows and monarchical iron whiskers of cowcatchers front and rear. They lumbered and clanged, and their brake tanks panted in the slushy brown of a winter afternoon or the bare stone brown of a summer's, salted with ash, smoke, and prairie dust, with long stops at the clinics to let off clumpers, cripples, hunchbacks, brace-legs, crutch-wielders, tooth and eye sufferers, and all the rest.

So before going with my mother for the glasses I was always instructed by the old woman and had to sit and listen with profound care. My mother too had to be present, for there must be no slip-up. She must be coached to say nothing. "Remember, Rebecca," Grandma would re-repeat, "let him answer everything." To which Mama was too obedient even to say yes, but only sat and kept her long hands folded on the bottle-fly iridescence of the dress the old woman had picked for her to wear. Very healthy and smooth, her color; none of us inherited this high a color from her, or the form of her nose with nostrils turned back and showing a little of the partition. "You keep out of it. If they ask you something, you look at Augie like this." And she illustrated how Mama was to turn to me, terribly exact, if she had only been able to drop her habitual grandeur. "Don't tell anything. Only answer questions," she said to me. My mother was anxious that I should be worthy and faithful. Simon and I were her miracles or accidents; Georgie was her own true work in which she returned to her fate after blessed and undeserved success. "Augie, listen to Grandma. Hear what she says," was all she ever dared when the old woman unfolded her plan.

"When they ask you, 'Where is your father?' you say, 'I don't know where, miss.' No matter how old she is, you shouldn't forget to say 'miss.' If she wants to know where he was the last time you heard from him, you must tell her that the last time he sent a money order was about two years ago from Buffalo, New York. Never say a word about the Charity. The Charity you should never mention, you hear that? Never. When she asks you how much the rent is, tell her eighteen dollars. When she asks where the money comes from, say you have boarders. How many? Two boarders. Now, say to me, how much rent?"

"Eighteen dollars."

"And how many boarders?"

"Two."

"And how much do they pay?"

"How much should I say?"

"Eight dollars each a week."

"Eight dollars."

"So you can't go to a private doctor, if you get sixty-four dollars a month. The eyedrops alone cost me five when I went, and he scalded my eyes. And these specs"—she tapped the case—"cost ten dollars the frames and fifteen the glasses."

Never but at such times, by necessity, was my father mentioned. I claimed to remember him; Simon denied that I did, and Simon was right. I liked to imagine it.

"He wore a uniform," I said. "Sure I remember. He was a soldier."

"Like hell he was. You don't know anything about it."

"Maybe a sailor."

"Like hell. He drove a truck for Hall Brothers laundry on Marshfield, that's what he did. *I* said he used to wear a uniform. Monkey sees, monkey does; monkey hears, monkey says." Monkey was the basis of much thought with us. On the sideboard, on the Turkestan runner, with their eyes, ears, and mouth covered, we had see-no-evil, speak-no-evil, hear-no-evil, a lower trinity of the house. The advantage of lesser gods is that you can take their names any way you like. "Silence in the courthouse, monkey wants to speak; speak, monkey, speak." "The monkey and the bamboo were playing in the grass . . ." Still the monkeys could be potent, and awesome besides, and deep social critics when the old woman, like a great lama—for she is Eastern to me, in the end—would point to the squatting brown three, whose mouths and nostrils were drawn in sharp blood-red, and with profound wit, her unkindness finally touching greatness, say, "Nobody asks you to love the whole world, only to be honest, *ehrlich.* Don't have a loud mouth. The more you love people the more they'll mix you up. A child loves, a person respects. Respect is better than love. And that's respect, the middle monkey." It never occurred to us that she sinned mischievously herself against that convulsed speak-no-evil who hugged his lips with his hands; but no criticism of her came near our minds at any time, much less when the resonance of a great principle filled the whole kitchen. She used to read us lessons off poor

Georgie's head. He would kiss the dog. This bickering hand-maiden of the old lady, at one time. Now a dozy, long-sighing crank and proper object of respect for her years of right-minded but not exactly lovable busyness. But Georgie loved her—and Grandma, whom he would kiss on the sleeve, on the knee, taking knee or arm in both hands and putting his underlip forward, chaste, lummoxy, caressing, gentle and dili-gent when he bent his narrow back, blouse bagging all over it, whitish hair pointy and close as a burr or sunflower when the seeds have been picked out of it. The old lady let him embrace her and spoke to him in the following way: "Hey, you, boy, clever *junge,* you like the old Grandma, my minister, my *cavalyer?* That's-a-boy. You know who's good to you, who gives you gizzards and necks? Who? Who makes noodles for you? Yes. Noodles are slippery, hard to pick up with a fork and hard to pick up with the fingers. You see how the little bird pulls the worm? The little worm wants to stay in the ground. The little worm doesn't want to come out. Enough, you're making my dress wet." And she'd sharply push his forehead off with her old prim hand, having fired off for Simon and me, mindful always of her duty to wise us up, one more animadversion on the trustful, loving, and simple surrounded by the cunning-hearted and tough, a fighting nature of birds and worms, and a desperate mankind without feelings. Illustrated by Georgie. But the principal illustration was not Georgie but Mama, in her love-originated servitude, simple-minded, abandoned with three children. This was what old lady Lausch was driving at, now, in the later wisdom of her life, that she had a second family to lead.

And what must Mama have thought when in any necessary connection my father was brought into the conversation? She sat docile. I conceive that she thought of some detail about him—a dish he liked, perhaps meat and potatoes, perhaps cabbage or cranberry sauce; perhaps that he disliked a starched collar, or a soft collar; that he brought home the *Evening American* or the *Journal*. She thought this because her thoughts were always simple; but she felt abandonment, and greater pains than conscious mental ones put a dark streak to her simplicity. I don't know how she made out before, when we were alone after the desertion, but Grandma came and put a regulating hand on the family life. Mama surrendered powers to her that maybe she had never known she had and took her punishment in drudgery; occupied a place, I suppose, among women conquered by a superior force of love, like those women whom Zeus got the better of in animal form and who next had to take cover from his furious wife. Not that I can see my big, gentle, dilapidated, scrubbing, and lugging mother as a fugitive of immense beauty from such classy wrath, or our father as a marble-legged Olympian. She had sewed buttonholes in a coat factory in a Wells Street loft and he was a laundry driver—there wasn't even so much as a picture of him left when he blew. But she does have a place among such women by the deeper right of continual payment. And as for vengeance from a woman, Grandma Lausch was there to administer the penalties under the standards of legitimacy, representing the main body of married womankind.

Still the old lady had a heart. I don't mean to say she didn't. She was tyrannical and a snob about her Odessa luster and her servants and governesses, but though she had been a success herself she knew what it was to fall through susceptibility. I began to realize this when I afterward read some of the novels she used to send me to the library for. She taught me the Russian alphabet so that I could make out the titles. Once a year she read *Anna*

Karenina and *Eugene Onegin.* Occasionally I got into hot water by bringing a book she didn't want. "How many times do I have to tell you if it doesn't say *roman* I don't want it? You didn't look inside. Are your fingers too weak to open the book? Then they should be too weak to play ball or pick your nose. For that you've got strength! *Bozhe moy!* God in Heaven! You haven't got the brains of a cat, to walk two miles and bring me a book about religion because it says Tolstoi on the cover."

The old *grande dame,* I don't want to be misrepresenting her. She was suspicious of what could have been, given one wrong stitch of heredity, a family vice by which we could have been exploited. She didn't want to read Tolstoi on religion. She didn't trust him as a family man because the countess had had such trouble with him. But although she never went to the synagogue, ate bread on Passover, sent Mama to the pork butcher where meat was cheaper, loved canned lobster and other forbidden food, she was not an atheist and free-thinker. Mr. Anticol, the old junky she called (search me why) "Rameses"—after the city named with Pithom in the Scriptures maybe; no telling what her inspirations were—was that. A real rebel to God. Icy and canny, she would listen to what he had to say and wouldn't declare herself. He was ruddy, and gloomy; his leathery serge cap made him flat-headed, and his alley calls for rags, old iron—"recks aline," he sung it—made him gravel-voiced and gruff. He had tough hair and brows and despising brown eyes; he was a studious, shaggy, meaty old man. Grandma bought a set of the *Encyclopedia Americana*—edition of 1892, I think—from him and saw to it that Simon and I read it; and he too, whenever he met us, asked, "How's the set?" believing, I reckon, that it taught irreverence to religion. What had made him an atheist was a massacre of Jews in his town. From the cellar where he was hidden he saw a laborer pissing on the body of his wife's younger brother, just killed. "So don't talk to me about God," he said. But it was he that talked about God, all the time. And while Mrs. Anticol stayed pious, it was his idea of grand apostasy to drive to the reform synagogue on the high holidays and park his pink-eye nag among the luxurious, whirl-wired touring cars of the rich Jews who bared their heads inside as if they were attending a theater, a kind of abjectness in them that gave him grim entertainment to the end of his life. He caught a cold in the rain and died of pneumonia.

Grandma, all the same, burned a candle on the anniversary of Mr. Lausch's death, threw a lump of dough on the coals when she was baking, as a kind of offering, had incantations over baby teeth and stunts against the evil eye. It was kitchen religion and had nothing to do with the giant God of the Creation who turned back the waters and exploded Gomorrah, but it was on the side of religion at that. And while we're on that side I'll mention the Poles—we were just a handful of Jews among them in the neighborhood—and the swollen, bleeding hearts on every kitchen wall, the pictures of saints, baskets of death flowers tied at the door, communions, Easters, and Christmases. And sometimes we were chased, stoned, bitten, and beat up for Christ-killers, all of us, even Georgie, articled, whether we liked it or not, to this mysterious trade. But I never had any special grief from it, or brooded, being by and large too larky and boisterous to take it to heart, and looked at it as needing no more special explanation than the stone-and-bat wars of the street gangs or the swarming on a fall evening of parish punks to rip up fences, screech and bawl at girls, and beat up strangers. It wasn't in my nature to fatigue myself with worry over being born to this occult work, even though some of my friends and playmates would turn up in the middle of these mobs to trap you between houses from both ends of a passageway. Simon had less truck with them. School absorbed him more, and he had his sentiments anyway, a mixed extract from Natty Bumppo, Quentin Durward, Tom Brown, Clark at Kaskaskia, the messenger who brought the good news from Ratisbon, and so on, that kept him more to himself. I was just a slow understudy to this, just as he never got me to put in hours on his Sandow muscle builder and the gimmick for developing the sinews of the wrist. I was an easy touch for friendships, and most of the time they were cut short by older loyalties. I was pals longest with Stashu Kopecs, whose mother was a midwife graduated from the Aesculapian School of Midwifery on Milwaukee Avenue. Well to do, the Kopecses had an electric player piano and linoleums in all the rooms, but Stashu was a thief, and to run with him I stole too: coal off the cars, clothes from the lines, rubber balls from the dime store, and pennies off the newsstands. Mostly for the satisfaction of dexterity, though Stashu invented the game of stripping in the cellar and putting on girls' things swiped from the clotheslines. Then he too showed up in a gang that caught me one cold afternoon of very little snow while I was sitting on a crate frozen into the mud, eating Nabisco wafers, my throat full of the sweet dust. Foremost, there was a thug of a kid, about thirteen but undersized, hard and grieved-looking. He came up to accuse me, and big Moonya Staplanski, just out of the St. Charles Reformatory and headed next for the one at Pontiac, backed him up.

"You little Jew bastard, you hit my brother," Moonya said.

"I never did. I never even saw him before."

"You took away a nickel from him. How did you buy them biscuits else, you?"

"I got them at home."

Then I caught sight of Stashu, hayheaded and jeering, pleased to sickness with his deceit and his new-revealed brotherhood with the others, and I said, "Hey, you lousy bedwetter, Stashu, you know Moon ain't even got a brother."

Here the kid hit me and the gang jumped me, Stashu with the rest, tearing the buckles from my sheepskin coat and bloodying my nose.

"Who is to blame?" said Grandma Lausch when I came home. "You know who? You are, Augie, because that's all the brains you have to go with that piss-in-bed *accoucherka*'s son. Does Simon hang around with them? Not Simon. He has too much sense." I thanked God she didn't know about the stealing. And in a way, because that was her schooling temperament, I suspect she was pleased that I should see where it led to give your affections too easily. But Mama, the prime example of this weakness, was horrified. Against the old lady's authority she didn't dare to introduce her feelings during the hearing, but when she took me into the kitchen to put a compress on me she nearsightedly pored over my scratches, whispering and sighing to me, while Georgie tottered around behind her, long and white, and Winnie lapped water under the sink.

(1953)

CUNT CRAZY

from *Portnoy's Complaint*

PHILIP ROTH

D id I mention that when I was fifteen I took it out of my pants and whacked off on the 107 bus from New York? I had been treated to a perfect day by my sister and Morty Feibish, her fiancé—a double-header at Ebbets Field, followed afterward by a seafood dinner at Sheepshead Bay. An exquisite day. Hannah and Morty were to stay overnight in Flatbush with Morty's family, and so I was put on a subway to Manhattan about ten o'clock—and there boarded the bus for New Jersey, upon which I took not just my cock in my hands but my whole life, when you think about it. The passengers were mostly drowsing off before we had even emerged from the Lincoln Tunnel—including the girl in the seat beside me, whose tartan skirt folds I had begun to press up against with the corduroy of my trouser legs—and I had it out in my fist by the time we were climbing onto the Pulaski Skyway.

You might have thought that given the rich satisfactions of

the day, I'd have had my fill of excitement and my dick would have been the last thing on my mind heading home that night. Bruce Edwards, a new catcher up from the minors—and just what we needed (we being Morty, myself, and Burt Shotton, the Dodger manager)—had gone something like six for eight in his first two games in the majors (or was it Furillo? at any rate, how insane whipping out my joint like that! imagine what would have been had I been caught red-handed! imagine if I had gone ahead and come all over that sleeping *shikse's* golden arm!) and then for dinner Morty had ordered me a lobster, the first of my life.

Now, maybe the lobster is what did it. That taboo so easily and simply broken, confidence may have been given to the whole slimy, suicidal Dionysian side of my nature; the lesson may have been learned that to break the law, all you have to do is—just go ahead and break it! All you have to do is stop trembling and quaking and finding it unimaginable and beyond you: all you have to do, *is do it!* What else, I ask you, were all those prohibitive dietary rules and regulations all about to begin with, what else but to give us little Jewish children practice in being repressed? Practice, darling, practice, practice, practice. Inhibition doesn't grow on trees, you know—takes patience, takes concentration, takes a dedicated and self-sacrificing parent and a hard-working attentive little child to create in only a few years' time a really constrained and tight-ass human being. Why else the two sets of dishes? Why else the kosher soap and salt? Why else, I ask you, but to remind us three times a day that life is boundaries and restrictions if it's anything, hundreds of thousands of little rules laid down by none other than None Other, rules which either you obey without question, regardless of how idiotic they may appear (and thus remain, by obeying, in His good graces), or you transgress, most likely in the name of outraged common sense—which you transgress because even a child doesn't like to go around feeling like an absolute moron and schmuck—yes, you trangress, only with the strong likelihood (my father assures me) that comes next Yom Kippur and the names are written in the big book where He writes the names of those who are going to get to live until the following September (a scene which manages somehow to engrave itself upon my imagination), and lo, your own precious name ain't among them. Now who's the schmuck, huh? And it doesn't make any difference either (this I understand from the outset, about the way this God, Who runs things, reasons) how big or how small the rule is that you break: it's the breaking alone that gets His goat—it's the simple fact of waywardness, and that alone, that He absolutely cannot stand, and which He does not forget either, when He sits angrily down (fuming probably, and surely with a smashing miserable headache, like my father at the height of his constipation) and begins to leave the names out of that book.

When duty, discipline, and obedience give way—ah, here, *here* is the message I take in each Passover with my mother's *matzoh brei*—what follows, there is no predicting. Renunciation is all, cries the koshered and bloodless piece of steak my family and I sat down to eat at dinner time. Self-control, sobriety, sanctions—this is the key to a human life, saith all those endless dietary laws. Let the *goyim* sink *their* teeth into whatever lowly creature crawls and grunts across the face of the dirty earth, we will not contaminate our humanity thus. Let *them* (if you know who I mean) gorge themselves upon anything and everything that moves, no matter how odious and abject the animal, no matter how grotesque or *shmutzig* or dumb the creature in question happens to be. Let them eat eels and frogs and pigs and crabs and lobsters; let them eat vulture, let them eat ape-meat and skunk if they like—a diet of abominable creatures well befits a breed of mankind so hopelessly shallow and empty-headed as to drink, to divorce, and to fight with their fists. All they know, these imbecilic eaters of the execrable, is to swagger, to insult, to sneer, and sooner or later to hit. Oh, also they know how to go out into the woods with a gun, these geniuses, and kill innocent wild deer, deer who themselves *nosh* quietly on berries and grasses and then go on their way, bothering no one. You stupid *goyim!* Reeking of beer and empty of ammunition, home you head, a dead animal (formerly *alive*) strapped to each fender, so that all the motorists along the way can see how strong and manly you are: and then, in your houses, you take these deer—who have done you, who have done nothing in all of nature, not the least bit of harm—you take these deer, cut them up into pieces, and cook them in a pot. There isn't enough to eat in this world, they have to eat up the *deer* as well! They will eat *anything,* anything they can get their big *goy* hands on! And the terrifying corollary, *they will do anything as well.* Deer eat what deer eat, and Jews eat what Jews eat, but not these *goyim.* Crawling animals, wallowing animals, leaping and angelic animals—it makes no difference to them—what they want they take, and to hell with the other thing's feelings (let alone kindness and compassion). Yes, it's all written down in history, what they have done, our illustrious neighbors who own the world and know absolutely nothing of human boundaries and limits.

. . . Thus saith the kosher laws, at least to the child I was, growing up under the tutelage of Sophie and Jack P., and in a school district of Newark where in my entire class there are only two little Christian children, and they live in houses I do not enter, on the far fringes of our neighborhood . . . thus saith the kosher laws, and who am I to argue that they're wrong? For look at Alex himself, the subject of *our* every syllable—age fifteen, he sucks one night on a lobster's claw and within the hour his cock is out and aimed at a *shikse* on a Public Service bus. And his superior Jewish brain might as well be *made* of *matzoh brei!*

Such a creature, needless to say, has never been boiled alive in our house—the lobster, I refer to. A *shikse* has never been in our house period, and so it's a matter of conjecture in what condition she might emerge from my mother's kitchen. The cleaning lady is obviously a *shikse,* but she doesn't count because she's black.

Ha ha. A *shikse* has never been in our house because I have brought her there, is what I mean to say. I do recall one that my own father brought home with him for dinner one night when I was still a boy: a thin, tense, shy, deferential, soft-spoken, aging cashier from his office named Anne McCaffery.

Doctor, could he have been slipping it to her? I can't believe it! Only it suddenly occurs to me. Could my father have been slipping it to this lady on the side? I can still remember how she sat down beside me on the sofa, and in her nervousness made a lengthy to-do of spelling her first name, and of pointing out to me how it ended with an E, which wasn't always the case with someone called Anne— and so on and so forth . . . and meanwhile, though her arms were long and white and skinny and freckled (Irish arms, I thought) inside her smooth white blouse, I could see she had breasts that were nice and substantial—and I kept taking peeks at her legs, too. I was only eight or nine, but she really did have such a terrific pair of legs that I couldn't keep my eyes away from them, the kind of legs that every once in a while it surprises you to find some pale spinster with a pinched face walking around on top of . . . With those legs—why, *of course* he was *shtupping* her . . . *Wasn't* he?

Why he brought her home, *he* said, was "for a real Jewish meal." For weeks he had been jabbering about the new *goyische* cashier ("a very plain drab person," he said, "who dresses in *shmattas*") who had been pestering him—so went the story he couldn't stop telling us—for a real Jewish meal from the day she had come to work in the Boston & Northeastern office. Finally my mother couldn't take any more. "All right, bring her already—she needs it so bad, so I'll give her one." Was he caught a little by surprise? Who will ever know.

At any rate, a Jewish meal is what she got all right. I don't think I have ever heard the word "Jewish" spoken so many times in one evening in my life, and let me tell you, I am a person who has heard the word "Jewish" spoken.

"This is your real Jewish chopped liver, Anne. Have you ever had real Jewish chopped liver before? Well, my wife makes the real thing, you can bet your life on that. Here, you eat it with a piece of bread. This is real Jewish rye bread, with seeds. That's it, Anne, you're doing very good, ain't she doing good, Sophie, for her first time? That's it, take a nice piece of real Jewish rye, now take a big fork full of the real Jewish chopped liver"—and on and on, right down to the jello—"that's right, Anne, the jello is kosher too, sure, of course, has to be—oh no, oh no, no cream in your coffee, not after meat, ha ha, hear what Anne wanted, Alex—?"

But babble-babble all you want, Dad dear, a question has just occurred to me, twenty-five years later (not that I have a single shred of evidence, not that until this moment I have ever imagined my father capable of even the slightest infraction of domestic law . . . but since infraction seems to hold for me a certain fascination), a question has arisen in the audience: why *did* you bring a *shikse,* of all things, into our home? Because you couldn't bear that a gentile woman should go through life without the experience of eating a dish of Jewish jello? Or because you could no longer live your own life without making Jewish confession? Without confronting your wife with your crime, so she might accuse, castigate, humiliate, punish, and thus bleed you forever of your forbidden lusts! Yes, a regular Jewish desperado, my father. I recognize the syndrome perfectly. Come, someone, anyone, find me out and condemn me—I did the most terrible thing you can think of: I took what I am not supposed to have! Chose pleasure for myself over duty to my loved ones! Please, catch me, incarcerate me, before God forbid I get away with it completely—and go out and do again something I actually like!

And did my mother oblige? Did Sophie put together the two tits and the two legs and come up with four? Me it seems to have taken two and a half decades to do such steep calculation. Oh, I must be making this up, really. My father . . . and a *shikse?* Can't be. Was beyond his ken. My own father— fucked *shikses?* I'll admit under duress that he fucked my mother . . . but *shikses?* I can no more imagine him knocking over a gas station.

But then why is she shouting at him so, what is this scene of accusation and denial, of castigation and threat and unending tears . . . what is this all about except that he has done something that is very bad and maybe even unforgivable? The scene itself is like some piece of heavy furniture that sits in my mind and will not budge—which leads me to believe that, yes, it actually did happen. My sister, I see, is hiding behind my mother: Hannah is clutching her around the middle and whimpering, while my mother's own tears are tremendous and fall from her face all the way to the linoleum floor. Simultaneously with the tears she is screaming so loud at him that her veins stand out—and screaming at me, too, because, looking further into this thing, I find that while Hannah hides behind my mother, *I take refuge behind the culprit himself.* Oh, this is pure fantasy, this is right out of the casebook, is it not? No, no, that is nobody else's father but my own who now brings his fist down on the kitchen table and shouts back at her, "I did no such thing! That is a lie and wrong!" Only wait a minute—it's *me* who is screaming "I didn't do it!" *The culprit is me!* And why my mother weeps so is because my father refuses to potch my behind, which she promised would be *potched*, "and good," when he found out the terrible thing *I* had done.

When I am bad and rotten in small ways she can manage me herself: she has, you recall—I know I recall!—only to put me in my coat and galoshes—oh, nice touch, Mom, those galoshes!—lock me out of the house *(lock me out of the house!)* and announce through the door that she is never going to let me in again, so I might as well be off and into my new life; she has only to take that simple and swift course of action to get instantaneously a confession, a self-scorification, and, if she should want it, a signed warranty that I will be one hundred percent pure and good for the rest of my life—all this if only I am allowed back inside that door, where they happen to have my bed and my clothes and *the refrigerator.* But when I am really wicked, so evil that she can only raise her arms to God Almighty to ask Him what she has done to deserve such a child, at such times my father is called in to mete out justice; my mother is herself too sensitive, too fine a creature, it turns out, to administer corporal punishment: "It hurts me," I hear her explain to my Aunt Clara, "more than it hurts him. That's the kind of person I am. I can't do it, and that's that." Oh, poor Mother.

But look, what is going on here after all? Surely, Doctor, we can figure this thing out, two smart Jewish boys like ourselves . . . A terrible act has been committed, and it has been committed by either my father or me. The wrongdoer, in other words, is one of the two members of the family who owns a penis. Okay. So far so good. Now: did he fuck between those luscious legs the gentile cashier from the office, or have I eaten my sister's chocolate pudding? You see, she *didn't* want it at dinner, but apparently *did* want it saved so she could have it before she went to bed. Well, good Christ, how was I supposed to know all that, Hannah? Who looks into the fine points when he's hungry? I'm eight years old and chocolate pudding happens to get me hot. All I have to do is see that deep chocolatey surface gleaming out at me from the refrigerator, and my life isn't my own. Furthermore, I *thought* it was *left over!* and that's the truth! Jesus Christ, is that what this screaming and *shrying* is all about, that I ate that sad sack's chocolate pudding? Even if I did, I didn't mean it! I thought it was something else! I swear, I swear, I didn't mean to do it! . . . But *is* that me—or my father hollering out his defense before the jury? Sure, that's him—he did it, okay, okay, Sophie, leave me alone already, I did it, *but I didn't mean it!* Shit, the next thing he'll tell her is why he should be forgiven is because he didn't *like* it either. What do you mean, you didn't *mean* it, schmuck—you stuck it in there, didn't you? Then stick up for yourself now, like a man!

Tell her, tell her: "That's right, Sophie, I slipped it to the *shikse,* and what you think and don't think on the subject don't mean shit to me. Because the way it works, in case you ain't heard, is that I am the man around here, *and I call the shots!"* And slug her if you have to! Deck her, Jake! Surely that's what a *goy* would do, would he not? Do you think one of those big-shot deer hunters with a gun collapses in a chair when he gets caught committing the seventh and starts weeping and begging his wife to be *forgiven?*—forgiven for *what?* What after all does it consist of? You put your dick some place and moved it back and forth and stuff came out the front. So, Jake, what's the big deal? How long did the whole thing last that you should suffer such damnation from her mouth—such guilt, such recrimination and self-loathing! Poppa, why do we have to have such guilty deference to women, you and me—when we don't! We mustn't! Who should run the show, Poppa, is *us!* "Daddy has done a terrible terrible thing," cries my mother—or is that my imagination? Isn't what she is saying more like, "Oh, little Alex has done a terrible thing again, Daddy—" Whatever, she lifts Hannah (of all people, Hannah!), who until that moment I had never really taken seriously as a genuine object of anybody's love, takes her up into her arms and starts kissing her all over her sad and unloved face, saying that her little girl is the only one in the whole wide world she can really trust . . . But if I am eight, Hannah is twelve, and nobody is picking her up, I assure you, because the poor kid's problem is that she is overweight, "and how," my mother says. She's not even sup-posed to *eat* chocolate pudding. Yeah, *that's* why I took it! Tough shit, Hannah, it's what the *doctor* ordered, not me. I can't help it if you're fat and "sluggish" and I'm skinny and brilliant. I can't help it that I'm so beautiful they stop Mother when she is wheeling me in my carriage so as to get a good look at my gorgeous *punim*—you hear her tell that story, it's something I myself had nothing to do with, it's a simple fact of nature, that I was born beautiful and you were born, if not ugly, certainly not something people wanted to take special looks at. And is that my fault, too? How you were born, four whole years before I even entered the world? Apparently this is the way God wants it to be, Hannah! In the big book!

But the fact of the matter is, she doesn't seem to hold me responsible for anything: she just goes on being good to her darling little baby brother, and never once strikes me or calls me a dirty name. I take her chocolate pudding, and she takes my shit, and never says a word in protest. Just kisses me before I go to bed, and carefully crosses me going to school, and then stands back and obligingly allows herself to be swallowed up by the wall (I guess that's where she is) when I am imitating for my beaming parents all the voices on "Allen's Alley," or being heralded to relatives from one end of North Jersey to the other for my perfect report card. Because when I am not being punished, Doctor, I am being carried around the house like the Pope through the streets of Rome . . .

You know, I can really come up with no more than a dozen memories involving my sister from those early years of my childhood. Mostly, until she emerges in my adolescence as the only sane person in that lunatic asylum whom I can talk to, it is as though she is someone we see maybe once or twice a year—for a night or two she visits with us, eating at our table, sleeping in one of our beds, and then, poor fat thing, she just blessedly disappears.

(1969)

THE GUEST

from *Criers and Kibitzers, Kibitzers and Criers*

STANLEY ELKIN

O n Sunday, Bertie walked into an apartment building in St. Louis, a city where, in the past, he had changed trains, waited for buses, or thought about Klaff, and where, more recently, truckers dropped him, or traveling salesmen stopped their Pontiacs downtown just long enough for him to reach into the back seat for his trumpet case and get out. In the hallway he stood before the brass mailboxed wall seeking the name of his friend, his friends' friend really, and his friends' friend's wife. The girl had danced with him at parties in the college town, and one night—he imagined he must have been particularly pathetic, engagingly pathetic—she had kissed him. The man, of course, patronized him, asked him questions that would have been more vicious had they been less naïve. He remembered he rather enjoyed making his long, patient answers. Condescension always brought the truth out of him. It was more appealing than indifference at least, and more necessary to him now. He supposed he didn't care for either of them, but he couldn't go further. He had to rest or he would die.

He found the name on the mailbox—Mr. and Mrs. Richard Preminger—the girl's identity, as he might have guessed, swallowed up in the husband's. It was no way to treat women, he thought gallantly.

He started up the stairs. Turning the corner at the second landing, he saw a man moving cautiously downward, burdened by boxes and suitcases and loose bags. Only as they passed each other did Bertie, through a momentary clearing in the boxes, recognize Richard Preminger.

"Old man, old man," Bertie said.

"Just a minute," Preminger said, forcing a package aside with his chin. Bertie stood, half a staircase above him, leaning against the wall. He grinned in the shadows, conscious of his ridiculous fedora, his eye patch rakishly black against the soft whiteness of his face. Black-suited, tiny, white-fleshed, he posed above Preminger, dapper as a scholarly waiter in a restaurant. He waited until he was recognized.

"Bertie? Bertie? Let me get rid of this stuff. Give me a hand, will you?" Preminger said.

"Sure," Bertie said. "It's on my family crest. One hand washing the other. Here, wait a minute." He passed Preminger on the stairs and held the door for him. He followed him outside.

"Take the key from my pocket, Bertie, and open the trunk. It's the blue convertible."

Bertie put his hand in Preminger's pocket. "You've got nice thighs," he said. To irritate Preminger he pretended to try to force the house key into the trunk lock. Preminger stood impatiently behind him, balancing his heavy burdens.

"I've been to Dallas, lived in a palace," Bertie said over his shoulder. "There's this great Eskimo who blows down there. Would you believe he's cut the best side ever recorded of 'Mood Indigo'?" Bertie shook the key ring as if it were a castanet.

Preminger dumped his load on the hood of the car and took the keys from Bertie. He opened the trunk and started to throw things into it. "Going somewhere?" Bertie asked.

"Vacation," Preminger said.

"Oh," Bertie said.

Preminger looked toward the apartment house. "I've got to go up for another suitcase, Bertie."

"Sure," Bertie said.

He went up the stairs behind Preminger. About halfway up he stopped to catch his breath. Preminger watched him curiously. He pounded his chest with his tiny fist and grinned weakly. *"Mea culpa,"* he said. "Mea booze. Mea sluts. Mea pot. Me-o-mea."

"Come on," Preminger said.

They went inside and Bertie heard a toilet flushing. Through a hall, through an open door, he saw Norma, Preminger's wife, staring absently into the bowl. "If she moves them now you won't have to stop at God knows what kind of place along the road," Bertie said brightly.

Norma lifted a big suitcase easily in her big hands and came into the living room. She stopped when she saw Bertie. "Bertie! Richard, it's Bertie."

"We bumped into each other in the hall," Preminger said.

Bertie watched the two of them look at each other.

"You sure picked a time to come visiting, Bertie," Preminger said.

"We're leaving on our vacation, Bertie," Norma said.

"We're going up to New England for a couple of weeks," Preminger told him.

"We can chat for a little with Bertie, can't we, Richard, before we go?"

"Of course," Preminger said. He sat down and pulled the suitcase next to him.

"It's very lovely in New England." Bertie sat down and crossed his legs. "I don't get up there very regularly. Not my territory. I've found that when a man makes it in the Ivy League he tends to forget about old Bertie," he said sadly.

"What are you doing in St. Louis, Bertie?" Preminger's wife asked him.

"It's my Midwestern swing," Bertie said. "I've been down South on the southern sponge. Opened up a whole new territory down there." He heard himself cackle.

"Who did you see, Bertie?" Norma asked him.

"You wouldn't know her. A cousin of Klaff's."

"Were you living with her?" Preminger asked.

Bertie shook his finger at him. The Premingers stared glumly at each other. Richard rubbed the plastic suitcase handle. In a moment, Bertie thought, he would probably say, "Gosh, Bertie, you should have written. You should have let us know." He should have written! Did the Fuller Brush man write? Who would be home? Who *wouldn't* be on vacation? They were commandos, the Fuller Brush man and he. He was tired, sick. He couldn't move on today. Would they kill him because of their lousy vacation?

Meanwhile the Premingers weren't saying anything. They stared at each other openly, their large eyes in their large heads on their large necks largely. He thought he could wait them out. It was what he *should* do. It should have been the easiest thing in the world to wait out the Premingers, to stare them down. Who was he kidding? It wasn't his forte. He had no forte. *That* was his forte. He could already hear himself begin to speak.

"Sure," he said. "I almost married that girl. Klaff's lady cousin. The first thing she ever said to me was, 'Bertie, they never build drugstores in the middle of the block. Always on corners.' It was the truth. Well, I thought, this was the woman for me. One time she came out of the ladies' john of a Greyhound bus station and she said, 'Bertie, have you ever noticed how public toilets often smell like bubble gum?' That's what it was like all the time. She had all these institutional insights. I was sure we could make it together. It didn't work out." He sighed.

Preminger stared at him, but Norma was beginning to soften. He wondered randomly what she would be like in bed. He looked coolly at her long legs, her wide shoulders. Like Klaff's cousin: institutional.

"Bertie, how are your eyes now?" she asked.

"Oh," he said, "still seeing double." He smiled. "Two for one. It's all right when there's something to look at. Other times I use the patch."

Norma seemed sad.

"I have fun with it," he said. "It doesn't make any difference which eye I cover. I'm ambidexterous." He pulled the black elastic band from his forehead. Instantly there were two large Richards, two large Normas. The Four Premingers like a troupe of Jewish acrobats. He felt surrounded. In the two living rooms his four hands fumbled with the two patches. He felt sick to his stomach. He closed one eye and hastily replaced the patch. "I shouldn't try that on an empty stomach," he said.

Preminger watched him narrowly. "Gee, Bertie," he said finally, "maybe we could drop you some place."

It was out of the question. He couldn't get into a car again. "Do you go through Minneapolis, Minnesota?" he asked indifferently.

Preminger looked confused, and Bertie liked him for a moment. "We were going to catch the Turnpike up around Chicago, Bertie."

"Oh, Chicago," Bertie said. "I can't go back to Chicago yet." Preminger nodded.

"Don't you know anybody else in St. Louis?" Norma asked.

"Klaff used to live across the river, but he's gone," Bertie said.

"Look, Bertie . . ." Preminger said.

"I'm fagged," Bertie said helplessly, "locked out."

"Bertie," Preminger said, "do you need any money? I could let you have twenty dollars."

Bertie put his hand out mechanically.

"This is stupid," Norma said suddenly. "Stay *here*."

"Oh, well—"

"No, I mean it. Stay *here*. We'll be gone for two weeks. What difference does it make?"

Preminger looked at his wife for a moment and shrugged. "Sure," he said, "there's no reason you *couldn't* stay here. As a matter of fact you'd be doing us a favor. I forgot to cancel the newspaper, the milk. You'd keep the burglars off. They don't bother a place if it looks lived in." He put twenty dollars on the coffee table. "There might be something you need," he explained.

Bertie looked carefully at them both. They seemed to mean it. Preminger and his wife grinned at him steadily, relieved at how easily they had come off. He enjoyed the idea himself. At last he had a real patron, a real matron. "Okay," he said.

"Then it's settled," Preminger said, rising.

"It's all right?" Bertie said.

"Certainly it's all right," Preminger said. "What harm could you do?"

"I'm harmless," Bertie said.

Preminger picked up the suitcase and led his wife toward the door. "Have a good time," Bertie said, following them. "I'll watch things for you. Rrgghh! Rrrgghhhfff!"

Preminger waved back at him as he went down the stairs. "Hey," Bertie called, leaning over the banister, "did I tell you about that crazy Klaff? You know what nutty Klaff did out at U.C.L.A.? He became a second-story man." They were already down the stairs.

Bertie pressed his back against the door and turned his head slowly across his left shoulder. He imagined himself photographed from underneath. "Odd man in," he said. He bounded into the center of the living room. I'll bet there's a lease, he thought. I'll bet there's a regular lease that goes with this place. He considered this respectfully, a little awed. He couldn't remember ever having been in a place where the tenants actually had to sign a lease. In the dining room he turned on the chandelier lights. "Sure there's a lease," Bertie said. He hugged himself. "How the fallen are mighty," he said.

In the living room he lay down on the couch without taking off his shoes. He sat up and pulled them off, but when he lay down again he was uneasy. He had gotten out of the habit, living the way he did, of sleeping without shoes. In his friends' leaseless basements the nights were cold and he wore them for warmth. He put the shoes on again, but found that he wasn't tired any more. It was a fact that dependence gave him energy. He was never so alert as when people did him favors. It was having to be on your own that made you tired.

"Certainly," Bertie said to the committee, "it's scientific. We've suspected it for years, but until our researchers divided up the town of Bloomington, Indiana, we had no proof. What our people found in that community was that the orphans and bastards were sleepy and run down, while the housewives and people on relief were wide awake, alert, raring to go. We can't positively state the link yet, but we're fairly certain that it's something to do with dependency—in league perhaps with a particularly virulent form of gratitude. Ahem. Ahem."

As he lectured the committee he wandered around the apartment, touring from right to left. He crossed from the living room into the dining room and turned right into the kitchen and then right again into Preminger's small study. "Here's where all the magic happens," Bertie said, glancing at the contour chair near Preminger's desk. He went back into the kitchen. "Here's where all the magic happens," he said, looking at Norma's electric stove. He stepped into the dining room and continued on, passing Norma's paintings of picturesque side streets in Mexico, of picturesque side streets in Italy, of picturesque side streets in Puerto Rico, until he came to a door that led to the back sun parlor. He went through it and found himself in a room with an easel, with paints in sexy little tubes, with brushes, with palettes and turpentine and rags. "Here's where all the magic happens," Bertie said and walked around the room to another door. He opened it and was in the Premingers' master bedroom. He looked at the bed. "Here's where all the magic happens," he said. Through a door at the other end of the room was another small hall. On the right was the toilet. He went in and flushed it. It was one of those toilets with instantly renewable tanks. He flushed it again. And again. "The only kind to have," he said out of the side of his mouth, imagining a rental agent. "I mean, it's like this. Supposing the missus has diarrhea or something. You don't want to have to wait until the tank fills up. Or suppose you're sick. Or suppose you're giving a party and it's mixed company. Well, it's just corny to whistle to cover the noise, know what I mean? 'S jus' corny. On the other hand, you flush it once suppose you're not through, then what happens? There's the damn noise after the water goes down. What have you accomplished? This way"—he reached across and jiggled the little lever and then did it a second time, a third, a fourth—"you never have any embarrassing interim, what we in the trade call 'flush lag.' "

He found the guest bedroom and knew at once that he would never sleep in it, that he would sleep in the Premingers' big bed.

"Nice place you got here," he said when he had finished the tour.

"Dooing de woh eet ees all I tink of, what I fahting foe," the man from the Underground said. "Here ees eet fahrproof, air-condizione and safe from Nazis."

"Stay out of Volkswagens, kid," Bertie said.

He went back into the living room. He wanted music, but it was a cardinal principle with him never to blow alone. He would drink alone, take drugs alone, but somehow for him the depths of depravity were represented by having to play jazz alone. He had a vision of himself in a cheap hotel room sitting on the edge of an iron bedstead. Crumpled packages of cigarettes were scattered throughout the room. Bottles of gin were on top of the Gideon Bible, the Western Union blanks. His trumpet was in his lap. "Perfect," Bertie said. "Norma Preminger could paint it in a picture." He shuddered.

The phonograph was in the hall between the dining room and living room. It was a big thing, with the AM and the FM and the short wave and the place where you plugged in the color television when it was perfected. He found records in Preminger's little room and went through them rapidly. "Ahmad Jamahl, for Christ's sake." Bertie took the record out of its sleeve and broke it across his knee. He stood up slowly and kicked the fragments of the broken recording into a neat pile.

He turned around and scooped up as many of Preminger's recordings as he could carry and brought them to the machine. He piled them on indiscriminately and listened with visible, professional discomfort. He listened to *The New World Symphony,* to Beethoven's *Fifth,* to *My Fair Lady.* The more he listened the more he began to dislike the Premingers. When he could stand it no longer he tore the playing arm viciously away from the record and looked around him. He saw the Premingers' bookcase.

"I'll read," Bertie said.

He took down the Marquis de Sade and Henry Miller and Ronald Firbank and turned the pages desultorily. Nothing happened. He tried reading aloud in front of a mirror. He went back to the bookcase and looked for *The Egg and I* and *Please Don't Eat the Daisies.* The prose of a certain kind of bright housewife always made Bertie feel erotic. But the Premingers owned neither book. He browsed through Rachel Carson's *Silent Spring* with his fly unzipped, but he felt only a mild lasciviousness.

He went into their bedroom and opened the closet. He found a pair of Norma's shoes and put them on. Although he was no fetishist, he had often promised himself that if he ever had the opportunity he would see what it was like. He got into drag and walked around the apartment in Norma's high heels. All he experienced was a pain in his calves.

In the kitchen he looked into the refrigerator. There were some frozen mixed vegetables in the freezer compartment. "I'll starve first," Bertie said.

He found a Billie Holiday record and put it on the phonograph. He hoped that out in Los Angeles, Klaff was being beaten with rubber hoses by the police. He looked up at the kitchen clock. "Nine," he said. "Only seven in L.A. They probably don't start beating them up till later."

"Talk, Klaff," he snarled, "or we'll drag you into the Blood Room."

"Flake off, copper," Klaff said.

"That's enough of that, Klaff. Take that and that and that."

"Bird lives!" Bertie screamed suddenly, invoking the dead Charlie Parker. It was his code cry.

"Mama may have," Billie Holiday wailed, "Papa may have, but God Bless the child who's got his own, who—oo—zz—"

"Who—oo—zz," Bertie wailed.

"Got his own," Billie said.

"I'll tell him when he comes in, William," Bertie said.

He waited respectfully until Billie was finished and then turned off the music.

He wondered why so many people felt that Norman Mailer was the greatest living American novelist.

He sat down on the Premingers' coffee table and marveled at his being alone in so big and well-furnished an apartment. The Premingers were probably the most substantial people he knew. Though plenty of the others wanted to, Bertie thought bitterly, Preminger was the only one from the old crowd who might make it. Of course he was Jewish, and that helped. Some Jews swung pretty good, but he always suspected that in the end they would hold out on you. But then who wouldn't, Bertie wondered. Kamikaze pilots, maybe. Anyway, this was Bertie's special form of anti-Semitism and he cherished it. Melvin Gimpel, for example, his old roommate. Every time Melvin tried to kill himself by sticking his head in the oven he left the kitchen window open. One time he found Gimpel on his knees with his head on the oven door, oddly like the witch in Hansel and Gretel. Bertie closed the window and shook Gimpel awake.

"Mel," he yelled, slapping him. *"Mel."*

"Bertie, go way. Leave me alone, I want to kill myself."

"Thank God," Bertie said. "Thank God I'm in time. When I found that window closed I thought it was all over."

"What, the window was closed? My God, was the *window* closed?"

"Melvin Gimpel is so simple
Thinks his nipple is a pimple,"

Bertie recited.

He hugged his knees, and felt again a wave of the nauseous sickness he had experienced that morning. "It's foreshadowing. One day as I am shoveling my walk I will collapse and die."

When the nausea left him he thought again about his situation. He had friends everywhere and made his way from place to place like an old-time slave on the Underground Railway. For all the pathos of the figure he knew he deliberately cut, there were always people to do him favors, give him money, beer, drugs, to nurse him back to his normal state of semi-invalidism, girls to kiss him in the comforting way he liked. This was probably the first time he had been alone in months. He felt like a dog whose master has gone away for the weekend. Just then he heard some people coming up the stairs and he growled experimentally. He went down on his hands and knees and scampered to the door, scratching it with his nails. "Rrrgghhf," he barked. "Rrgghhfff!" He heard whoever it was fumbling to open a door on the floor below him. He smiled, "Good dog," he said. "Good dog, goodog, gudug, gudugguduggudug."

He whined. He missed his master. A tear formed in the corner of his left eye. He crawled to a full-length mirror in the bathroom. "Ahh," he said. "Ahh." Seeing the patch across his eye, he had an inspiration. "Here, Patch," he called. "Come on, Patch." He romped after his own voice.

He moved beside Norma Preminger's easel in the sun parlor. He lowered his body carefully, pushing himself slightly backward with his arms. He yawned. He touched his chest to the wooden floor. He wagged his tail and then let himself fall heavily on one side. He pulled his legs up under him and fell asleep.

When Bertie awoke he was hungry. He fingered the twenty dollars in his pocket that Preminger had given him. He could order out. The light in the hall where the phone and phone books were was not good, so he tore "Restaurants" from the Yellow Pages and brought the sheets with him into the living room. Only two places delivered after one a.m. It was already one-thirty. He dialed the number of a pizza place across the city.

"Pal, bring over a big one, half shrimp, half mushroom. And two six-packs." He gave the address. The man explained that the truck had just gone out and that he shouldn't expect delivery for at least another hour and a half.

"Put it in a cab," Bertie said. "While Bird lives Bertie spends."

He took out another dozen or so records and piled them on the machine. He sat down on the couch and drummed his trumpet case with his fingers. He opened the case and fit the mouthpiece to the body of the horn. He put the trumpet to his lips and experienced the unpleasant shock of cold metal he always felt. He still thought it strange that men could mouth metal this way, ludicrous that his professional attitude should be a kiss. He blew a few bars in accompaniment to the record and then put the trumpet back in the case. He felt in the side pockets of the trumpet case and took out two pairs of dirty underwear, some handkerchiefs and three pairs of socks. He unrolled one of the pairs of socks and saw with pleasure that the drug was still there. He took out the bottle of carbon tetrachloride. This was what he cleaned his instrument with, and it was what he would use to kill himself when he had finally made the decision.

He held the bottle to the light. "If nothing turns up," he said, "I'll drink this. And to hell with the kitchen window."

The cab driver brought the pizza and Bertie gave him the twenty dollars.

"I can't change that," the driver said.

"Did I ask you to change it?" Bertie said.

"That's twenty bucks there."

"Bird lives. Easy come, easy go go go," Bertie said.

The driver started to thank him.

"Go." He closed the door.

He spread Norma Preminger's largest tablecloth over the dining-room table and then, taking china and silver from the big breakfront, laid several place settings. He found champagne glasses.

Unwrapping the pizza, he carefully plucked all the mush-rooms from it ("American mushrooms," he said. "Very square. No visions.") and laid them in a neat pile on the white linen. ("Many mushloom," he said. "Mushloom crowd.") He poured some beer into a champagne glass and rose slowly from his chair.

"Gentlemen," he said, "to the absent Klaff. May the police in Los Angeles, California, beat his lousy ass off." He drank off all the beer in one gulp and tossed the glass behind him over his shoulder. He heard it shatter and then a soft sizzling sound. Turning around, he saw that he had hit one of Norma's paintings right in a picturesque side street. Beer dripped ignobly down a donkey's leg. "Goddamn," Bertie said appreciatively, "*action* painting."

He ate perhaps a quarter of the pizza before rising from the table, wiping the corner of his lips with a big linen napkin. "Gentlemen," he said. "I propose that the ladies retire to the bedroom while we men enjoy our cigars and port and some good talk."

"I propose that we men retire to the bedroom and enjoy the ladies," he said in Gimpel's voice.

"Here, here," he said in Klaff's voice. "Here, here. Good talk. Good talk."

"If you will follow me, gentlemen," Bertie said in his own voice. He began to walk around the apartment. "I have often been asked the story of my life. These requests usually follow a personal favor someone has done me, a supper shared, a bed made available, a ride in one of the several directions. Indeed, I have become a sort of troubadour who does not sing so much as whine for his supper. Most of you—"

"Whine is very good with supper," Gimpel said.

"Gimpel, my dear, why don't you run into the kitchen and

play?" Bertie said coolly. "Many of you may know the humble beginnings, the sordid details, the dark Freudian patterns, and those of you who are my friends—"

Klaff belched.

"Those of you who are my *friends,* who do not run off to mix it up with the criminal element in the far West, have often wondered what will ultimately happen to me, to 'Poor Bertie' as I am known in the trade."

He unbuttoned his shirt and let it fall to the floor. In his undershirt he looked defenseless, his skin pale as something seen in moonlight. "Why, you wonder, doesn't he do something about himself, pull himself up by his bootstraps? Why, for example, doesn't he get his eyes fixed? Well, I've tried."

He kicked off his shoes. "You have all admired my bushy mustache. Do you remember that time two years ago I dropped out of sight for four months? Well, let me tell you what happened that time."

He took off his black pants. "I had been staying with Royal Randle, the distinguished philologist and drunk. You will recall what Royal, Klaff, Myers, Gimpel and myself once were to each other. Regular Whiffenpoofs we were. Damned from here to eternity. Sure, sure." He sighed. "You remember Randle's promises: 'It won't make any difference, Bertie. It won't make any difference, Klaff. It won't make any difference, fellas.' He married the girl in the muu-muu."

He was naked now except for his socks. He shivered once and folded his arms across his chest. "Do you know why the girl in the muu-muu married Randle?" He paused dramatically. "*To get at me, that's why!* The others she didn't care about. She knew even before I did what they were like. Even what *Klaff* was like. She knew they were corrupt, that they had it in them to sell me out, to settle down—that all anyone had to do was wave their deaths in front of them and they'd come running, that reason and fucking money and getting it steady would win again. But in me she recognized the real enemy, the last of the go-to-hell-goddamn-its. Maybe the first.

"They even took me with them on their honeymoon. At the time I thought it was a triumph for dependency, but it was just a trick, that's all. The minute they were married, this girl in the muu-muu was after Randle to do something about Bertie. And it wasn't 'Poor' Bertie this time. It was she who got me the appointment with the mayor. Do you know what His Honor said to me? 'Shave your mustache and I'll give you a job clerking in one of my supermarkets.' Christ, friends, do you know I *did* it? Well, I'm not made of stone. They had taken me on their honeymoon, for God's sake."

He paused.

"I worked in that supermarket *for three hours*. Clean-shaved. My mustache sacrificed as an earnest to the mayor. Well, I'm telling you, you don't know what square *is* till you've worked in a supermarket for three hours. They pipe in Mantovani. Mantovani! I cleared out for four months to raise my mustache again and to forget. What you see now isn't the original, you understand. It's all second growth, and believe me it's not the same."

He drew aside the shower curtain and stepped into the tub. He paused with his hand on the tap. "But I tell you this, friends. I would rather be a mustached bum than a clean-shaved clerk. I'll work. Sure I will. When they pay anarchists! When they subsidize the hip! When they give grants to throw bombs! When they shell out for gainsaying!"

Bertie pulled the curtain and turned on the faucet. The rush of water was like applause.

After his shower Bertie went into the second bedroom and carefully removed the spread from the cot. Then he punched the pillow and mussed the bed. "Very clever," he said. "It wouldn't do to let them think I never slept here." He had once realized with sudden clarity that he would never, so long as he lived, make a bed.

Then he went into the other bedroom and ripped the spread from the big double bed. For some time, in fact since he had first seen it, Bertie had been thinking about this bed. It was the biggest bed he would ever sleep in. He thought invariably in such terms. One cigarette in a pack would suddenly become distinguished in his mind as the best, or the worst, he would smoke that day. A homely act, such as tying his shoelaces, if it had occurred with unusual ease, would be remembered forever. This lent to his vision an oblique sadness, conscious as he was that he was forever encountering experiences which would never come his way again.

He slipped his naked body between the sheets, but no sooner had he made himself comfortable than he became conscious of the phonograph, still playing in the little hall. He couldn't hear it very well. He thought about turning up the volume, but he had read somewhere about neighbors. Getting out of bed, he moved the heavy machine through the living room, pushing it with difficulty over the seamed, bare wooden floor, trailing deep scratches. Remember not to walk barefoot there, he thought. At one point one of the legs caught in a loop of the Premingers' shag rug and Bertie strained to free it, finally breaking the thick thread and producing an interesting pucker along one end of the rug, not unlike the pucker in raised theatrical curtains. At last he had maneuvered the machine into the hall just outside the bedroom and plugged it in. He went back for the Billie Holiday recording he had heard earlier and put it on the phonograph. By fiddling with the machine, he fixed it so that the record would play all night.

Bertie got back into the bed. "Ah," he said, "the *sanctum sanctorum.*" He rolled over and over from one side of the bed to the other. He tucked his knees into his chest and went under the covers. "It makes you feel kind of small and insignificant," he said.

"Ladies and gentlemen, this is Graham Macnamee speaking to you from the Cave of the Winds. I have made my way into the heart of this darkness to find my friend, Poor Bertie, who, as you know, entered the bed eight weeks ago. Bertie is with me now, and while there isn't enough light for me to be able to see his condition, his voice may tell us something about his physical state. Bertie, just what *is* the official record?"

"Well, Graham, some couples have been known to stick it out for seventy-five years. Of course, your average is much less than that, but still—"

"Seventy-five years."

"Seventy-five, yes sir. It's amazing, isn't it, Graham, when you come to think? All that time in one bed."

"It certainly is," Graham Macnamee said. "Do you think you'll be able to go the distance, Bert?"

"Who, me? No, no. A lot of folks have misunderstood my purpose in coming here. I'm rather glad you've given me the opportunity to clear that up. Actually my work here is scientific. This isn't a stunt or anything like that. I'm here to learn."

"Can you tell us about it, Bert?"

"Graham, it's been a fascinating experience, if you know what I mean, but frankly there are many things we still don't understand. *I* don't know why they do it. All that licit love, that regularity. Take the case of Richard and Norma, for example—and incidentally, you don't want to overlook the significance of that name 'Norma.' Norma/Normal, you see?"

"Say, I never thought of that."

"Well, I'm trained to think like that, Graham. In my work you have to."

"Say," Graham Macnamee said.

"Sure. Well, the thing is this, buddy, when I first came into this bed I felt the aura, know what I mean, the *power.* I think it's built into the mattress or something."

"Say."

"Shut your face, Graham, and let me speak, will you please? Well, anyway, you feel surrounded. Respectable. Love is made here, of course, but it's not love as we know it. There are things that must remain mysteries until we have more facts. I mean, Graham, checks could be cashed in this bed, for Christ's sake, credit cards honored. It's ideal for family reunions, high teas. Graham, it's the kind of place you wouldn't be ashamed to take your mother."

"Go to sleep, Bert," Graham Macnamee said.

"Say," Bertie said.

Between the third and fourth day of his stay in the Premingers' apartment Bertie became restless. He had not been outside the house since the Sunday he arrived, even to bring in the papers Preminger had told him about. (Indeed, it was by counting the papers that he knew how long he had been there, though he couldn't be sure, since he didn't know whether the Premingers had taken the Sunday paper along with them.) He could see them on the back porch through the window of Norma's sun parlor. With the bottles of milk they made a strange little pile. After all, he was not a caretaker; he was a guest. Preminger could bring in his own papers, drink his own damn milk. For the same reasons he had determined not even to answer the phone when it rang.

One evening he tried to call Klaff at the Los Angeles County Jail, but the desk sergeant wouldn't get him. He wouldn't even take a message.

Although he had not been outside since Sunday, Bertie had only a vague desire to leave the apartment. He weighed this against his real need to rest and his genuine pleasure in being alone in so big a place. Like the man in the joke who does not leave his Miami hotel room because it is costing him thirty-five dollars a day, Bertie decided he had better remain inside.

With no money left he was reduced to eating the dry, cold remainder of the pizza, dividing it mathematically into a week's provisions, like someone on a raft. (He actually fancied himself, not on a raft perhaps, but set alone and drifting on, say, the *Queen Mary*.) To supplement the pizza he opened some cans of soup he found in the pantry and drank the contents straight, without heating it or even adding water. Steadily he drank away at the Premingers' modest stock of liquor. The twelve cans of beer had been devoured by the second morning, of course.

After the second full day in the apartment his voices began to desert him. It was only with difficulty that he could manage his imitations, and only for short lengths of time. The glorious discussions that had gone on long into the night were now out of the question. He found he could not do Gimpel's voice any more, and even Klaff's was increasingly difficult and largely confined to his low, caressing obscenities. Mostly he talked with himself, although it was a real strain to keep up his end of the conversation, and it always made him cry when he said how pathetic he was and asked himself where do you go from here. Oh, to be like Bird, he thought. Not to have to be a bum. To ask, as it were, no quarter.

At various times during the day he would call out "Bird lives" in seeming stunning triumph. But he didn't believe it.

He watched a lot of television. "I'm getting ammunition," he said. "It's scientific."

Twice a day he masturbated in the Premingers' bed.

He settled gradually, then, into restlessness. He knew, of course, that he had it always in his power to bring himself back up to the heights he had known in those wonderful first two days. He was satisfied, however, not to use this power, and thought of himself as a kind of soldier, alone in a foxhole, in enemy territory, at night, at a bad time in the war, with one bullet in his pistol. Oddly, he derived more pride—and comfort, and a queer security—from this single bullet than others might have from whole cases of ammunition. It was his *strategic* bullet, the one he would use to get the big one, turn the tide, make the difference. The Premingers would be away two weeks. He would not waste his ammunition. Just as he divided the stale pizza, cherishing each piece as much for the satisfaction he took from possessing it during a time of emergency as for any sustenance it offered, so he enjoyed his knowledge that at any time he could recoup his vanishing spirits. He shared with the squares ("Use their own weapons to beat them, Bertie") a special pride in adversity, in having to do without, in having to expose whatever was left of his character to the narrower straits. It was strange, he thought seriously, it was the paradox of the world and an institutional insight that might have come right out of the mouth of that slut in Dallas, but the most peculiar aspect of the squares wasn't their lack of imagination or their bland bad taste, but their ability, like the wildest fanatics, like the furthest out of the furthest out, to cling to the illogical, finally untenable notion that they must have and have in order to live, at the same time that they realized that it was better not to have. What seemed so grand to Bertie, who admired all impossible positions, was that they believed both things with equal intensity, never suspecting for a moment any inconsistency. And here was Bertie, Bertie thought, here was Bertie inside their capitol, on the slopes of their mountains, on their smooth shores, who believed neither of these propositions, who believed in not having and in not suffering too, who yet realized the very same pleasure that they would in having and not using. It was the strangest thing that would ever happen to him, he thought.

"Are you listening, Klaff, you second-story fink?" Bertie yelled. "Do you see how your old pal is developing what is called character?"

And so, master of himself for once, he resolved—feeling what someone taking a vow feels—not to use the last of his drugs until the strategic moment of strategic truth.

That was Wednesday evening. By Thursday morning he had decided to break his resolution. He had not yielded to temptation, had not lain fitfully awake all night—indeed, his resolution had given him the serenity to sleep well—in the sweaty throes of withdrawal. There had been no argument or rationalization, nor had he decided that he had reached his limit or that this was the strategic moment he had been waiting for. He yielded as he always yielded: spontaneously, suddenly, unexpectedly, as the result neither of whim nor of calculation. His important decisions were almost always reached without his knowledge, and he was often as surprised as the next one to see what he was going to do—to see, indeed, that he was already doing it. (Once someone had asked him whether he believed in Free Will, and after considering this for a moment as it applied to himself, Bertie had answered "Free? Hell, it's positively *loose*.")

Having discovered his new intention, he was eager to realize it. As often as he had taken drugs (he never called it anything but drugs, never used the cute or obscene names, never even said "dope"; to him it was always "drugs," medicine for his spirit), they were still a major treat for him. "It's a rich man's game," he had once told Klaff, and then he had leaned back philosophically. "You know, Klaff, it's a good thing I'm poor. When I think of the snobbish ennui of your wealthy junkies, I realize that they don't know how to appreciate their blessings. God keep me humble, Klaff. Abstinence makes the heart grow fonder, a truer word was never spoken."

Nor did a drug ever lose its potency for him. If he graduated from one to another, it was not in order to recover some fading jolt, but to experience a new and different one. He held in contempt all those who professed disenchantment with the drugs they had been raised on, and frequently went back to rediscover the old pleasures of marijuana, as a sentimental father might chew some of his boy's bubble gum. "Loyalty, Gimpel," he exclaimed, "loyalty, do you know what *that* is?"

Bertie would and did try anything, though currently his favorite was mescaline for the visions it induced. Despite what he considered his eclectic tastes in these matters, there were one or two things he would not do, however. He never introduced any drug by hypodermic needle. This he found disgusting and, frankly, painful. He often said he could stand anything but pain and was very proud of his clear, unpunctured skin. "Not a mark on me," he would say, waving his arms like a professional boxer. The other thing he would not do was take his drugs in the presence of other users, for he found the company of addicts offensive. However, he was not above what he called "seductions." A seduction for him was to find some girl and talk her into letting him share his drugs with her. Usually it ended in their lying naked in a bed together, both of them serene, absent of all desire and what Bertie called "unclean thoughts."

"You know," he would say to the girl beside him, "I think that if all the world's leaders would take drugs and lie down on the bed naked like this without any unclean thoughts, the cause of world peace would be helped immeasurably. What do you think?"

"I think so too," she would say.

Once he knew he was going to take the drug, Bertie made his preparations. He went first to his trumpet case and took out the last small packet of powder. He opened it carefully, first closing all the windows so that no sudden draft could blow any of it away. This had once happened to a friend of his, and Bertie had never forgotten the warning.

"I am not one on whom a lesson is lost," Bertie said.

"You're okay, Bertie," a Voice said. "Go save France."

He placed the packet on the Premingers' coffee table and carefully spread the paper, exactly like the paper wrapper around a stick of chewing gum, looking almost lustfully at the soft, flat layer of ground white powder. He held out his hand to see how steady it was, and although he was not really shaky he did not trust himself to lift the paper from the table. He brought a water tumbler from the kitchen and gently placed it upside down on top of the powder. He was not yet ready to take it. Bertie was a man who postponed his pleasures as long as he possibly could; he let candy dissolve in his mouth and played with the threads on his tangerine before eating the fruit. It was a weakness in his character perhaps, but he laid it lovingly at the feet of his poverty.

He decided to wait until sundown to take the drug, reasoning that when it wore off, it would be early next morning and he would be ready for bed. Sleep was one of his pleasures too, and he approved of regularity in small things, taking a real pride in being able to keep hours. To pass the time until sundown he looked for something to do. First he found some tools and busied himself by taking Norma's steam iron apart. There was still time left after that, so he took a canvas and painted a picture. Because he did not know how to draw he simply covered the canvas first with one color and then with another, applying layer after layer of the paint thickly. Each block of color he made somewhat smaller than the last, so that the finished painting portrayed successive jagged margins of color. He stepped back and considered his work seriously.

"Well, it has texture, Bertie," Hans Hoffman said.

"Bertie," the Voice said suddenly, "I don't like to interrupt when you're working, but it's sundown."

"So it is," he said, looking up.

He went back into the living room and removed the tumbler. Taking up the paper in his fingers and creasing it as if he were a cowboy rolling a cigarette, Bertie tilted his head far back and inhaled the powder deeply. This part was always uncomfortable for him. "Ooo," he said, "the bubbles." He stuffed the last few grains up his nose with his fingers. "Waste not, want not," he said.

He sat down to wait. After half an hour in which nothing

happened, Bertie became uneasy. "It's been cut," he said. "Sure, depend upon friends to do you favors." He was referring to the fact that the mescaline had been a going-away present from friends in Oklahoma City. He decided to give it fifteen more minutes. "Nothing," he said at last, disappointed. "Nothing."

The powder, as it always did, left his throat scratchy, and there was a bitter taste in his mouth. His soft palate prickled. He seized the water tumbler from the coffee table and walked angrily into the kitchen. He ran the cold water, then gargled and spit in the sink. In a few minutes the bitter taste and the prickly sensation subsided and he felt about as he had before he took the drug. He was conscious, however, of a peculiar smell, unpleasant, unfamiliar, nothing like the odor of rotting flowers he associated with the use of drugs. He opened a window and leaned out, breathing the fresh air. But as soon as he came away from the window, the odor was again overpowering. He went to see if he could smell it in the other rooms. When he had made his tour he realized that the stench *must* be coming from the kitchen. Holding his breath, he came back to see if he could locate its source. The kitchen was almost as Norma had left it. He had done no cooking, and although there were some empty soup and beer cans in the sink he knew *they* couldn't be causing the odor. He shrugged. Then he noticed the partially closed door to Preminger's study.

"Of course," Bertie said. "Whatever it is must be in there." He pushed the door open. In the middle of the floor were two blackish mounds that looked like dark sawdust. Bertie stepped back in surprise.

"Camel shit," he said. "My God, how did *that* get in here?" He went closer to investigate. "That's what it is, all right." He had never seen it before but a friend had, and had described it to him. This stuff fitted the description perfectly. He considered what to do.

"I can't leave it there," he said. He found a dustpan and a broom, and propping the pan against the leg of Preminger's chair, began to sweep the stuff up. He was surprised at how remarkably gummy it seemed. When he finished he washed the spot on the floor with a foaming detergent and stepped gingerly to the back door. He lifted the lid of the garbage can and shoved the broom and the contents of the dustpan and the dustpan itself into the can. Then he went to the bathroom and washed his hands.

In the living room he saw the Chinaman. "Jesus," Bertie said breathlessly.

The Chinaman lowered his eyes in a shy, almost demure smile. He said nothing, but motioned Bertie to sit in the chair across from him. Bertie, too frightened to disobey, sat down.

He waited for the Chinaman to tell him what he wanted. After an hour (he heard the chime clock strike nine times and then ten times), when the Chinaman still had not said anything, he began to feel a little calmer. Maybe he was just tired, Bertie thought, and came in to rest. He realized that perhaps he and the Chinaman had more in common than had at first appeared. He looked at the fellow in this new light and saw that he had been foolish to fear him. The Chinaman was small, smaller even than Bertie. In fact, he was only two feet tall. Perhaps what made him seem larger was the fact that he was wrapped in wide, voluminous white silk robes. Bertie stared at the robes, fascinated by the delicate filigree trim up and down their length. To see this closer he stood up and walked tentatively toward the Chinaman.

The Chinaman gazed steadily to the front, and Bertie, seeing no threat, continued toward him. He leaned down over the Chinaman, and gently grasping the delicate lace-work between his forefinger and his thumb, drew it toward his eye. "May I?" Bertie asked. "I know a good deal about this sort of thing."

The Chinaman lowered his eyes.

Bertie examined the weird symbols and designs, and although he did not understand them, recognized at once their cabalistic origin.

"Magnificent," Bertie said at last. "My God, the man hours that must have gone into this. *The sheer craftsmanship!* That's really a terrific robe you've got there."

The Chinaman lowered his eyes still further.

Bertie sat down in his chair again. He heard the clock strike eleven and he smiled at the Chinaman. He was trying to be sympathetic, patient. He knew the fellow had his reasons for coming and that in due time they would be revealed, but he couldn't help being a little annoyed. First the failure of the drug and then the camel shit on the floor and now this. However, he remained very polite.

There was nothing else to do, so he concentrated on the Chinaman's face.

Then a strange thing happened.

He became aware, as he scrutinized the face, of some things he hadn't noticed before. First he realized that it was the oldest face he had ever seen. He knew that this face was old enough to have looked on Buddha's. It was only *faintly* yellow, really, and he understood with a sweeping insight that originally it must have been white, as it still largely was, a striking, flat white, naked as a sheet, bright as teeth, that its yellowness was an intrusion, the intruding yellowness of

fantastic age, of pages in ancient books. As soon as he per-
ceived this he understood the origin and mystery of the
races. All men had at first been white; their different tints
were only the shades of their different wisdoms. Of course,
he thought. Of course. It's beautiful. Beautiful!

The second thing Bertie noticed was that the face seemed
extraordinarily wise. The longer he stared at it the wiser it
seemed. Clearly this was the wisest Chinaman, and thus the
wisest man, in the history of the world. Now he was impatient for the Chinaman to speak, to tell him his secrets, but
he also understood that so long as he was impatient the Chinaman would *not* speak, that he must become serene, as
serene as the Chinaman himself, or else the Chinaman would
go away. As this occurred to him the Chinaman smiled and
Bertie knew he had been right. He was aware that if he just
sat there, deliberately trying to become serene, nothing
would happen. He decided that the best way to become
serene was to ignore the Chinaman, to go on about his business as if the Chinaman weren't even there.

He stood up. "Am I getting warm?" Bertie asked.

The Chinaman lowered his eyes and smiled.

"Well, then," Bertie said, rubbing his hands, "let's see."

He went into the kitchen to see if there was anything he
could do there to make him serene.

He washed out the empty cans of soup.

He strolled into the bedroom and made the bed. This took
him an hour. He heard the clock strike twelve and then one.

He took a record off the machine, and starting from the
center hole and working to the outer edge, counted all the
ridges. This took him fourteen seconds.

He found a suitcase in one of the closets and packed all of
Norma's underwear into it.

He got a pail of water and some soap and washed all the walls in the small bedroom.

It was in the dining room, however, that he finally achieved serenity. He studied Norma's pictures of side streets throughout the world and with sudden insight understood what was wrong with them. He took some tubes of white paint and with a brush worked over the figures, painting back into the flesh all their original whiteness. He made the Mexicans white, the Negroes white, feeling as he worked an immense satisfaction, the satisfaction not of the creator, nor even of the reformer, but of the restorer.

Swelling with serenity, Bertie went back into the living room and sat down in his chair. For the first time the Chinaman met his gaze directly, and Bertie realized that something important was going to happen.

Slowly, very slowly, the Chinaman began to open his mouth. Bertie watched the slow parting of the Chinaman's thin lips, the gleaming teeth, white and bright as fence pickets. Gradually the rest of the room darkened and the thinly padded chair on which Bertie sat grew incredibly soft. He knew that they had been transported somehow, that they were now in a sort of theater. The Chinaman was seated on a kind of raised platform. Meanwhile the mouth continued to open, slowly as an ancient drawbridge. Tiny as the Chinaman was, the mouth seemed enormous. Bertie gazed into it, seeing nothing. At last, deep back in the mouth, he saw a brief flashing, as of a small crystal on a dark rock suddenly illuminated by the sun. In a moment he saw it again, brighter now, longer sustained. Soon it was so bright that he had to force himself to look at it. Then the mouth went black. Before he could protest, the brightness was overwhelming again and he saw a cascade of what seemed like diamonds tumble out of the Chinaman's mouth. It was the Chinaman's tongue.

Twisting, turning over and over like magicians' silks pulled endlessly from a tube, the tongue continued to pour from the Chinaman's mouth. Bertie saw that it had the same whiteness as the rest of his face, and that it was studded with bright, beautiful jewels. On the tongue, long now as an unfurled scroll, were thick black Chinese characters. It was the secret of life, of the world, of the universe. Bertie could barely read for the tears of gratitude in his eyes. Desperately he wiped the tears away with his fists. He looked back at the tongue and stared at the strange words, realizing that he could not read Chinese. He was sobbing helplessly now because he knew there was not much time. The presence of the Chinaman gave him courage and strength and he *forced* himself to read the Chinese. As he concentrated it became easier, the characters somehow re-forming, translating themselves into a sort of decipherable Chinesey script, like the words "Chop Suey" on the neon sign outside a Chinese restaurant. He was breathless from his effort and the stunning glory of what was being revealed to him. Frequently he had to pause, punctuating his experience with queer little squeals. "Oh," he said. "Oh. Oh."

Then it was over.

He was exhausted, but his knowledge glowed in him like fire. "So *that's* it" was all he could say. "So *that's* it. So *that's* it."

Bertie saw that he was no longer in the theater. The Chinaman was gone and Bertie was back in the Premingers' living room. He struggled for control of himself. He knew it was urgent that he tell someone what had happened to him. Desperately he pulled open his trumpet case. Inside he had pasted sheets with the names, addresses and phone numbers of all his friends.

"Damn Klaff," he said angrily. "Damn Second-Story Klaff in his lousy jail."

He spotted Gimpel's name and the phone number of his boarding house in Cincinnati. Tearing the sheet from where it was pasted inside the lid, he rushed to the phone and placed the call. "Life and death," he screamed at Gimpel's bewildered landlady. "Life and death."

When Gimpel came to the phone Bertie began to tell him, coherently, but with obvious excitement, all that had happened. Gimpel was as excited as himself.

"Then the Chinaman opened his mouth and this tongue with writing on it came out."

"Yeah?" Gimpel said. "Yeah? Yeah?"

"Only it was in Chinese," Bertie shouted.

"Chinese," Gimpel said.

"But I could read it, Gimpel! *I could read it!*"

"I didn't know you could read Chinese," Gimpel said.

"It was the meaning of life."

"Yeah?" Gimpel said. "Yeah? What'd it say? What'd it say?"

"What?" Bertie said.

"What'd it say? What'd the Chink's tongue say was the meaning of life?"

"I forget," Bertie said and hung up.

He slept until two the next afternoon, and when he awoke he felt as if he had been beaten up. His tongue was something that did not quite fit in his mouth, and throughout his body he experienced a looseness of the bones, as though his skeleton were a mobile put together by an amateur. He groaned dispiritedly, his eyes still closed. He knew he had to get up out of the bed and take a shower and shave and dress, that only by making extravagant demands on it would his body give him any service at all. "You *will* make the Death March," he warned it ruthlessly.

He opened his eyes and what he saw disgusted him and turned his stomach. His eye patch had come off during the night and now there were two of everything. He saw one eye patch on one pillow and another eye patch on another pillow. Hastily he grabbed for it, but he had chosen the wrong pillow. He reached for the other eye patch and the other pillow, but somehow he had put out one of his illusory hands. It did not occur to him to shut one eye. At last, by covering all visible space, real or illusory, with all visible fingers, real or illusory—like one dragging a river—he recovered the patch and pulled it quickly over one of his heads.

He stood stunned in his hot shower, and then shaved, cutting his neck badly. He dressed.

"Whan 'e iz through his toilette, *Monsieur* will see how much better 'e feel," his valet said. He doubted it and didn't answer.

In the dining room he tried not to look at Norma's paintings, but could not help noticing that overnight many of her sunny side streets had become partial snow scenes. He had done that, he remembered, though he could not now recall exactly why. It seemed to have something to do with a great anthropological discovery he had made the night before. He finished the last of the pizza, gagging on it briefly.

Considering the anguish of his body, it suddenly occurred to him that perhaps he was hooked. Momentarily this appealed to his sense of the dramatic, but then he realized that it would be a terrible thing to have happen to him. He could not afford to be hooked, for he knew with a sense of calm sadness that his character could no more sustain the responsibility of a steady drug habit than it could sustain the responsibility of any other kind of pattern.

"Oh, what a miserable bastard I am," Bertie said.

In near-panic he considered leaving the Premingers' apartment immediately, but he knew that he was in no condition to travel. "You wouldn't make it to the corner," he said.

He felt massively sorry for himself. The more he considered it the more certain it appeared that he was hooked. It was terrible. Where would he get the money to buy the drugs? What would they do to his already depleted physical resources? "Oh, what a miserable bastard I am," he said again.

To steady himself he took a bottle of Scotch from the shelf in the pantry. Bertie did not like hard liquor. Though he drank a lot, it was beer he drank, or, when he could get them, the sweeter cordials. Scotch and bourbon had always seemed vaguely square to him. But he had already finished the few liqueurs that Preminger had, and now nothing was left but Scotch. He poured himself an enormous drink.

Sipping it calmed him—though his body still ached— and he considered what to do. If he *was* hooked, the first thing was to tell his friends. Telling his friends his latest failure was something Bertie regarded as a sort of responsibility. Thus his rare letters to them usually brought Bertie's intimates—he laughed at the word—nothing but bad news. He would write that a mistress had given him up, and, with his talent for mimicry, would set down her last long disappointed speech to him, in which she exposed in angry, honest language the hollowness of his character, his infinite weakness as a man, his vileness. When briefly he had turned to homosexuality to provide himself with funds, the first thing he did was write his friends about it. Or he wrote of being fired from bands when it was discovered how bad a trumpeter he really was. He spared neither himself nor his friends in his passionate self-denunciations.

Almost automatically, then, he went into Preminger's study and began to write all the people he could think of. As he wrote he pulled heavily at the whiskey remaining in the bottle. At first the letters were long, detailed accounts of symptoms and failures and dashed hopes, but as evening came on and he grew inarticulate he realized that it was more important—and, indeed, added to the pathos of his situation—for him just to get the facts to them.

"Dear Klaff," he wrote at last, "I am hooked. I am at the bottom, Klaff. I don't know what to do." Or "Dear Randle, I'm hooked. Tell your wife. I honestly don't know where to turn." And "Dear Myers, how are your wife and kids? Poor Bertie is hooked. He is thinking of suicide."

He had known for a long time that one day he would have to kill himself. It would happen, and even in the way he had imagined. One day he would simply drink the bottle of carbon tetrachloride. But previously he had been in no hurry. Now it seemed like something he might have to do before he had meant to, and what he resented most was the idea of having to change his plans.

He imagined what people would say.

"I let him down, Klaff," Randle said.

"Everybody let him down," Klaff said.

"Everybody let him down," Bertie said. "Everybody let him down."

Weeping, he took a last drink from Preminger's bottle, stumbled into the living room and passed out on the couch.

• • •

That night Bertie was awakened by a flashlight shining in his eyes. He threw one arm across his face defensively and struggled to sit up. So clumsy were his efforts that whoever was holding the flashlight started to laugh.

"Stop that," Bertie said indignantly, and thought, I have never been so indignant in the face of danger.

"You said they were out of town," a voice said. The voice did not come from behind the flashlight, and Bertie wondered how many there might be.

"Jesus, I thought so. Nobody's answered the phone for days. I never seen a guy so plastered. He stinks."

"Kill him," the first voice said.

Bertie stopped struggling to get up.

"Kill him," the voice repeated.

"What is this?" Bertie said thickly. "What is this?"

"Come on, he's so drunk he's harmless," the second voice said.

"Kill him," the first voice said again.

"You kill him," the second voice said.

The first voice giggled.

They were playing with him, Bertie knew. Nobody who did not know him could want him dead.

"Turn on the lights," Bertie said.

"Screw that," the second voice said. "You just sit here in the dark, sonny, and you won't get hurt."

"We're wasting time," the first voice said.

A beam from a second flashlight suddenly intersected the beam from the first.

"Say," Bertie said nervously, "it looks like the opening of a supermarket."

Bertie could hear them working in the dark, moving boxes, pulling drawers.

"Are you folks Negroes?" Bertie called. No one answered him. "I mean I dig Negroes, man—*men.* Miles. Jay Jay. Bird lives." He heard a closet door open.

"You *are* robbing the place, right? I mean you're actually *stealing,* aren't you? This isn't just a social call. Maybe you know my friend Klaff."

The men came back into the living room. From the sound of his footsteps Bertie knew one of them was carrying something heavy.

"I've got the TV," the first voice said.

"There are some valuable paintings in the dining room," Bertie said.

"Go see," the first voice said.

One of Norma's pictures suddenly popped out of the darkness as the man's light shone on it.

"Crap," the second voice said.

"You cats can't be all bad," Bertie said.

"Any furs?" It was a third voice, and it startled Bertie. Someone flashed a light in Bertie's face. "Hey, you," the voice repeated, "does your wife have any furs?"

"Wait a minute," Bertie said as though it were a fine point they must be made to understand, "you've got it wrong. This isn't *my* place. I'm just taking care of it while my friends are gone." The man laughed.

Now all three flashlights were playing over the apartment. Bertie hoped a beam might illuminate one of the intruders, but this never happened. Then he realized that he didn't want it to happen, that he was safe as long as he didn't recognize any of them. Suddenly a light caught one of the men behind the ear. "Watch that light. Watch that light," Bertie called out involuntarily.

"I found a trumpet," the second voice said.

"Hey, that's mine," Bertie said angrily. Without thinking, he got up and grabbed for the trumpet. In the dark he was able to get his fingers around one of the valves, but the man snatched it away from him easily. Another man pushed him back down on the couch.

"Could you leave the carbon tetrachloride?" Bertie asked miserably.

In another ten minutes they were ready to go. "Shouldn't we do something about the clown?" the third voice said.

"Nah," the second voice said.

They went out the front door.

Bertie sat in the darkness. "I'm drunk," he said after a while. "I'm hooked and drunk. It never happened. It's still the visions. The apartment is a vision. The darkness is. Everything."

In a few minutes he got up and wearily turned on the lights. Magicians, he thought, seeing even in a first glance all that they had taken. Lamps were gone, curtains. He walked through the apartment. The TV was gone. Suits were missing from the closets. Preminger's typewriter was gone, the champagne glasses, the silver. His trumpet was gone.

Bertie wept. He thought of phoning the police, but then wondered what he could tell them. The thieves had been in the apartment for twenty minutes and he hadn't even gotten a look at their faces.

Then he shuddered, realizing the danger he had been in. "Crooks," he said. "Killers." But even as he said it he knew it was an exaggeration. He had never been in any danger. He had the fool's ancient protection, his old immunity against consequence.

He wondered what he could say to the Premingers. They would be furious. Then, as he thought about it, he realized that this too was an exaggeration. They would not be furious. Like the thieves they would make allowances for him, as people always made allowances for him. They would forgive him; possibly they would even try to give him something toward the loss of his trumpet.

Bertie began to grow angry. They had no right to patronize him like that. If he was a clown it was because he had chosen to be. It was a way of life. Why couldn't they respect it? He should have been hit over the head like other men. How dare they forgive him? For a moment it was impossible for him to distinguish between the thieves and the Premingers.

Then he had his idea. As soon as he thought of it he knew it would work. He looked around the apartment to see what he could take. There was some costume jewelry the thieves had thrown on the bed. He scooped it up and stuffed it in his pockets. He looked at the apartment one more time and then got the hell out of there. "Bird lives," he sang to himself as he raced down the stairs. "He lives and lives."

It was wonderful. How they would marvel! He couldn't get away with it. Even the far West wasn't far enough. How they hounded you if you took something from them! He would be back, no question, and they would send him to jail, but first there would be the confrontation, maybe even in the apartment itself: Bertie in handcuffs, and the Premingers staring at him, not understanding and angry at last, and something in their eyes like fear.

(1965)

IN DREAMS BEGIN RESPONSIBILITIES

from *In Dreams Begin Responsibilities*

DELMORE SCHWARTZ

I think it is the year 1909. I feel as if I were in a motion picture theatre, the long arm of light crossing the darkness and spinning, my eyes fixed on the screen. This is a silent picture as if an old Biograph one, in which the actors are dressed in ridiculously old-fashioned clothes, and one flash succeeds another with sudden jumps. The actors too seem to jump about and walk too fast. The shots themselves are full of dots and rays, as if it were raining when the picture was photographed. The light is bad.

It is Sunday afternoon, June 12th, 1909, and my father is walking down the quiet streets of Brooklyn on his way to visit my mother. His clothes are newly pressed and his tie is too tight in his high collar. He jingles the coins in his pockets, thinking of the witty things he will say. I feel as if I had by now relaxed entirely in the soft darkness of the theatre; the organist peals out the obvious and approximate emotions on which the audience rocks unknowingly. I am anonymous, and

I have forgotten myself. It is always so when one goes to the movies, it is, as they say, a drug.

My father walks from street to street of trees, lawns and houses, once in a while coming to an avenue on which a streetcar skates and gnaws, slowly progressing. The conductor, who has a handle-bar mustache helps a young lady wearing a hat like a bowl with feathers on to the car. She lifts her long skirts slightly as she mounts the steps. He leisurely makes change and rings his bell. It is obviously Sunday, for everyone is wearing Sunday clothes, and the streetcar's noises emphasize the quiet of the holiday. Is not Brooklyn the City of Churches? The shops are closed and their shades drawn, but for an occasional stationery store or drug-store with great green balls in the window.

My father has chosen to take this long walk because he likes to walk and think. He thinks about himself in the future and so arrives at the place he is to visit in a state of mild exaltation. He pays no attention to the houses he is passing, in which the Sunday dinner is being eaten, nor to the many trees which patrol each street, now coming to their full leafage and the time when they will room the whole street in cool shadow. An occasional carriage passes, the horse's hooves falling like stones in the quiet afternoon, and once in a while an automobile, looking like an enormous upholstered sofa, puffs and passes.

My father thinks of my mother, of how nice it will be to introduce her to his family. But he is not yet sure that he wants to marry her, and once in a while he becomes panicky about the bond already established. He reassures himself by thinking of the big men he admires who are married: William Randolph Hearst, and William Howard Taft, who has just become President of the United States.

My father arrives at my mother's house. He has come too early and so is suddenly embarrassed. My aunt, my mother's sister, answers the loud bell with her napkin in her hand, for the family is still at dinner. As my father enters, my grandfather rises from the table and shakes hands with him. My mother has run upstairs to tidy herself. My grandmother asks my father if he has had dinner, and tells him that Rose will be downstairs soon. My grandfather opens the conversation by remarking on the mild June weather. My father sits uncomfortably near the table, holding his hat in his hand. My grandmother tells my aunt to take my father's hat. My uncle, twelve years old, runs into the house, his hair tousled. He shouts a greeting to my father, who has often given him a nickel, and then runs upstairs. It is evident that the respect in which my father is held in this household is tempered by a good deal of mirth. He is impressive, yet he is very awkward.

Finally my mother comes downstairs, all dressed up, and my father being engaged in conversation with my grandfather becomes uneasy, not knowing whether to greet my mother or continue the conversation. He gets up from the chair clumsily and says "hello" gruffly. My grandfather watches, examining their congruence, such as it is, with a critical eye, and meanwhile rubbing his bearded cheek roughly, as he always does when he reflects. He is worried; he is afraid that my father will not make a good husband for his oldest daughter. At this point something happens to the film, just as my father is saying something funny to my mother; I am awakened to myself and my unhappiness just as my interest was rising. The audience begins to clap impatiently. Then the trouble is cared for but the film has been returned to a portion just shown, and once more I see my grandfather rubbing his bearded cheek and pondering my father's character. It is difficult to get back into the picture once more and forget myself, but as my mother giggles at my father's words, the darkness drowns me.

My father and mother depart from the house, my father shaking hands with my mother once more, out of some unknown uneasiness. I stir uneasily also, slouched in the hard chair of the theatre. Where is the older uncle, my mother's older brother? He is studying in his bedroom upstairs, studying for his final examination at the College of the City of New York, having been dead of rapid pneumonia for the last twenty-one years. My mother and father walk down the same quiet streets once more. My mother is holding my father's arm and telling him of the novel which she has been reading; and my father utters judgments of the characters as the plot is made clear to him. This is a habit which he very much enjoys, for he feels the utmost superiority and confidence when he approves and condemns the behavior of other people. At times he feels moved to utter a brief "Ugh"—whenever the story becomes what he would call sugary. This tribute is paid to his manliness. My mother feels satisfied by the interest which she has awakened; she is showing my father how intelligent she is, and how interesting.

They reach the avenue, and the streetcar leisurely arrives. They are going to Coney Island this afternoon, although my mother considers that such pleasures are inferior. She has made up her mind to indulge only in a walk on the boardwalk and a pleasant dinner, avoiding the riotous amusements as being beneath the dignity of so dignified a couple.

My father tells my mother how much money he has made

in the past week, exaggerating an amount which need not have been exaggerated. But my father has always felt that actualities somehow fall short. Suddenly I begin to weep. The determined old lady who sits next to me in the theatre is annoyed and looks at me with an angry face, and being intimidated, I stop. I drag out my handkerchief and dry my face, licking the drop which has fallen near my lips. Meanwhile I have missed something, for here are my mother and father alighting at the last stop, Coney Island.

They walk toward the boardwalk, and my father commands my mother to inhale the pungent air from the sea. They both breathe in deeply, both of them laughing as they do so. They have in common a great interest in health, although my father is strong and husky, my mother frail. Their minds are full of theories of what is good to eat and not good to eat, and sometimes they engage in heated discussions of the subject, the whole matter ending in my father's announcement, made with a scornful bluster, that you have to die sooner or later anyway. On the boardwalk's flagpole, the American flag is pulsing in an intermittent wind from the sea.

My father and mother go to the rail of the boardwalk and look down on the beach where a good many bathers are casually walking about. A few are in the surf. A peanut whistle pierces the air with its pleasant and active whine, and my father goes to buy peanuts. My mother remains at the rail and stares at the ocean. The ocean seems merry to her; it pointedly sparkles and again and again the pony waves are released. She notices the children digging in the wet sand, and the bathing costumes of the girls who are her own age. My father returns with the peanuts. Overhead the sun's lightning strikes and strikes, but neither of them are at all aware of it. The boardwalk is full of people dressed in their Sunday clothes and idly strolling. The tide does not reach as far as the boardwalk, and the strollers would feel no danger if it did. My mother and father lean on the rail of the boardwalk and absently stare at the ocean. The ocean is becoming rough; the waves come in slowly, tugging strength from far back. The moment before they somersault, the moment when they arch their backs so beautifully, showing green and white veins amid the black, that moment is intolerable. They finally crack, dashing fiercely upon the sand, actually driving, full force downward, against the sand, bouncing upward and forward, and at last petering out into a small stream which races up the beach and then is recalled. My parents gaze absentmindedly at the ocean, scarcely interested in its harshness. The sun overhead does not disturb them. But I stare at the terrible sun which breaks up sight, and the fatal, merciless, passionate ocean, I forget my parents. I stare fascinated and finally, shocked by the indifference of my father and mother, I burst out weeping once more. The old lady next to me pats me on the shoulder and says "There, there, all of this is only a movie, young man, only a movie," but I look up once more at the terrifying sun and the terrifying ocean, and being unable to control my tears, I get up and go to the men's room, stumbling over the feet of the other people seated in my row.

When I return, feeling as if I had awakened in the morning sick for lack of sleep, several hours have apparently passed and my parents are riding on the merry-go-round. My father is on a black horse, my mother on a white one, and they seem to be making an eternal circuit for the single purpose of snatching the nickel rings which are attached to the arm of one of the posts. A hand-organ is playing; it is one with the ceaseless circling of the merry-go-round.

For a moment it seems that they will never get off the merry-go-round because it will never stop. I feel like one who looks down on the avenue from the fiftieth story of a building. But at length they do get off; even the music of the hand-organ has ceased for a moment. My father has acquired ten rings, my mother only two, although it was my mother who really wanted them.

They walk on along the boardwalk as the afternoon descends by imperceptible degrees into the incredible violet of dusk. Everything fades into a relaxed glow, even the ceaseless murmuring from the beach, and the revolutions of the merry-go-round. They look for a place to have dinner. My father suggests the best one on the boardwalk and my mother demurs, in accordance with her principles.

However they do go to the best place, asking for a table near the window, so that they can look out on the boardwalk and the mobile ocean. My father feels omnipotent as he places a quarter in the waiter's hand as he asks for a table. The place is crowded and here too there is music, this time from a kind of string trio. My father orders dinner with a fine confidence.

As the dinner is eaten, my father tells of his plans for the future, and my mother shows with expressive face how interested she is, and how impressed. My father becomes exultant. He is lifted up by the waltz that is being played, and his own future begins to intoxicate him. My father tells my mother that he is going to expand his business, for there is a great deal of money to be made. He wants to settle down. After all, he is twenty-nine, he has lived by himself since he was thirteen, he is making more and more money, and he is envious of his married friends when he visits them in the cozy security of their homes, surrounded, it seems, by the calm domestic pleasures, and by delightful children, and then, as the waltz reaches the moment when all the dancers swing madly, then, then with awful daring, then he asks my mother to marry him, although awkwardly enough and puzzled, even in his excitement, at how he had arrived at the proposal, and she, to make the whole business worse, begins to cry, and my father looks nervously about, not knowing at all what to do now, and my mother says: "It's all I've wanted from the moment I saw you," sobbing, and he finds all of this very difficult, scarcely to his taste, scarcely as he had thought it would be, on his long walks over Brooklyn Bridge in the revery of a fine cigar, and it was then that I stood up in the theatre and shouted: "Don't do it. It's not too late to change your minds, both of you. Nothing good will come of it, only remorse, hatred, scandal, and two children whose characters are monstrous." The whole audience turned to look at me, annoyed, the usher came hurrying down the aisle flashing his searchlight, and the old lady next to me tugged me down into my seat, saying: "Be quiet. You'll be put out, and you paid thirty-five cents to come in." And so I shut my eyes because I could not bear to see what was happening. I sat there quietly.

But after awhile I begin to take brief glimpses, and at length I watch again with thirsty interest, like a child who wants to maintain his sulk although offered the bribe of candy. My parents are now having their picture taken in a photographer's booth along the boardwalk. The place is shadowed in the mauve light which is apparently necessary. The camera is set to the side on its tripod and looks like a Martian man. The photographer is instructing my parents in how to pose. My father has his arm over my mother's shoulder, and both of them smile emphatically. The photographer brings my mother a bouquet of flowers to hold in her hand but she holds it at the wrong angle. Then the photographer covers himself with the black cloth which drapes the camera and all that one sees of him is one protruding arm and his hand which clutches the rubber ball which he will squeeze when the picture is finally taken. But he is not satisfied with their appearance. He feels with certainty that somehow there is something wrong in their pose. Again and again he issues from his hidden place with new directions. Each suggestion merely makes matters worse. My father is becoming impatient. They try a seated pose. The photographer explains that he has pride, he is not interested in all of this for the money, he wants to make beautiful pictures. My father says: "Hurry up, will you? We haven't got all night." But the photographer only scurries about apologetically, and issues new directions. The photographer charms me. I approve of him with all my heart, for I know just how he feels, and as he criticizes each revised pose according to some unknown idea of rightness, I become quite hopeful. But then my father says angrily: "Come on, you've had enough time, we're not going to wait any longer." And the photographer, sighing unhappily, goes back under his black covering, holds out his hand, says: "One, two, three, Now!", and the picture is taken, with my father's smile turned to a grimace and my mother's bright and false. It takes a few minutes for the picture to be developed and as my parents sit in the curious light they become quite depressed.

They have passed a fortune-teller's booth, and my mother wishes to go in, but my father does not. They begin to argue about it. My mother becomes stubborn, my father once more impatient, and then they begin to quarrel, and what my father would like to do is walk off and leave my mother there, but he knows that that would never do. My mother refuses to budge. She is near to tears, but she feels an uncontrollable desire to hear what the palm-reader will say. My father consents angrily, and they both go into a booth which is in a way like the photographer's, since it is draped in black cloth and its light is shadowed. The place is too warm, and my father keeps saying this is all nonsense, pointing to the crystal ball on the table. The fortuneteller, a fat, short woman, garbed in what is supposed to be Oriental robes, comes into the room from the back and greets them, speaking with an accent. But suddenly my father feels that the whole thing is intolerable; he tugs at my mother's arm, but my mother refuses to budge. And then, in terrible anger, my father lets go of my mother's arm and strides out, leaving my mother stunned. She moves to go after my father, but the fortune-teller holds her arm tightly and begs her not to do so, and I in my seat am shocked more than can ever be said, for I feel as if I were walking a tight-rope a hundred feet over a circus-audience and suddenly the rope is showing signs of breaking, and I get up from my seat and begin to shout once more the first words I can think of to communicate my terrible fear and once more the usher comes hurrying down the aisle flashing his searchlight, and the old lady pleads with me, and the shocked audience has turned to stare at me, and I keep shouting: "What are they doing? Don't they know what they are doing? Why doesn't my mother go after my father? If she does not do that, what will she do? Doesn't my father know what he is doing?"—But the usher has seized my arm and is dragging me away, and as he does so, he says: "What are *you* doing? Don't you know that you can't do whatever you want to do? Why should a young man like you, with your whole life before you, get hysterical like this? Why don't you *think* of what you're doing? You can't act like this even if other people aren't around! You will be sorry if you do not do what you should do, you can't carry on like this, it is not right, you will find that out soon enough, everything you do matters too much," and he said that dragging me through the lobby of the theatre into the cold light, and I woke up into the bleak winter morning of my twenty-first birthday, the windowsill shining with its lip of snow, and the morning already begun.

(1938)

HESTER STREET

from *Red Ribbon on a White Horse*

ANZIA YEZIERSKA

I paused in front of my rooming house on Hester Street. This was 1920, when Hester Street was the pushcart center of the East Side. The air reeked with the smell of fish and overripe fruit from the carts in front of the house. I peeked into the basement window. The landlady was not there to nag me for the rent. I crept into her kitchen, filled my pitcher with water and hurried out. In my room I set the kettle boiling. There wasn't much taste to the stale tea leaves but the hot water warmed me. I was still sipping my tea, thankful for this short reprieve from my landlady, when I heard my name shouted outside the door.

The angel of death, I thought, my landlady had come to put me out! And Hester Street had gathered to watch another eviction. I opened the door with fear.

Mrs. Katz with her baby in her arms, Mrs. Rubin drying her wet hands on her apron, and Zalmon Shlomoh, the fish peddler, crowded into my room, pushing forward a Western Union messenger who handed me a yellow envelope.

"*Oi-oi weh!* A telegram!" Mrs. Rubin wailed. "Somebody died?"

Their eyes gleamed with prying curiosity. "Read—read already!" they clamored.

I ripped open the envelope and read:

TELEPHONE IMMEDIATELY FOR AN APPOINTMENT
TO DISCUSS MOTION PICTURE RIGHTS OF "HUNGRY HEARTS"

R. L. GIFFEN

"Who died?" they demanded.

"Nobody died. It's only a place for a job," I said, shooing them out of the room.

I reread the message. "Telephone immediately!" It was from one of the big moving-picture agents. In those days Hollywood was still busy with Westerns and Pollyanna romances. The studios seldom bought stories from life. This was like winning a ticket on a lottery.

Hungry Hearts had been my first book. It had been praised by the critics, esteemed as literature. That meant it didn't sell. After spending the two hundred dollars I had received in royalties, I was even poorer than when I had started writing.

And now movie rights! Money! Wealth! I could get the world for the price of a telephone call. But if I had had a nickel for a telephone call I wouldn't have fooled a starving stomach with stewed-over tea leaves. I needed a nickel for telephoning, ten cents for carfare—fifteen cents! What could I pawn to get fifteen cents?

I looked about my room. The rickety cot didn't belong to me. The rusty gas plate on the window sill? My typewriter? The trunk that was my table? Then I saw the shawl, my mother's shawl that served as a blanket and a cover for my cot.

Nobody in our village in Poland had had a shawl like it. It had been Mother's wedding present from her rich uncle in Warsaw. It had been her Sabbath, her holiday. . . . When she put it on she outshone all the other women on the way to the synagogue.

Old and worn—it held memories of my childhood, put space and color in my drab little room. It redeemed the squalor in which I had to live. But this might be the last time I'd have to pawn it. I seized the shawl and rushed with it to the pawnshop.

Zaretsky, the pawnbroker, was a bald-headed dwarf, grown gray with the years in the dark basement—tight-skinned and crooked from squeezing pennies out of despairing people.

I watched his dirty, bony fingers appraise the shawl. "An old rag!" he grunted, peering at me through his thick-rimmed glasses. He had always intimidated me before, but this time the telegram in my hand made me bold.

"See here, Zaretzky," I said, "this shawl is rarer than diamonds—an antique from Poland, pure wool. The older it gets, the finer—the softer the colors——"

He spread it out and held it up to the light. "A moth-eaten rag full of holes!"

"You talk as if I were a new customer. You make nothing of the best things. As you did with my samovar."

"A samovar is yet something. But this!" He pushed the shawl from him. "A quarter. Take it or leave it."

"This was the finest shawl in Plinsk. It's hand-woven, hand-dyed. People's lives are woven into it."

"For what is past nobody pays. Now it's junk—falling apart."

"I'm only asking a dollar. It's worth ten times that much. Only a dollar!"

"A quarter. You want it? Yes or no?"

I grabbed the quarter and fled.

Within a half-hour I was at the agent's office.

"I've great news for you," he said, drawing up a chair near his desk. "I've practically sold your book to Hollywood. Goldwyn wants it. Fox is making offers, too, but I think Goldwyn is our best bet. They offered five thousand dollars. I'm holding out for ten."

I had pawned Mother's shawl to get there, and this man talked of thousands of dollars. Five, ten thousand dollars was a fortune in 1920. I was suddenly aware of my hunger. I saw myself biting into thick, juicy steaks, dipping fresh rolls into mounds of butter, swallowing whole platters of French fried potatoes in one gulp.

"If we settle with Goldwyn," Mr. Giffen said, "he will want you to go to Hollywood to collaborate on the script."

I stood up to go, dizzy from lack of food and so much excitement.

"Maybe what you're saying is real," I said. "If it is, then can you advance me one dollar on all these thousands?"

Smiling, he handed me a bill.

I walked out of his office staring at the ten-dollar bill in my hand. Directly across the street was the white-tiled front of a Child's restaurant. How often I had stood outside this same restaurant, watching the waitresses clear away leftover food and wanting to cry out, "Don't throw it away! Give it to me. I'm hungry!" I stumbled through the door, sank into the first vacant chair and ordered the most expensive steak on the menu. A platter was set before me—porterhouse steak, onions, potatoes, rolls, butter. I couldn't eat fast enough. Before I was half through, my throat tightened. My head bent over my plate, tears rolled down my cheeks onto the uneaten food.

When I hadn't had a penny for a roll I had had the appetite of a wolf that could devour the earth. Now that I could treat myself to a dollar dinner, I couldn't take another bite. But just having something to eat, even though I could only half eat it, made me see the world with new eyes. If only Father and Mother were alive now! How I longed to be at peace with them!

I had not meant to abandon them when I left home—I had only wanted to get to the place where I belonged. To do it, I had to strike out alone.

If my mother could only have lived long enough to see that I was not the heartless creature I seemed to be! As for my father—would he forgive me even now?

Now that there was no longer reason to feel sorry for myself, my self-pity turned to regret for all that I did not do and might have done for them.

The waitress started to remove the dishes.

"I'm not through!" I held onto the plate, still starved for the steak and potatoes I could not eat. The agent's talk of Hollywood might have been only a dream. But steak was real. When no one was looking, I took out my handkerchief, thrust the meat and cold potatoes into it, covered it with my newspaper and sneaked out like a thief with the food for which I had paid.

Back in my room I opened the newspaper bundle, still too excited with the prospect of Hollywood to be able to eat. "God! What a hoarding creature I've become!" I cried out in self-disgust. In my purse was the change from the ten-dollar bill the agent had given me. More than enough for a dozen meals. And yet the hoarding habit of poverty was so deep in my bones that I had to bring home the food that I could not eat.

I leaned out of the window. Lily, the alley cat, was scavenging the garbage can as usual. I had named her Lily because she had nothing but garbage to eat and yet somehow looked white and beautiful like the lilies that rise out of dunghills.

"Lily!" I called to her, holding up the steak. The next moment she bounded up on my window sill, devouring the steak and potatoes in huge gulps.

"I've been a pauper all my life," I told Lily as I watched her eat. "But I'll be a pauper no longer. I'll have money, plenty of it. I'll not only have money to buy food when I'm hungry, but I'll have men who'll love me on my terms. An end to hoarding food, or hoarding love!"

I threw open the trunk, dug down and yanked out the box of John Morrow's letters, determined to tear them up and shed the memory of them once and for all. For years those letters had been to me music and poetry. I had stayed up nights to console my loneliness reading and rereading them, drugged with the opiate of his words.

But now, with the prospect of Hollywood, I began to hate those letters. Why hang on to words when the love that had inspired them was dead? In Hollywood there would be new people. There would be other men.

I seized the first letter and began tearing it. But a panicky fear of loss stopped me. Money could buy meat and mink, rye bread and rubies, but not the beauty of his words. Those letters were my assurance that I was a woman who could love and be loved. Without them, I was again the oddity of Hester Street, an object of pity and laughter.

"Poor thing! I can't stand the starved-dog look in her eyes," I had overheard one of the men in the shop say to another.

"Well, if you're so sorry for her, marry her," came the jeering retort.

"Marry her? Oi-i-i! Oi-yoi! That *meshugeneh?* That red-headed witch? Her head is on wheels, riding on air. She's not a woman. She has a *dybbuk,* a devil, a book for a heart."

But when I met John Morrow, the *dybbuk* that drove away other men had drawn him to me. He saw my people in me, struggling for a voice. I could no more tear up those letters than I could root out the memory of him!

I slipped the torn pieces of the letter into the envelope, put it back with the others in the box and stuck it at the bottom of my trunk, under my old clothes.

A week later Mr. Giffen asked me to lunch to talk over the movie contract I was to sign.

After I had signed a twenty-page contract, Giffen handed me a check—a check made out to me—a check for nine thousand dollars.

"I've deducted one thousand for my ten per cent," he explained.

I looked at the check. Nine thousand dollars!

"Riches for a lifetime!" I cried.

Giffen smiled. "It's only the beginning. When you're in Hollywood you'll see the more you have, the more you'll get."

He took out my railroad reservation from his wallet and handed it to me. "They want you to assist in the production of the book. You're to get two hundred a week and all your expenses while there."

He gave me another check for a hundred dollars. "This is for your incidentals on the train. Meals for three and a half days—one hundred dollars. Not so bad!" He patted my hand. "Young lady! You go on salary the moment you step on the train."

I told him I could be ready as soon as I got something out of a pawnshop.

With my purse full of money, I hurried to Zaretzky's to redeem my shawl.

"Zaretzky!" I charged into the basement. "I forgot to take my receipt for the shawl!"

"Forgot, nothing! I gave it to you in your hand."

"I swear to you, I left it on the counter."

"If you were crazy enough to lose it, it's not my fault."

I took out a five-dollar bill. "Here's five dollars for your quarter," I said. "What more do you want?"

He made no move. He stood like stone staring at me.

"Shylock! Here's ten dollars! I have no time to bargain with you. If that's not enough, here's twice ten dollars! Twenty dollars for your twenty-five cents!"

There was a flicker in the black pinpoints of his eyes. He took out a signed receipt from the money box. "I sold it the day you brought it here for five dollars," he groaned, his face distorted by frustrated greed.

The next day I packed my belongings without the shawl that had gone with me everywhere I went. The loss of that one beautiful thing which all my money could not reclaim shadowed my prospective trip to Hollywood.

The distrust of good fortune always in the marrow of my bones made me think of my father. While I was struggling with hunger and want, trying to write, I feared to go near him. I couldn't stand his condemnation of my lawless, godless, selfish existence. But now, with Hollywood ahead of me, I had the courage to face him. As I entered the dark hallway of the tenement where he lived, I heard his voice chanting.

"And a man shall be as a hiding place from the wind, and covert from the tempest; as rivers of water in a dry place, as the shadow of a great rock in a weary land . . ."

Since earliest childhood I had heard this chant of Isaiah. It was as familiar to me as Mother Goose rhymes to other children. Hearing it again after so many years, I was struck for the first time by the beauty of the words. Though my father was poor and had nothing, the Torah, the poetry of prophets, was his daily bread.

He was still chanting as I entered, a gray-bearded man in a black skullcap.

"And the eyes of them that see shall not be dim, and the ears of them that hear shall hearken. The heart of the rash shall understand knowledge, and the tongue of the stammerers shall be ready to speak plainly . . ."

As I stood there, waiting for him to see me, I noticed the aging stoop of his shoulders. He was getting paler, thinner. The frail body accused me for having been away so long. But in the same moment of guilt the smells of the musty room in which he wouldn't permit a window to be opened or a book to be dusted made me want to run. On the table piled high with his papers and dust-laden books were dishes with remains of his last meal—cabbage soup and pumpernickel. He was as unaware of the squalor around him as a medieval monk.

Dimly I realized that this new world didn't want his kind. He had no choice but to live for God. And I, his daughter, who abandoned him for the things of this world, had joined the world against him.

He looked up and saw me.

"So you've come at last? You've come to see your old father?"

"I was so busy. . . ." I mumbled. And then, hastily, to halt his reproaches, I reached into my bag and dropped ten ten-dollar bills on the open page of his book. He pushed aside the bills as if they would contaminate the holiness of the script.

"Months, almost a year, you've been away. . . ."

"Bessie, Fannie live right near here, they promised to look after you. . . ."

"They have their own husbands to look after. You're my only unmarried daughter. Your first duty to God is to serve your father. But what's an old father to an *Amerikanerin,* a daughter of Babylon?"

"Your daughter of Babylon brought you a hundred dollars."

"Can your money make up for your duty as a daughter? In America, money takes the place of God."

"But I earned that money with my writing." For all his scorn of my godlessness, I thought he would take a father's pride in my success. "Ten thousand they paid me. . . ."

He wouldn't let me finish. He shook a warning finger in my face. "Can you touch pitch without being defiled? Neither can you hold on to all that money without losing your soul."

Even in the street, his words still rang in my ears. "Daughter of Babylon! You've polluted your inheritance. . . . You'll wander in darkness and none shall be there to save you. . . ."

His old God could not save me in a new world, I told myself. Why did we come to America, if not to achieve all that had been denied us for centuries in Europe? Fear and poverty were behind me. I was going into a new world of plenty. I would learn to live in the now . . . not in the next world.

I had but to open my purse, look at my reservation for a drawing room on the fastest flyer to Hollywood, think of the fabulous salary I was to be paid even while traveling, and no hope in which I might indulge was too high, no longing too visionary.

Grand Central Station, where I waited for my train, seemed an unreal place. Within the vast marble structure people rushed in and out, meeting, parting and hurrying on, each in pursuit of his own dream. As I stood lost in my thoughts, every man I saw seemed John Morrow coming to see me off. If so incredible a thing could happen as my going to Hollywood, surely John Morrow could appear. He must know *Hungry Hearts* was written for him. He must sense my need to share my wealth with him even more than I had needed him in poverty.

The gates opened. My train was called. I picked up my bundle, started through the gate, still looking back, still expecting the miracle. I could not give up the hope that love as great as his had been could ever cease.

The first days and nights on the train I was too dazed by the sudden turn of events to notice the view from my window. Miles of beautiful country I saw, unaware of what I was seeing. Then one morning I woke up and saw the desert stretching out on both sides. The train raced through the wide monotonous landscape at a terrific pace to reach its destination on scheduled time.

It was getting hotter and hotter. Sand sifted through the screened air vents and closed doors. The train stopped at the station to refuel. Passengers stepped out to buy trinkets from the Indians squatting on the platform. Over the entrance of an adobe building I read in gilt letters the inscription:

THE DESERT WAITED, SILENT AND HOT AND FIERCE IN ITS DESOLATION, HOLDING ITS TREASURES UNDER SEAL OF DEATH AGAINST THE COMING OF THE STRONG ONE.

I looked across the vast space and thought of the time when all this silent sand was a rolling ocean. What eons had to pass for the ocean to dry into this arid waste! In the immensity of the desert the whirl of trivialities which I had so magnified all fell away. I was suspended in timelessness—sand, sky, and space. What a relief it was to let go—not to think—not to feel, but rest, silent—past, present and future stretching to infinity.

Slowly, imperceptibly, the dry desert air receded before the humid, subtropical warmth of southern California. The sense of time and the concern with self stirred again. Green hills, dazzling gardens and orange groves, towering date palms ushered in the great adventure ahead of me.

(1950)

CITY BOY

from *Going Places*

LEONARD MICHAELS

P hillip," she said, "this is crazy."

I didn't agree or disagree. She wanted some answer. I bit her neck. She kissed my ear. It was nearly three in the morning. We had just returned. The apartment was dark and quiet. We were on the living-room floor and she repeated, "Phillip, this is crazy." Her crinoline broke under us like cinders. Furniture loomed all around—settee, chairs, a table with a lamp. Pictures were cloudy blotches drifting above. But no lights, no things to look at, no eyes in her head. She was underneath me and warm. The rug was warm, soft as mud, deep. Her crinoline cracked like sticks. Our naked bellies clapped together. Air fired out like farts. I took it as applause. The chandelier clicked. The clock ticked as if to split its glass. "Phillip," she said, "this is crazy." A little voice against the grain and power. Not enough to stop me. Yet once I had been a man of feeling. We went to concerts, walked in the park, trembled in the maid's room. Now in the foyer, a flash of hair and claws. We stumbled to the living-room floor. She said, "Phillip, this is crazy." Then silence, except in my head where a conference table was set up, ashtrays scattered about. Priests, ministers and rabbis were rushing to take seats. I wanted their opinion, but came. They vanished. A voice lingered, faintly crying, "You could mess up the rug, Phillip, break something . . ." Her fingers pinched my back like ants. I expected a remark to kill good death. She said nothing. The breath in her nostrils whipped mucus. It cracked in my ears like flags. I dreamed we were in her mother's Cadillac, trailing flags. I heard her voice before I heard the words. "Phillip, this is crazy. My parents are in the next room." Her cheek jerked against mine, her breasts were knuckles in my nipples. I burned. Good death was killed. I burned with hate. A rabbi shook his finger, "You shouldn't hate." I lifted on my elbows, sneering in pain. She wrenched her hips, tightened muscles in belly and neck. She said, "Move." It was imperative to move. Her parents were thirty feet away. Down the hall between Utrillos and Vlamincks, through the door, flick the light and I'd see them. Maybe like us, Mr. Cohen adrift on the missus. Hair sifted down my cheek. "Let's go to the maid's room," she whispered. I was reassured. She tried to move. I kissed her mouth. Her crinoline smashed like sugar. Pig that I was, I couldn't move. The clock ticked hysterically. Ticks piled up like insects. Muscles lapsed in her thighs. Her fingers scratched on my neck as if looking for buttons. She slept. I sprawled like a bludgeoned pig, eyes open, loose lips. I flopped into sleep, in her, in the rug, in our scattered clothes.

Dawn hadn't shown between the slats in the blinds. Her breathing sissed in my ear. I wanted to sleep more, but needed a cigarette. I thought of the cold avenue, the lonely subway ride. Where could I buy a newspaper, a cup of coffee? This was crazy, dangerous, a waste of time. The maid might arrive, her parents might wake. I had to get started. My hand pushed along the rug to find my shirt, touched a brass lion's paw, then a lamp cord.

A naked heel humped wood.

She woke, her nails in my neck. "Phillip, did you hear?" I whispered, "Quiet." My eyes rolled like Milton's. Furniture loomed, whirled. "Dear God," I prayed, "save my ass." The steps ceased. Neither of us breathed. The clock ticked. She trembled. I pressed my cheek against her mouth to keep her from talking. We heard pajamas rustle, phlegmy breathing, fingernails scratching hair. A voice, "Veronica, don't you think it's time you sent Phillip home?"

A murmur of assent started in her throat, swept to my cheek, fell back drowned like a child in a well. Mr. Cohen had spoken. He stood ten inches from our legs. Maybe less. It was impossible to tell. His fingernails grated through hair. His voice hung in the dark with the quintessential question. Mr. Cohen, scratching his crotch, stood now as never in the light. Considerable. No tool of his wife, whose energy in business kept him eating, sleeping, overlooking the park. Pinochle change in his pocket four nights a week. But were they his words? Or was he the oracle of Mrs. Cohen, lying sleepless, irritated, waiting for him to get me out? I didn't breathe. I didn't move. If he had come on his own he would leave without an answer. His eyes weren't adjusted to the dark. He couldn't see. We lay at his feet like worms. He scratched, made smacking noises with his mouth.

The question of authority is always with us. Who is responsible for the triggers pulled, buttons pressed, the gas, the fire? Doubt banged my brain. My heart lay in the fist of intellect, which squeezed out feeling like piss out of kidneys. Mrs. Cohen's voice demolished doubt, feeling, intellect. It ripped from the bedroom.

"For God's sake, Morris, don't be banal. Tell the schmuck to go home and keep his own parents awake all night, if he has any."

Veronica's tears slipped down my cheeks. Mr. Cohen sighed, shuffled, made a strong voice. "Veronica, tell Phillip . . ." His foot came down on my ass. He drove me into his daughter. I drove her into his rug.

"I don't believe it," he said.

He walked like an antelope, lifting hoof from knee, but stepped down hard. Sensitive to the danger of movement, yet finally impulsive, flinging his pot at the earth in order to cross it. His foot brought me his weight and character, a hundred fifty-five pounds of stomping shlemiel, in a mode of apprehension so primal we must share it with bugs. Let armies stomp me to insensate pulp—I'll yell "Cohen" when he arrives.

Veronica squealed, had a contraction, fluttered, gagged a shriek, squeezed, and up like a frog out of the hand of a child I stood spread-legged, bolt naked, great with eyes. Mr. Cohen's face was eyes in my eyes. A secret sharer. We faced each other like men accidentally met in hell. He retreated flapping, moaning, "I will not believe it one bit."

Veronica said, "Daddy?"

"Who else you no good bum?"

The rug raced. I smacked against blinds, glass broke and I whirled. Veronica said, "Phillip," and I went off in streaks, a sparrow in the room, here, there, early American, baroque and rococo. Veronica wailed, "Phillip." Mr. Cohen screamed, "I'll kill him." I stopped at the door, seized the knob. Mrs.

Cohen yelled from the bedroom, "Morris, did something break? Answer me."

"I'll kill that bastid."

"Morris, if something broke you'll rot for a month."

"Mother, stop it," said Veronica. "Phillip, come back."

The door slammed. I was outside, naked as a wolf.

I needed poise. Without poise the street was impossible. Blood shot to my brain, thought blossomed, I'd walk on my hands. Beards were fashionable. I kicked up my feet, kicked the elevator button, faced the door and waited. I bent one elbow like a knee. The posture of a clothes model, easy, poised. Blood coiled down to my brain, weeds bourgeoned. I had made a bad impression. There was no other way to see it. But all right. We needed a new beginning. Everyone does. Yet how few of us know when it arrives. Mr. Cohen had never spoken to me before; this was a breakthrough. There had been a false element in our relationship. It was wiped out. I wouldn't kid myself with the idea that he had nothing to say. I'd had enough of his silent treatment. It was worth being naked to see how mercilessly I could think. I had his number. Mrs. Cohen's, too. I was learning every second. I was a city boy. No innocent shitkicker from Jersey. I was the A train, the Fifth Avenue bus. I could be a cop. My name was Phillip, my style New York City. I poked the elevator button with my toe. It rang in the lobby, waking Ludwig. He'd come for me, rotten with sleep. Not the first time. He always took me down, walked me through the lobby and let me out on the avenue. Wires began tugging him up the shaft. I moved back, conscious of my genitals hanging upside down. Absurd consideration; we were both men one way or another. There were social distinctions enforced by his uniform, but they would vanish at the sight of me. "The unaccommodated thing itself." "Off ye lendings!" The greatest play is about a naked man. A picture of Lear came to me, naked, racing through the wheat. I could be cool. I thought of Ludwig's uniform, hat, whipcord collar. It signified his authority. Perhaps he would be annoyed, in his authority, by the sight of me naked. Few people woke him at such hours. Worse, I never tipped him. Could I have been so indifferent month after month? In a crisis you discover everything. Then it's too late. Know yourself, indeed. You need a crisis every day. I refused to think about it. I sent my mind after objects. It returned with the chairs, settee, table and chandelier. Where were my clothes? I sent it along the rug. It found buttons, eagles stamped in brass. I recognized them as the buttons on Ludwig's coat. Eagles, beaks like knives, shrieking for tips. Fuck'm, I thought. Who's Ludwig? A big coat, a whistle, white gloves and a General MacArthur hat. I could understand him completely. He couldn't begin to understand me. A naked man is mysterious. But aside from that, what did he know? I dated Veronica Cohen and went home late. Did he know I was out of work? That I lived in a slum downtown? Of course not.

Possibly under his hat was a filthy mind. He imagined Veronica and I might be having sexual intercourse. He resented it. Not that he hoped for the privilege himself, in his coat and soldier hat, but he had a proprietary interest in the building and its residents. I came from another world. *The* other world against which Ludwig defended the residents. Wasn't I like a burglar sneaking out late, making him my accomplice? I undermined his authority, his dedication. He despised me. It was obvious. But no one thinks such thoughts. It made me laugh to think them. My genitals jumped. The elevator door slid open. He didn't say a word. I padded inside like a seal. The door slid shut. Instantly, I was ashamed of myself, thinking as I had about him. I had no right. A better man than I. His profile was an etching by Dürer. Good peasant stock. How had he fallen to such work? Existence precedes essence. At the controls, silent, enduring, he gave me strength for the street. Perhaps the sun would be up, birds in the air. The door slid open. Ludwig walked ahead of me through the lobby. He needed new heels. The door of the lobby was half a ton of glass, encased in iron vines and leaves. Not too much for Ludwig. He turned, looked down into my eyes. I watched his lips move.

"I vun say sumding. Yur bisniss vot you do. Bud vy you mek her miserable? Nod led her slip. She has beks unter her eyes."

Ludwig had feelings. They spoke to mine. Beneath the uniform, a man. Essence precedes existence. Even rotten with sleep, thick, dry bags under his eyes, he saw, he sympathized. The discretion demanded by his job forbade anything tangible, a sweater, a hat. "Ludwig," I whispered, "you're all right." It didn't matter if he heard me. He knew I said something. He knew it was something nice. He grinned, tugged the door open with both hands. I slapped out onto the avenue. I saw no one, dropped to my feet and glanced back through the door. Perhaps for the last time. I lingered, indulged a little melancholy. Ludwig walked to a couch in the rear of the lobby. He took off his coat, rolled it into a pillow and lay down. I had never stayed to see him do that before, but always rushed off to the subway. As if I were indifferent to the life of the building. Indeed, like a burglar. I seized the valuables and fled to the subway. I stayed another moment, watching good Ludwig, so I could hate myself. He assumed the modest, saintly posture of sleep. One leg here, the other there. His good head on his coat. A big arm across his stomach, the hand between his hips. He made a fist and punched up and down.

I went down the avenue, staying close to the buildings. Later I would work up a philosophy. Now I wanted to sleep, forget. I hadn't the energy for moral complexities: Ludwig cross-eyed, thumping his pelvis in such a nice lobby. Mirrors, glazed pots, rubber plants ten feet high. As if he were generating all of it. As if it were part of his job. I hurried. The buildings were on my left, the park on my right. There were doormen in all the buildings; God knows what was in the park. No cars were moving. No people in sight. Streetlights glowed in a receding sweep down to Fifty-ninth Street and beyond. A wind pressed my face like Mr. Cohen's breath. Such hatred. Imponderable under any circumstances, a father cursing his daughter. Why? A fright in the dark? Freud said things about fathers and daughters. It was too obvious, too hideous. I shuddered and went more quickly. I began to run. In a few minutes I was at the spit-mottled steps of the subway. I had hoped for vomit. Spit is no challenge for bare feet. Still, I wouldn't complain. It was sufficiently disgusting to make me live in spirit. I went down the steps flatfooted, stamping, elevated by each declension. I was a city boy, no mincing creep from the sticks.

A Negro man sat in the change booth. He wore glasses, a white shirt, black knit tie and a silver tie clip. I saw a mole on his right cheek. His hair had spots of grey, as if strewn with ashes. He was reading a newspaper. He didn't hear me approach, didn't see my eyes take him in, figure him out. Shirt, glasses, tie—I knew how to address him. I coughed. He looked up.

"Sir, I don't have any money. Please let me through the

turnstile. I come this way every week and will certainly pay you the next time."

He merely looked at me. Then his eyes flashed like fangs. Instinctively, I guessed what he felt. He didn't owe favors to a white man. He didn't have to bring his allegiance to the Transit Authority into question for my sake.

"Hey, man, you naked?"

"Yes."

"Step back a little."

I stepped back.

"You're naked."

I nodded.

"Get your naked ass the hell out of here."

"Sir," I said, "I know these are difficult times, but can't we be reasonable? I know that . . ."

"Scat, mother, go home."

I crouched as if to dash through the turnstile. He crouched, too. It proved he would come after me. I shrugged, turned back toward the steps. The city was infinite. There were many other subways. But why had he become so angry? Did he think I was a bigot? Maybe I was running around naked to get him upset. His anger was incomprehensible otherwise. It made me feel like a bigot. First a burglar, then a bigot. I needed a cigarette. I could hardly breathe. Air was too good for me. At the top of the steps, staring down, stood Veronica. She had my clothes.

"Poor, poor," she said.

I said nothing. I snatched my underpants and put them on. She had my cigarettes ready. I tried to light one, but the match failed. I threw down the cigarette and the matchbook. She retrieved them as I dressed. She lit the cigarette for me and held my elbow to help me keep my balance. I finished dressing, took the cigarette. We walked back toward her building. The words "thank you" sat in my brain like driven spikes. She nibbled her lip.

"How are things at home?" My voice was casual and morose, as if no answer could matter.

"All right," she said, her voice the same as mine. She took her tone from me. I liked that sometimes, sometimes not. Now I didn't like it. I discovered I was angry. Until she said that, I had no idea I was angry. I flicked the cigarette into the gutter and suddenly I knew why. I didn't love her. The cigarette sizzled in the gutter. Like truth. I didn't love her. Black hair, green eyes, I didn't love her. Slender legs. I didn't. Last night I had looked at her and said to myself, "I hate communism." Now I wanted to step on her head. Nothing less than that would do. If it was a perverted thought, then it was a perverted thought. I wasn't afraid to admit it to myself.

"All right? Really? Is that true?"

Blah, blah, blah. Who asked those questions? A zombie; not Phillip of the foyer and rug. He died in flight. I was sorry, sincerely sorry, but with clothes on my back I knew certain feelings would not survive humiliation. It was so clear it was thrilling. Perhaps she felt it, too. In any case she would have to accept it. The nature of the times. We are historical creatures. Veronica and I were finished. Before we reached her door I would say deadly words. They'd come in a natural way, kill her a little. Veronica, let me step on your head or we're through. Maybe we're through, anyway. It would deepen her looks, give philosophy to what was only charming in her face. The dawn was here. A new day. Cruel, but change is cruel. I could bear it. Love is infinite and one. Women are not. Neither are men. The human condition. Nearly unbearable.

"No, it's not true," she said.

"What's not?"

"Things aren't all right at home."

I nodded intelligently, sighed, "Of course not. Tell me the truth, please. I don't want to hear anything else."

"Daddy had a heart attack."

"Oh God," I yelled. "Oh God, no."

I seized her hand, dropped it. She let it fall. I seized it again. No use. I let it fall. She let it drift between us. We stared at one another. She said, "What were you going to say? I can tell you were going to say something."

I stared, said nothing.

"Don't feel guilty, Phillip. Let's just go back to the apartment and have some coffee."

"What can I say?"

"Don't say anything. He's in the hospital and my mother is there. Let's just go upstairs and not say anything."

"Not say anything. Like moral imbeciles go slurp coffee and not say anything? What are we, nihilists or something? Assassins? Monsters?"

"Phillip, there's no one in the apartment. I'll make us coffee and eggs . . ."

"How about a roast beef? Got a roast beef in the freezer?"

"Phillip, he's *my* father."

We were at the door. I rattled. I was in a trance. This was life. Death!

"Indeed, your father. I'll accept that. I can do no less."

"Phillip, shut up. Ludwig."

The door opened. I nodded to Ludwig. What did be know about life and death? Give him a uniform and a quiet lobby— that's life and death. In the elevator he took the controls. "Always got a hand on the controls, eh Ludwig?"

Veronica smiled in a feeble, grateful way. She liked to see me get along with the help. Ludwig said, "Dots right."

"Ludwig has been our doorman for years, Phillip. Ever since I was a little girl."

"Wow," I said.

"Dots right."

The door slid open. Veronica said, "Thank you, Ludwig." I said, "Thank you, Ludwig."

"Vulcum."

"Vulcum? You mean, 'welcome'? Hey, Ludwig, how long you been in this country?"

Veronica was driving her key into the door.

"How come you never learned to talk American, baby?"

"Phillip, come here."

"I'm saying something to Ludwig."

"Come here right now."

"I have to go, Ludwig."

"Vulcum."

She went directly to the bathroom. I waited in the hallway between Vlamincks and Utrillos. The Utrillos were pale and flat. The Vlamincks were thick, twisted and red. Raw meat on one wall, dry stone on the other. Mrs. Cohen had an eye for contrasts. I heard Veronica sob. She ran water in the sink, sobbed, sat down, peed. She saw me looking and kicked the door shut.

"At a time like this . . ."

"I don't like you looking."

"Then why did you leave the door open? You obviously don't know your own mind."

"Go away, Phillip. Wait in the living room."

"Just tell me why you left the door open."

"Phillip, you're going to drive me nuts. Go away. I can't do a damn thing if I know you're standing there."

The living room made me feel better. The settee, the chandelier full of teeth and the rug were company. Mr. Cohen was everywhere, a simple, diffuse presence. He jingled change in his pocket, looked out the window and was happy he could see the park. He took a little antelope step and tears came into my eyes. I sat among his mourners. A rabbi droned platitudes: Mr. Cohen was generous, kind, beloved by his wife and daughter. "How much did he weigh?" I shouted. The phone rang.

Veronica came running down the hall. I went and stood at her side when she picked up the phone. I stood dumb, stiff as a hatrack. She was whimpering, "Yes, yes . . ." I nodded my head yes, yes, thinking it was better than no, no. She put the phone down.

"It was my mother. Daddy's all right. Mother is staying with him in his room at the hospital and they'll come home together tomorrow."

Her eyes looked at mine. At them as if they were as flat and opaque as hers. I said in a slow, stupid voice, "You're allowed to do that? Stay overnight in a hospital with a patient? Sleep in his room?" She continued looking at my eyes. I shrugged, looked down. She took my shirt front in a fist like a bite. She whispered. I said, "What?" She whispered again, "Fuck me." The clock ticked like crickets. The Vlamincks spilled blood. We sank into the rug as if it were quicksand.

(1969)

Levitation

from *Levitation: Five Fictions*

Cynthia Ozick

A pair of novelists, husband and wife, gave a party. The husband was also an editor; he made his living at it. But really he was a novelist. His manner was powerless; he did not seem like an editor at all. He had a nice plain pale face, likable. His name was Feingold.

For love, and also because he had always known he did not want a Jewish wife, he married a minister's daughter. Lucy too had hoped to marry out of her tradition. (These words were hers. "Out of my tradition," she said. The idea fevered him.) At the age of twelve she felt herself to belong to the people of the Bible. ("A Hebrew," she said. His heart lurched, joy rocked him.) One night from the pulpit her father read a Psalm; all at once she saw how the Psalmist meant *her;* then and there she became an Ancient Hebrew.

She had huge, intent, sliding eyes, disconcertingly luminous, and copper hair, and a grave and timid way of saying honest things.

They were shy people, and rarely gave parties.

Each had published one novel. Hers was about domestic life; he wrote about Jews.

All the roil about the State of the Novel had passed them by. In the evening after the children had been put to bed, while the portable dishwasher rattled out its smell of burning motor oil, they sat down, she at her desk, he at his, and began to write. They wrote not without puzzlements and travail; nevertheless as naturally as birds. They were devoted to accuracy, psychological realism, and earnest truthfulness; also to virtue, and even to wit. Neither one was troubled by what had happened to the novel: all those declarations about the end of Character and Story. They were serene. Sometimes, closing up their notebooks for the night, it seemed to them that they were literary friends and lovers, like George Eliot and George Henry Lewes.

In bed they would revel in quantity and murmur distrustingly of theory. "Seven pages so far this week." "Nine-and-a-half, but I had to throw out four. A wrong tack." "Because you're doing first person. First person strangles. You can't get out of their skin." And so on. The one principle they agreed on was the importance of never writing about writers. Your protagonist always has to be someone *real,* with real work-in-the-world—a bureaucrat, a banker, an architect (ah, they envied Conrad his shipmasters!)—otherwise you fall into solipsism, narcissism, tedium, lack of appeal-to-the-common-reader; who knew what other perils.

This difficulty—seizing on a concrete subject—was mainly Lucy's. Feingold's novel—the one he was writing now—was about Menachem ben Zerach, survivor of a massacre of Jews in the town of Estella in Spain in 1328. From morning to midnight he hid under a pile of corpses, until a "compassionate knight" (this was the language of the history Feingold relied on) plucked him out and took him home to tend his wounds. Menachem was then twenty; his father and mother and four younger brothers had been cut down in the terror. Six thousand Jews died in a single day in March. Feingold wrote well about how the mild winds carried the salty fragrance of fresh blood, together with the ashes of Jewish houses, into the faces of the marauders. It was nevertheless a triumphant story: at the end Menachem ben Zerach becomes a renowned scholar.

"If you're going to tell about how after he gets to be a scholar he just sits there and *writes,*" Lucy protested, "then you're doing the Forbidden Thing." But Feingold said he meant to concentrate on the massacre, and especially on the life of the "compassionate knight." What had brought him to this compassion? What sort of education? What did he read? Feingold would invent a journal for the compassionate knight, and quote from it. Into this journal the compassionate knight would direct all his gifts, passions, and private opinions.

"Solipsism," Lucy said. "Your compassionate knight is only another writer. Narcissism. Tedium."

They talked often about the Forbidden Thing. After a while they began to call it the Forbidden City, because not only were they (but Lucy especially) tempted to write—solipsistically, narcissistically, tediously, and without common appeal—about writers, but, more narrowly yet, about writers in New York.

"The compassionate knight," Lucy said, "lived on the Upper West Side of Estella. He lived on the Riverside Drive, the West End Avenue, of Estella. He lived in Estella on Central Park West."

The Feingolds lived on Central Park West.

In her novel—the published one, not the one she was writing now—Lucy had described, in the first person, where they lived:

> By now I have seen quite a few of those West Side apartments. They have mysterious layouts. Rooms with doors that go nowhere—turn the knob, open: a wall. Someone is snoring behind it, in another apartment. They have made two and three or even four and five flats out of these palaces. The toilet bowls have antique cracks that shimmer with moisture like old green rivers. Fluted columns and fireplaces. Artur Rubinstein once paid rent here. On a gilt piano he raced a sonata by Beethoven. The sounds went spinning like mercury. Breathings all lettered now. Editors. Critics. Books, old, old books, heavy as centuries. Shelves built into the cold fireplace; Freud on the grate, Marx on the hearth, Melville, Hawthorne, Emerson. Oh God, the weight, the weight.

Lucy felt herself to be a stylist; Feingold did not. He believed in putting one sentence after another. In his publishing house he had no influence. He was nervous about his decisions. He rejected most manuscripts because he was afraid of mistakes; every mistake lost money. It was a small house panting after profits; Feingold told Lucy that the only books his firm respected belonged to the accountants. Now and then he tried to smuggle in a novel after his own taste, and then he would be brutal to the writer. He knocked the paragraphs about until they were as sparse as his own. "God knows what you would do to mine," Lucy said; "bald man, bald prose." The horizon of Feingold's head shone. She never showed him her work. But they understood they were lucky in each other. They pitied every writer who was not married to a writer. Lucy said: "At least we have the same premises."

Volumes of Jewish history ran up and down their walls; they belonged to Feingold. Lucy read only one book—it was *Emma*—over and over again. Feingold did not have a "philosophical" mind. What he liked was event. Lucy liked to speculate and ruminate. She was slightly more intelligent than Feingold. To strangers he seemed very mild. Lucy, when silent, was a tall copper statue.

They were both devoted to omniscience, but they were not acute enough to see what they meant by it. They thought of themselves as children with a puppet theater: they could make anything at all happen, speak all the lines, with gloved hands bring all the characters to shudders or leaps. They fancied themselves in love with what they called "imagination." It was not true. What they were addicted to was counterfeit pity, and this was because they were absorbed by power, and were powerless.

They lived on pity, and therefore on gossip: who had been childless for ten years, who had lost three successive jobs, who was in danger of being fired, which agent's prestige had fallen, who could not get his second novel published, who was *persona non grata* at this or that magazine, who was drinking seriously, who was a likely suicide, who was dreaming of divorce, who was secretly or flamboyantly sleeping with whom, who was being snubbed, who counted or did not count; and toward everyone in the least way victimized they appeared to feel the most immoderate tenderness. They were, besides, extremely "psychological": kind listeners, helpful, lifting hot palms they would gladly put to anyone's anguished temples. They were attracted to bitter lives.

About their own lives they had a joke: they were "secondary-level" people. Feingold had a secondary-level job with a secondary-level house. Lucy's own publisher was secondary-level; even the address was Second Avenue. The reviews of their books had been written by secondary-level reviewers. All their friends were secondary-level: not the presidents or partners of the respected firms, but copy editors and production assistants; not the glittering eagles of the intellectual organs, but the wearisome hacks of small Jewish journals; not the fiercely cold-hearted literary critics, but those wan and chattering daily reviewers of film. If they knew a playwright, he was off-off-Broadway in ambition and had not yet been produced. If they knew a painter, he lived in a loft and had exhibited only once, against the wire fence in the outdoor show at Washington Square in the spring. And this struck them as mean and unfair; they liked their friends, but other people—why not they?—were drawn into the deeper caverns of New York, among the lions.

New York! They risked their necks if they ventured out to Broadway for a loaf of bread after dark; muggers hid behind the seesaws in the playgrounds, junkies with knives hung upside down in the jungle gym. Every apartment a lit fortress; you admired the lamps and the locks, the triple locks on the caged-in windows, the double locks and the police rods on the doors, the lamps with timers set to make burglars think you were always at home. Footsteps in the corridor, the elevator's midnight grind; caution's muffled gasps. Their parents lived in Cleveland and St. Paul, and hardly ever dared to visit. All of this: grit and unsuitability (they might have owned a snowy lawn somewhere else); and no one said their names, no one had any curiosity about them, no one ever asked whether they were working on anything new. After half a year their books were remaindered for eighty-nine cents each. Anonymous mediocrities. They could not call themselves forgotten because they had never been noticed.

Lucy had a diagnosis: they were, both of them, sunk in a ghetto. Feingold persisted in his morbid investigations into Inquisitional autos-da-fé in this and that Iberian marketplace. She herself had supposed the inner life of a housebound woman—she cited *Emma*—to contain as much comedy as the cosmos. Jews and women! They were both beside the point. It was necessary to put aside pity; to look to the center; to abandon selflessness; to study power.

They drew up a list of luminaries. They invited Irving Howe, Susan Sontag, Alfred Kazin, and Leslie Fiedler. They invited Norman Podhoretz and Elizabeth Hardwick. They invited Philip Roth and Joyce Carol Oates and Norman Mailer and William Styron and Donald Barthelme and Jerzy Kosinski and Truman Capote. None of these came; all of them had unlisted numbers, or else machines that answered the telephone, or else were in Prague or Paris or out of town. Nevertheless the apartment filled up. It was a Saturday night in a chill November. Taxis whirled on patches of sleet. On the inside of the apartment door a mound of rainboots grew taller and taller. Two closets were packed tight with raincoats and fur coats; a heap of coats smelling of skunk and lamb fell tangled off a bed.

The party washed and turned like a sluggish tub; it lapped at all the walls of all the rooms. Lucy wore a long skirt, violet-colored, Feingold a lemon shirt and no tie. He looked paler than ever. The apartment had a wide center hall, itself the breadth of a room; the dining room opened off it to the left, the living room to the right. The three party-rooms shone like a triptych: it was as if you could fold them up and enclose everyone into darkness. The guests were freestanding figures in the niches of a cathedral; or else dressed-up cardboard dolls, with their drinks, and their costumes all meticulously hung with sashes and draped collars and little capes, the women's hair variously bound, the men's sprouting and spilling: fashion stalked, Feingold moped. He took in how it all flashed, manhattans and martinis, earrings and shoe-tips—he marveled, but knew it was a falsehood, even a figment. The great world was somewhere else. The conversation could fool you: how these people talked! From the conversation itself—grains of it, carried off, swallowed by new eddyings, swirl devouring swirl, every moment a permutation in the tableau of those freestanding figures or dolls, all of them afloat in a tub— from this or that hint or syllable you could imagine the whole universe in the process of ultimate comprehension. Human nature, the stars, history—the voices drummed and strummed. Lucy swam by blank-eyed, pushing a platter of mottled cheeses. Feingold seized her: "It's a waste!" She gazed back. He said, "No one's here!" Mournfully she rocked a stump of cheese; then he lost her.

He went into the living room: it was mainly empty, a few lumps on the sofa. The lumps wore business suits. The dining room was better. Something in formation: something around the big table: coffee cups shimmering to the brim, cake cut onto plates (the mock-Victorian rosebud plates from Boots's drug store in London: the year before their first boy was born Lucy and Feingold saw the Brontës' moors;

Coleridge's house in Highgate; Lamb House, Rye, where Edith Wharton had tea with Henry James; Bloomsbury; the Cambridge stairs Forster had lived at the top of)—it seemed about to become a regular visit, with points of view, opinions; a discussion. The voices began to stumble; Feingold liked that, it was nearly human. But then, serving round the forks and paper napkins, he noticed the awful vivacity of their falsetto phrases: actors, theater chatter, who was directing whom, what was opening where; he hated actors. Shrill puppets. Brainless. A double row of faces around the table; gurgles of fools.

The center hall—swept clean. No one there but Lucy, lingering.

"Theater in the dining room," he said. "Junk."

"Film. I heard film."

"Film too," he conceded. "Junk. It's mobbed in there."

"Because they've got the cake. They've got all the food. The living room's got nothing."

"My God," he said, like a man choking, "do you realize *no one came?*"

The living room had—had once had—potato chips. The chips were gone, the carrot sticks eaten, of the celery sticks nothing left but threads. One olive in a dish; Feingold chopped it in two with vicious teeth. The business suits had disappeared. "It's awfully early," Lucy said; "a lot of people had to leave." "It's a cocktail party, that's what happens," Feingold said. "It isn't *exactly* a cocktail party," Lucy said. They sat down on the carpet in front of the fireless grate. "Is that a real fireplace?" someone inquired. "We never light it," Lucy said. "Do you light those candlesticks ever?" "They belonged to Jimmy's grandmother," Lucy said, "we never light them."

She crossed no-man's-land to the dining room. They were serious in there now. The subject was Chaplin's gestures.

In the living room Feingold despaired; no one asked him, he began to tell about the compassionate knight. A problem of ego, he said: compassion being superconsciousness of one's own pride. Not that he believed this; he only thought it provocative to say something original, even if a little muddled. But no one responded. Feingold looked up. "Can't you light that fire?" said a man. "All right," Feingold said. He rolled a paper log made of last Sunday's *Times* and laid a match on it. A flame as clear as a streetlight whitened the faces of the sofa-sitters. He recognized a friend of his from the Seminary—he had what Lucy called "theological" friends—and then and there, really very suddenly, Feingold wanted to talk about God. Or, if not God, then certain historical atrocities, abominations: to wit, the crime of the French nobleman Draconet, a proud Crusader, who in the spring of the year 1247 arrested all the Jews of the province of Vienne, castrated the men, and tore off the breasts of the women; some he did not mutilate, and only cut in two. It interested Feingold that Magna Carta and the Jewish badge of shame were issued in the same year, and that less than a century afterward all the Jews were driven out of England, even families who had been settled there seven or eight generations. He had a soft spot for Pope Clement IV, who absolved the Jews from responsibility for the Black Death. "The plague takes the Jews themselves," the Pope said. Feingold knew innumerable stories about forced conversions, he felt at home with these thoughts, comfortable, the chairs seemed dense with family. He wondered whether it would be appropriate—at a cocktail party, after all!—to inquire after the status of the Seminary friend's agnosticism: was it merely that God had stepped out of history, left the room for a moment, so to speak, without a pass, or was there no Creator to begin with, nothing had been created, the world was a chimera, a solipsist's delusion?

Lucy was uneasy with the friend from the Seminary; he was the one who had administered her conversion, and every encounter was like a new stage in a perpetual examination. She was glad there was no Jewish catechism. Was she a backslider? Anyhow she felt tested. Sometimes she spoke of Jesus to the children. She looked around—her great eyes wheeled—and saw that everyone in the living room was a Jew.

There were Jews in the dining room too, but the unruffled, devil-may-care kind: the humorists, the painters, film reviewers who went off to studio showings of *Screw on Screen* on the eve of the Day of Atonement. Mostly there were Gentiles in the dining room. Nearly the whole cake was gone. She took the last piece, cubed it on a paper plate, and carried it back to the living room. She blamed Feingold, he was having one of his spasms of fanaticism. Everyone normal, everyone with sense—the humanists and humorists, for instance—would want to keep away. What was he now, after all, but one of those boring autodidacts who spew out everything they read? He was doing it for spite, because no one had come. There he was, telling about the blood-libel. Little Hugh of Lincoln. How in London, in 1279, Jews were torn to pieces by horses, on a charge of having crucified a Christian child. How in 1285, in Munich, a mob burned down a synagogue on the same pretext. At Eastertime in Mainz two years earlier. Three centuries of beatified child martyrs, some of them figments, all called "Little Saints." The Holy Niño of LaGuardia. Feingold was crazed by these tales, he drank them like a vampire. Lucy stuck a square of chocolate cake in his mouth to shut him up. Feingold was waiting for a voice. The friend from the Seminary, pragmatic, licked off his bit of cake hungrily. It was a cake sent from home, packed by his wife in a plastic bag, to make sure there was something to eat. It was a guaranteed no-lard cake. They were all ravenous. The fire crumpled out in big paper cinders.

The friend from the Seminary had brought a friend. Lucy examined him: she knew how to give catechisms of her own, she was not a novelist for nothing. She catechized and catalogued: a refugee. Fingers like long wax candles, snuffed at the nails. Black sockets: was he blind? It was hard to tell where the eyes were under that ledge of skull. Skull for a head, but such a cushioned mouth, such lips, such orderly expressive teeth. Such a bone in such a dry wrist. A nose like a saint's. The face of Jesus. He whispered. Everyone leaned over to hear. He was Feingold's voice: the voice Feingold was waiting for.

"Come to modern times," the voice urged. "Come to yesterday." Lucy was right: she could tell a refugee in an instant, even before she heard any accent. They all reminded her of her father. She put away this insight (the resemblance of Presbyterian ministers to Hitler refugees) to talk over with Feingold later: it was nicely analytical, it had enough mystery to satisfy. "Yesterday," the refugee said, "the eyes of God were shut." And Lucy saw him shut his hidden eyes in their tunnels. "Shut," he said, "like iron doors"—a voice of such nobility that Lucy thought immediately of that eerie passage in Genesis where the voice of the Lord God walks in the Garden in the cool of the day and calls to Adam, "Where are you?"

They all listened with a terrible intensity. Again Lucy looked around. It pained her how intense Jews could be, though she too was intense. But she was intense because her brain was roiling with ardor, she wooed mind-pictures, she was a novelist. *They* were intense all the time; she supposed the grocers among them were as intense as any novelist; was it because they had been Chosen, was it because they pitied themselves every breathing moment?

Pity and shock stood in all their faces.

The refugee was telling a story. "I witnessed it," he said, "I am the witness." Horror; sadism; corpses. As if—Lucy took the image from the elusive wind that was his voice in its whisper—as if hundreds and hundreds of Crucifixions were all happening at once. She visualized a hillside with multitudes of crosses, and bodies dropping down from big bloody nails. Every Jew was Jesus. That was the only way Lucy could get hold of it: otherwise it was only a movie. She had seen all the movies, the truth was she could feel nothing. That same bulldozer shoveling those same sticks of skeletons, that same little boy in a cap with twisted mouth and his hands in the air—if there had been a camera at the Crucifixion Christianity would collapse, no one would ever feel anything about it. Cruelty came out of the imagination, and had to be witnessed by the imagination.

All the same, she listened. What he told was exactly like the movies. A gray scene, a scrubby hill, a ravine. Germans in helmets, with shining tar-black belts, wearing gloves. A ragged bundle of Jews at the lip of the ravine—an old grandmother, a child or two, a couple in their forties. All the faces stained with grayness, the stubble on the ground stained gray, the clothes on them limp as shrouds but immobile, as if they were already under the dirt, shut off from breezes, as if they were already stone. The refugee's whisper carved them like sculptures—there they stood, a shadowy stone asterisk of Jews, you could see their nostrils, open as skulls, the stony round ears of the children, the grandmother's awful twig of a neck, the father and mother grasping the children but strangers to each other, not a touch between them, the grandmother cast out, claiming no one and not claimed, all prayerless stone gums. There they stood. For a long while the refugee's voice pinched them and held them, so that you had to look. His voice made Lucy look and look. He pierced the figures through with his whisper. Then he let the shots come. The figures never teetered, never shook: the stoniness broke all at once and they fell cleanly, like sacks, into the ravine. Immediately they were in a heap, with random limbs all tangled together. The refugee's voice like a camera brought a German boot to the edge of the ravine. The boot kicked sand. It kicked and kicked, the sand poured over the family of sacks.

Then Lucy saw the fingers of the listeners—all their fingers were stretched out.

The room began to lift. It ascended. It rose like an ark on waters. Lucy said inside her mind, "This chamber of Jews." It seemed to her that the room was levitating on the little grains of the refugee's whisper. She felt herself alone at the bottom, below the floorboards, while the room floated upward, carrying Jews. Why did it not take her too? Only Jesus could take her. They were being kidnapped, these Jews, by a messenger from the land of the dead. The man had a power. Already he was in the shadow of another tale: she promised herself she would not listen, only Jesus could make her listen. The room was ascending. Above her head it grew smaller and smaller, more and more remote, it fled deeper and deeper into upwardness.

She craned after it. Wouldn't it bump into the apartment

upstairs? It was like watching the underside of an elevator, all dirty and hairy, with dust-roots wagging. The black floor moved higher and higher. It was getting free of her, into loftiness, lifting Jews.

The glory of their martyrdom.

Under the rising eave Lucy had an illumination: she saw herself with the children in a little city park. A Sunday afternoon early in May. Feingold has stayed home to nap, and Lucy and the children find seats on a bench and wait for the unusual music to begin. The room is still levitating, but inside Lucy's illumination the boys are chasing birds. They run away from Lucy, they return, they leave. They surround a pigeon. They do not touch the pigeon; Lucy has forbidden it. She has read that city pigeons carry meningitis. A little boy in Red Bank, New Jersey, contracted sleeping sickness from touching a pigeon; after six years, he is still asleep. In his sleep he has grown from a child to an adolescent; puberty has come on him in his sleep, his testicles have dropped down, a benign blond beard glints mildly on his cheeks. His parents weep and weep. He is still asleep. No instruments or players are visible. A woman steps out onto a platform. She is an anthropologist from the Smithsonian Institution in Washington, D.C. She explains that there will be no "entertainment" in the usual sense; there will be no "entertainers." The players will not be artists; they will be "real peasants." They have been brought over from Messina, from Calabria. They are shepherds, goatherds. They will sing and dance and play just as they do when they come down from the hills to while away the evenings in the taverns. They will play the instruments that scare away the wolves from the flock. They will sing the songs that celebrate the Madonna of Love. A dozen men file onto the platform. They have heavy faces that do not smile. They have heavy dark skins, cratered and leathery. They have ears and noses that look like dried twisted clay. They have gold teeth. They have no teeth. Some are young; most are in their middle years. One is very old; he wears bells on his fingers. One has an instrument like a butter churn: he shoves a stick in and out of a hole in a wooden tub held under his arm, and a rattling screech spurts out of it. One blows on two slender pipes simultaneously. One has a long strap, which he rubs. One has a frame of bicycle bells; a descendant of the bells the priests used to beat in the temple of Minerva.

The anthropologist is still explaining everything. She explains the "male" instrument: three wooden knockers; the innermost one lunges up and down between the other two. The songs, she explains, are mainly erotic. The dances are suggestive.

The unusual music commences. The park has filled with Italians—greenhorns from Sicily, settled New Yorkers from Naples. An ancient people. They clap. The old man with the bells on his fingers points his dusty shoe-toes and slowly follows a circle of his own. His eyes are in trance, he squats, he ascends. The anthropologist explains that up-and-down dancing can also be found in parts of Africa. The singers wail like Arabs; the anthropologist notes that the Arab conquest covered the southernmost portion of the Italian boot for two hundred years. The whole chorus of peasants sings in a dialect of archaic Greek; the language has survived in the old songs, the anthropologist explains. The crowd is laughing and stamping. They click their fingers and sway. Lucy's boys are bored. They watch the man with the finger-bells; they watch the wooden male pump up and down. Everyone is clapping, stamping, clicking, swaying, thumping. The wailing goes on and on, faster and faster. The singers are dancers, the dancers are singers, they turn and turn, they are smiling the drugged smiles of dervishes. At home they grow flowers. They follow the sheep into the deep grass. They drink wine in the taverns at night. Calabria and Sicily in New York, sans wives, in sweat-blotched shirts and wrinkled dusty pants, gasping before strangers who have never smelled the sweetness of their village grasses!

Now the anthropologist from the Smithsonian has vanished out of Lucy's illumination. A pair of dancers seize each other. Leg winds over leg, belly into belly, each man hopping on a single free leg. Intertwined, they squat and rise, squat and rise. Old Hellenic syllables fly from them. They send out high elastic cries. They celebrate the Madonna, giver of fertility and fecundity. Lucy is glorified. She is exalted. She comprehends. Not that the musicians are peasants, not that their faces and feet and necks and wrists are blown grass and red earth. An enlightenment comes on her: she sees what is eternal: before the Madonna there was Venus; before Venus, Aphrodite; before Aphrodite, Astarte. The womb of the goddess is garden, lamb, and babe. She is the river and the waterfall. She causes grave men of business—goatherds are men of business—to cavort and to flash their gold teeth. She induces them to blow, beat, rub, shake and scrape objects so that music will drop out of them.

Inside Lucy's illumination the dancers are seething. They are writhing. For the sake of the goddess, for the sake of the womb of the goddess, they are turning into serpents. When they grow still they are earth. They are from always to always. Nature is their pulse. Lucy sees: she understands: the gods are God. How terrible to have given up Jesus, a man like these, made of earth like these, with a pulse like these, God entering nature to become god! Jesus, no more miraculous than an ordinary goatherd; is a goatherd miracle? Is a leaf? A nut, a pit, a core, a seed, a stone? Everything is miracle! Lucy sees how she has abandoned nature, how she has lost true religion on account of the God of the Jews. The boys are on their bellies on the ground, digging it up with sticks. They dig and dig: little holes with mounds beside them. They fill them with peach pits, cherry pits, cantaloupe rinds. The Sicilians and Neapolitans pick up their baskets and purses and shopping bags and leave. The benches smell of eaten fruit, running juices, insect-mobbed. The stage is clean.

The living room has escaped altogether. It is very high and extremely small, no wider than the moon on Lucy's thumbnail. It is still sailing upward, and the voices of those on board are so faint that Lucy almost loses them. But she knows which word it is they mainly use. How long can they go on about it? How long? A morbid cud-chewing. Death and death and death. The word is less a human word than an animal's cry; a crow's. Caw caw. It belongs to storms, floods, avalanches. Acts of God. "Holocaust," someone caws dimly from above; she knows it must be Feingold. He always says this word over and over and over. History is bad for him: how little it makes him seem! Lucy decides it is possible to become jaded by atrocity. She is bored by the shootings and the gas and the camps, she is not ashamed to admit this. They are as tiresome as prayer. Repetition diminishes conviction; she is thinking of her father leading the same hymns week after week. If you said the same prayer over and over again, wouldn't your brain turn out to be no better than a prayer wheel?

In the dining room all the springs were running down. It was stale in there, a failed party. They were drinking beer or Coke or whiskey-and-water and playing with the cake crumbs on the tablecloth. There was still some cheese left on a plate, and half a bowl of salted peanuts. "The impact of Romantic Individualism," one of the humanists objected. "At the Frick?" "I never saw that." "They certainly are deliberate, you have to say that for them." Lucy, leaning abandoned against the door, tried to tune in. The relief of hearing atheists. A jacket designer who worked in Feingold's art department came in carrying a coat. Feingold had invited her because she was newly divorced; she was afraid to live alone. She was afraid of being ambushed in her basement while doing laundry. "Where's Jimmy?" the jacket designer asked. "In the other room." "Say goodbye for me, will you?" "Goodbye," Lucy said. The humanists—Lucy saw how they were all compassionate knights—stood up. A puddle from an overturned saucer was leaking onto the floor. "Oh, I'll get that," Lucy told the knights, "don't think another thought about it."

Overhead Feingold and the refugee are riding the living room. Their words are specks. All the Jews are in the air.

(1982)

GOODBYE AND GOOD LUCK

from *The Little Disturbances of Man*

GRACE PALEY

I was popular in certain circles, says Aunt Rose. I wasn't no thinner then, only more stationary in the flesh. In time to come, Lillie, don't be surprised—change is a fact of God. From this no one is excused. Only a person like your mama stands on one foot, she don't notice how big her behind is getting and sings in the canary's ear for thirty years. Who's listening? Papa's in the shop. You and Seymour, thinking about yourself. So she waits in a spotless kitchen for a kind word and thinks—poor Rosie. . . .

Poor Rosie! If there was more life in my little sister, she would know my heart is a regular college of feelings and there is such information between my corset and me that her whole married life is a kindergarten.

Nowadays you could find me any time in a hotel, uptown or downtown. Who needs an apartment to live like a maid with a dustrag in the hand, sneezing? I'm in very good with the bus boys, it's more interesting than home, all kinds of people, everybody with a reason. . . .

And my reason, Lillie, is a long time ago I said to the forelady, "Missus, if I can't sit by the window, I can't sit." "If you can't sit, girlie," she says politely, "go stand on the street corner." And that's how I got unemployed in novelty wear.

For my next job I answered an ad which said: "Refined young lady, medium salary, cultural organization." I went by trolley to the address, the Russian Art Theater of Second Avenue where they played only the best Yiddish plays. They needed a ticket seller, someone like me, who likes the public but is very sharp on crooks. The man who interviewed me was the manager, a certain type.

Immediately he said: "Rosie Lieber, you surely got a build on you!"

"It takes all kinds, Mr. Krimberg."

"Don't misunderstand me, little girl," he said. "I appreciate, I appreciate. A young lady lacking fore and aft, her blood is so busy warming the toes and the finger tips, it don't have time to circulate where it's most required."

Everybody likes kindness. I said to him: "Only don't be fresh, Mr. Krimberg, and we'll make a good bargain."

We did: Nine dollars a week, a glass of tea every night, a free ticket once a week for Mama, and I could go watch rehearsals any time I want.

My first nine dollars was in the grocer's hands ready to move on already, when Krimberg said to me, "Rosie, here's a great gentleman, a member of this remarkable theater, wants to meet you, impressed no doubt by your big brown eyes."

And who was it, Lillie? Listen to me, before my very eyes was Volodya Vlashkin, called by the people of those days the Valentino of Second Avenue. I took one look, and I said to myself: Where did a Jewish boy grow up so big? "Just outside Kiev," he told me.

How? "My mama nursed me till I was six. I was the only boy in the village to have such health."

"My goodness, Vlashkin, six years old! She must have had shredded wheat there, not breasts, poor woman."

"My mother was beautiful," he said. "She had eyes like stars."

He had such a way of expressing himself, it brought tears.

To Krimberg, Vlashkin said after this introduction: "Who is responsible for hiding this wonderful young person in a cage?"

"That is where the ticket seller sells."

"So, David, go in there and sell tickets for a half hour. I have something in mind in regards to the future of this girl and this company. Go, David, be a good boy. And you, Miss Lieber, please, I suggest Feinberg's for a glass of tea. The rehearsals are long. I enjoy a quiet interlude with a friendly person."

So he took me there, Feinberg's, then around the corner, a place so full of Hungarians, it was deafening. In the back room was a table of honor for him. On the tablecloth embroidered by the lady of the house was "Here Vlashkin Eats." We finished one glass of tea in quietness, out of thirst, when I finally made up my mind what to say.

"Mr. Vlashkin, I saw you a couple weeks ago, even before I started working here, in *The Sea Gull*. Believe me, if I was that girl, I wouldn't look even for a minute on the young bourgeois fellow. He could fall out of the play altogether. How Chekhov could put him in the same play as you, I can't understand."

"You liked me?" he asked, taking my hand and kindly patting it. "Well, well, young people still like me . . . so, and you like the theater too? Good. And you, Rose, you know you have such a nice hand, so warm to the touch, such a fine skin, tell me, why do you wear a scarf around your neck? You only hide your young, young throat. These are not olden times, my child, to live in shame."

"Who's ashamed?" I said, taking off the kerchief, but my hand right away went to the kerchief's place, because the truth is, it really was olden times, and I was still of a nature to melt with shame.

"Have some more tea, my dear."

"No, thank you, I am a samovar already."

"Dorfmann!" he hollered like a king. "Bring this child a seltzer with fresh ice!"

In weeks to follow I had the privilege to know him better and better as a person—also the opportunity to see him in his profession. The time was autumn; the theater full of coming and going. Rehearsing without end. After *The Sea Gull* flopped *The Salesman from Istanbul* played, a great success.

Here the ladies went crazy. On the opening night, in the middle of the first scene, one missus—a widow or her husband worked too long hours—began to clap and sing out, "Oi, oi, Vlashkin." Soon there was such a tumult, the actors had to stop acting. Vlashkin stepped forward. Only not Vlashkin to the eyes . . . a younger man with pitch-black hair, lively on restless feet, his mouth clever. A half a century later at the end of the play he came out again, a gray philosopher, a student of life from only reading books, his hands as smooth as silk. . . . I cried to think who I was—nothing—and such a man could look at me with interest.

Then I got a small raise, due to he kindly put in a good word for me, and also for fifty cents a night I was given the pleasure together with cousins, in-laws, and plain stagestruck kids to be part of a crowd scene and to see like he saw every single night the hundreds of pale faces waiting for his feelings to make them laugh or bend down their heads in sorrow.

The sad day came, I kissed my mama goodbye. Vlashkin helped me to get a reasonable room near the theater to be more free. Also my outstanding friend would have a place to recline away from the noise of the dressing rooms. She cried and she cried. "This is a different way of living, Mama," I said. "Besides, I am driven by love."

"You! You, a nothing, a rotten hole in a piece of cheese, are you telling me what is life?" she screamed.

Very insulted, I went away from her. But I am good-natured—you know fat people are like that—kind, and I thought to myself, poor Mama . . . it is true she got more of an idea of life than me. She married who she didn't like, a sick man, his spirit already swallowed up by God. He never washed. He had an unhappy smell. His teeth fell out, his hair disappeared, he got smaller, shriveled up little by little, till goodbye and good luck he was gone and only came to Mama's mind when she went to the mailbox under the stairs to get the electric bill. In memory of him and out of respect for mankind, I decided to live for love.

Don't laugh, you ignorant girl.

Do you think it was easy for me? I had to give Mama a little something. Ruthie was saving up together with your papa for linens, a couple knives and forks. In the morning I had to do piecework if I wanted to keep by myself. So I made flowers. Before lunch time every day a whole garden grew on my table.

This was my independence, Lillie dear, blooming, but it didn't have no roots and its face was paper.

Meanwhile Krimberg went after me too. No doubt observing the success of Vlashkin, he thought, "Aha, open sesame . . ." Others in the company similar. After me in those years were the following: Krimberg I mentioned. Carl Zimmer, played innocent young fellows with a wig. Charlie Peel, a Christian who fell in the soup by accident, a creator of beautiful sets. "Color is his middle name," says Vlashkin, always to the point.

I put this in to show you your fat old aunt was not crazy out of loneliness. In those noisy years I had friends among interesting people who admired me for reasons of youth and that I was a first-class listener.

The actresses—Raisele, Marya, Esther Leopold—were only interested in tomorrow. After them was the rich men, producers, the whole garment center; their past is a pincushion, future the eye of a needle.

Finally the day came, I no longer could keep my tact in my mouth. I said: "Vlashkin, I hear by carrier pigeon you have a wife, children, the whole combination."

"True, I don't tell stories. I make no pretense."

"That isn't the question. What is this lady like? It hurts me to ask, but tell me, Vlashkin . . . a man's life is something I don't clearly see."

"Little girl, I have told you a hundred times, this small room is the convent of my troubled spirit. Here I come to your innocent shelter to refresh myself in the midst of an agonized life."

"Ach, Vlashkin, serious, serious, who is this lady?"

"Rosie, she is a fine woman of the middle classes, a good mother to my children, three in number, girls all, a good cook, in her youth handsome, now no longer young. You see, could I be more frank? I entrust you, dear, with my soul."

It was some few months later at the New Year's ball of the Russian Artists Club, I met Mrs. Vlashkin, a woman with black hair in a low bun, straight and too proud. She sat at a small table speaking in a deep voice to whoever stopped a moment to converse. Her Yiddish was perfect, each word cut like a special jewel. I looked at her. She noticed me like she noticed everybody, cold like Christmas morning. Then she got tired. Vlashkin called a taxi and I never saw her again. Poor woman, she did not know I was on the same stage with her. The poison I was to her role, she did not know.

Later on that night in front of my door I said to Vlashkin, "No more. This isn't for me. I am sick from it all. I am no home breaker."

"Girlie," he said, "don't be foolish."

"No, no, goodbye, good luck," I said. "I am sincere."

So I went and stayed with Mama for a week's vacation and cleaned up all the closets and scrubbed the walls till the paint came off. She was very grateful, all the same her hard life made her say, "Now we see the end. If you live like a bum, you are finally a lunatic."

After this few days I came back to my life. When we met, me and Vlashkin, we said only hello and goodbye, and then for a few sad years, with the head we nodded as if to say, "Yes, yes, I know who you are."

Meanwhile in the field was a whole new strategy. Your mama and your grandmama brought around—boys. Your own father had a brother, you never even seen him. Ruben. A serious fellow, his idealism was his hat and his coat. "Rosie, I offer you a big new free happy unusual life." How? "With me, we will raise up the sands of Palestine to make a nation. That is the land of tomorrow for us Jews." "Ha-ha, Ruben, I'll go tomorrow then." "Rosie!" says Ruben. "We need strong women like you, mothers and farmers." "You don't fool me, Ruben, what you need is dray horses. But for that you need more money." "I don't like your attitude, Rose." "In that case, go and multiply. Goodbye."

Another fellow: Yonkel Gurstein, a regular sport, dressed to kill, with such an excitable nature. In those days—it looks to me like yesterday—the youngest girls wore undergarments like Battle Creek, Michigan. To him it was a matter of seconds. Where did he practice, a Jewish boy? Nowadays I suppose it is easier, Lillie? My goodness, I ain't asking you nothing—touchy, touchy. . . .

Well, by now you must know yourself, honey, whatever you do, life don't stop. It only sits a minute and dreams a dream.

While I was saying to all these silly youngsters "no, no, no," Vlashkin went to Europe and toured a few seasons . . . Moscow, Prague, London, even Berlin—already a pessimistic place. When he came back he wrote a book, you could get from the library even today, *The Jewish Actor Abroad.* If someday you're interested enough in my lonesome years, you could read it. You could absorb a flavor of the man from the book. No, no, I am not mentioned. After all, who am I?

When the book came out I stopped him in the street to say congratulations. But I am not a liar, so I pointed out, too, the egotism of many parts—even the critics said something along such lines.

"Talk is cheap," Vlashkin answered me. "But who are the critics? Tell me, do they create? Not to mention," he continues, "there is a line in Shakespeare in one of the plays from the great history of England. It says, 'Self-loving is not so vile a sin, my liege, as self-neglecting.' This idea also appears in modern times in the moralistic followers of Freud. . . . Rosie, are you listening? You asked a question. By the way, you look very well. How come no wedding ring?"

I walked away from this conversation in tears. But this talking in the street opened the happy road up for more discussions. In regard to many things. . . . For instance, the management—very narrow-minded—wouldn't give him any more certain young men's parts. Fools. What youngest man knew enough about life to be as young as him?

"Rosie, Rosie," he said to me one day, "I see by the clock on your rosy, rosy face you must be thirty."

"The hands are slow, Vlashkin. On a week before Thursday I was thirty-four."

"Is that so? Rosie, I worry about you. It has been on my mind to talk to you. You are losing your time. Do you understand it? A woman should not lose her time."

"Oi, Vlashkin, if you are my friend, what is time?"

For this he had no answer, only looked at me surprised. We went instead, full of interest but not with our former speed, up to my new place on Ninety-fourth Street. The same pictures on the wall, all of Vlashkin, only now everything painted red and black, which was stylish, and new upholstery.

A few years ago there was a book by another member of that fine company, an actress, the one that learned English very good and went uptown—Marya Kavkaz, in which she says certain things regarding Vlashkin. Such as, he was her lover for eleven years, she's not ashamed to write this down. Without respect for him, his wife and children, or even others who also may have feelings in the matter.

Now, Lillie, don't be surprised. This is called a fact of life. An actor's soul must be like a diamond. The more faces it got the more shining is his name. Honey, you will no doubt love and marry one man and have a couple kids and be happy forever till you die tired. More than that, a person like us don't have to know. But a great artist like Volodya Vlashkin . . . in order to make a job on the stage, he's got to practice. I understand it now, to him life is like a rehearsal.

Myself, when I saw him in *The Father-in-law*—an older man in love with a darling young girl, his son's wife, played by Raisele Maisel—I cried. What he said to this girl, how he whispered such sweetness, how all his hot feelings were on his face . . . Lillie, all this experience he had with me. The very words were the same. You can imagine how proud I was.

So the story creeps to an end.

I noticed it first on my mother's face, the rotten handwriting of time, scribbled up and down her cheeks, across her forehead back and forth—a child could read—it said, old, old, old. But it troubled my heart most to see these realities scratched on Vlashkin's wonderful expression.

First the company fell apart. The theater ended. Esther Leopold died from being very aged. Krimberg had a heart attack. Marya went to Broadway. Also Raisele changed her name to Roslyn and was a big comical hit in the movies. Vlashkin himself, no place to go, retired. It said in the paper, "an actor without peer, he will write his memoirs and spend his last years in the bosom of his family among his thriving grandchildren, the apple of his wife's doting eye."

This is journalism.

We made for him a great dinner of honor. At this dinner I said to him, for the last time, I thought, "Good-bye, dear friend, topic of my life, now we part." And to myself I said further: Finished. This is your lonesome bed. A lady what they call fat and fifty. You made it personally. From this lonesome bed you will finally fall to a bed not so lonesome, only crowded with a million bones.

And now comes? Lillie, guess.

Last week, washing my underwear in the basin, I get a

buzz on the phone. "Excuse me, is this the Rose Lieber formerly connected with the Russian Art Theater?"

"It is."

"Well, well, how do you do, Rose? This is Vlashkin."

"Vlashkin! Volodya Vlashkin?"

"In fact. How are you, Rose?"

"Living, Vlashkin, thank you."

"You are all right? Really, Rose? Your health is good? You are working?"

"My health, considering the weight it must carry, is first-class. I am back for some years now where I started, in novelty wear."

"Very interesting."

"Listen, Vlashkin, tell me the truth, what's on your mind?"

"My mind? Rosie, I am looking up an old friend, an old warmhearted companion of more joyful days. My circumstances, by the way, are changed. I am retired, as you know. Also I am a free man."

"What? What do you mean?"

"Mrs. Vlashkin is divorcing me."

"What come over her? Did you start drinking or something from melancholy?"

"She is divorcing me for adultery."

"But, Vlashkin, you should excuse me, don't be insulted, but you got maybe seventeen, eighteen years on me, and even me, all this nonsense—this daydreams and nightmares—is mostly for the pleasure of conversation alone."

"I pointed all this out to her. My dear, I said, my time is past, my blood is as dry as my bones. The truth is, Rose, she isn't accustomed to have a man around all day, reading out loud from the papers the interesting events of our time, waiting for breakfast, waiting for lunch. So all day she gets madder and madder. By nighttime a furious old lady gives me my supper. She has information from the last fifty years to pepper my soup. Surely there was a Judas in that theater, saying every day, 'Vlashkin, Vlashkin, Vlashkin . . .' and while my heart was circulating with his smiles he was on the wire passing the dope to my wife."

"Such a foolish end, Volodya, to such a lively story. What is your plans?"

"First, could I ask you for dinner and the theater—uptown, of course? After this . . . we are old friends. I have money to burn. What your heart desires. Others are like grass, the north wind of time has cut out their heart. Of you, Rosie, I recreate only kindness. What a woman should be to a man, you were to me. Do you think, Rosie, a couple of old pals like us could have a few good times among the material things of this world?"

My answer, Lillie, in a minute was altogether. "Yes, yes, come up," I said. "Ask the room by the switchboard, let us talk."

So he came that night and every night in the week, we talked of his long life. Even at the end of time, a fascinating man. And like men are, too, till time's end, trying to get away in one piece.

"Listen, Rosie," he explains the other day. "I was married to my wife, do you realize, nearly half a century. What good was it? Look at the bitterness. The more I think of it, the more I think we would be fools to marry."

"Volodya Vlashkin," I told him straight, "when I was young I warmed your cold back many a night, no questions asked. You admit it, I didn't make no demands. I was softhearted. I didn't want to be called Rosie Lieber, a breaker up of homes. But now, Vlashkin, you are a free man. How could you ask me to go with you on trains to stay in strange hotels, among Americans, not your wife? Be ashamed."

So now, darling Lillie, tell this story to your mama from your young mouth. She don't listen to a word from me. She only screams, "I'll faint, I'll faint." Tell her after all I'll have a husband, which, as everybody knows, a woman should have at least one before the end of the story.

My goodness, I am already late. Give me a kiss. After all, I watched you grow from a plain seed. So give me a couple wishes on my wedding day. A long and happy life. Many years of love. Hug Mama, tell her from Aunt Rose, goodbye and good luck.

(1959)

DEATH IN MIAMI BEACH

from *The Age of Happy Problems*

HERBERT GOLD

The state of madness can be defined partly as an extreme of isolation of one human being from everyone else. It provides a model for dying. Only an intermittent and fragmentary awareness of others interrupts the black folding of the layers of self upon each other—this also defines the state of that dilemma known as "mental health."

There is a false madness induced by the accidents of isolation which prisoners, travelers, and the very ill may sometimes experience without giving up their return ticket. Surely you out there all know what I mean from your own troubles and painful decisions. To say that it is false madness does not soften its extremity. The mask of existence fits harshly on your skin, but it is in fact your only skin; and when harshly your skin is peeled off—beneath it you are naked and your naked isolation is no joy to you.

During a period of work on a long job of writing in the winter of 1958, I deliberately withdrew myself from all those who knew my name and traveled by automobile in slow stages through the deep South to Miami Beach, Key West, Havana, and finally back up toward Detroit. No one asked me to write a novel, no one asked me to go away; but I did anyway. I was tempted by the prospect of dreaming through my story amid a pleasant chaos of sun and sea, all other responsibilities suspended, and so I arranged it for myself.

Work is very fine, but after the day's work, isolation, silence, and death seemed to follow me through the zazzy carnival of Miami, the casual resort indolence of Key West, and the smoky, blistered elegance of a tourist's Havana. In Havana, from the rooftop of the Ambos Mundos Hotel, I could see Batista's police loafing with their weapons in front of public buildings; occasionally there were bombs; once a body happened to be left in the street and people hurried by as if they knew nothing, nothing, nothing at all but the next step before them.

At Key West, a few days before Christmas, I visited the turtle slaughterhouse. It is one of the few tourist attractions on this spot of island, "North Havana," raised far out into the sea off the coast of Florida. Visitors take their kiddies by the hand and lead them to see the nice turtles.

Before being killed and canned, the turtles swim in dense kraals, bumping each other in the murky water, armor clashing, dully lurching against the high pens. Later, trussed on a plank dock, they lie unblinking in the sun, their flippers pierced and tied. The tough leather of their skin does not disguise their present helplessness and pain. They wear thick, sun-hardened accumulations of blood at their wounds. Barbados turtles, as large as children, they belong to a species which has been eliminated locally by ardent harvesting of the waters near Key West, but the commercial tradition still brings them here to be slaughtered. Crucified like thieves, they breathe in little sighs, they gulp, they wait.

At a further stage, in the room where the actual slaughtering occurs, the butchers stride through gore in heavy boots. The visitor must proceed on a catwalk; a misstep will plunge him into a slow river of entrails and blood. Because it was near Christmastime, the owners of the plant had installed a speaker system for musical divertissement of the butchers, and while the turtles dried under the sun or lay exposed to the butchers' knives, Christmas bells tolled out, electronically amplified, "God Rest Ye Merry, Gentlemen," or the Bing Crosby recording of *"Adeste Fideles."*

These commercial details are not intended to support a special plea on behalf of the humane harvesting of Barbados turtles. In fact, let me grant that I sought out this scene and visited the abattoir without having any proper business there at all: merely curiosity and the need to confirm my imagination about it. I should be judged for vulgarity by the man who chooses out of purity not to follow me, not by the man I saw lurking outside, with a face ravaged by the horrified fascination which makes it impossible for him to visit his dreams. What had I done which he could not permit himself? Was I filthied, was I weakened by pleasure but obscurely nourished, was I fed on coveted turtle joys after trampling in turtle blood? Had I asked permission from the butcher and plied a knife with my own hands on the belly of one of the slow, unblinking, dragon-headed, ancient sea-beasts? And did it arch its graceful dragon neck in reproach as I stabbed? He stared at me like a jealous lover, imagining my wickedness, rabid and hopeless, wanting to bury his head in the reek on my hands.

Most of us turn from the vision of death only out of

weakness, and this is no turning from death. Serve up your turtle steak, gourmet friend, with no protest from me; I'll eat at your table. ("A nice rendition," one gentleman said of Bing Crosby to his wife. Turtle is tasty, somewhat gamy meat. Protein nourishes the brain—brings oxygen and freedom.)

A few days later, in Miami Beach, I participated in two trivial accidents. My hotel was in one of the oldest, therefore least expensive, parts of the town, only a short block from the sea and a short block from restaurants and therefore very convenient to my casual schedule: breakfast at Whelan's, a stretch of writing, a long swim, lunch, a pleasant bit of loafing on the beach, then perhaps some sunbaked work at my typewriter on the tar roof ("solarium"), and another swim before dinner. I had the habit in the morning of disregarding the elevator, hurrying down a back stairway of the Webster Hotel, through an alley, and so shortcutting to the drugstore. One day, wearing tennis shoes, I felt an evil slide and crunch underfoot, and knew first by the shrinking in my heart and then by simple inspection that I had stepped on a small animal.

It seemed to be a variety of cockroach. It had been perhaps an inch and a half long, longer with its wings spread, and it had strayed from the raised platform nearby where the hotel stored its rubbish. Now it lay twitching, legs scrambling in the air without moving, and a yellow ooze seeped from its body within the crushed carapace. I suppose it was already dead despite all this nervous movement. I went for a walk, told myself that this was a silly matter to be fretful about (I was merely isolated), and finally took my habitual breakfast: orange juice, scrambled eggs, toast, coffee.

An hour later the dead beast was glued by its own innards to the paving of the alley; the Florida sun was moving through the sky above it. But now there was also a row of ants leading to it, another leading away, like twin caterpillars dissembling their unity of purpose. They were not merely eating, of course, they were carrying off the meat to their hill someplace. But the dead roach still twitched, and when the tickling jaws struck, it fluttered, squeezed, blindly pushed in its place. The ants went scrambling away, each carrying its minuscule steak.

All afternoon the shell of the roach lay there. Its row of legs no longer waved of their own power, but there were still tremors as the eating ants tugged at it. Unfatigued and busy, they were determined to wipe this slate clean.

Shortly before dark I again came down the back stairway. Now the familiar arena had changed. Another foot had struck, more strange and haphazard than my own. The shell of the roach was destroyed; there were also dead ants freckling the stone; stillness and death. The ants were suddenly individual in death; the undulating columns were erased. And the work of eating was permanently interrupted for both eaters and eaten.

The next morning when I walked through the alley no sign remained. A sweeper had done her work; there were straight, mechanical striations—a friendly broom. Good. But I bent to look for some sign or memorial to the departed beast on this stretch of alley which I now knew very well. There was none. Marks of broom; new arrangements of pebbles and dust; history here had entered upon an epoch which was strange to me.

Then finally a homely death entered what might pass for society in my isolated Miami Beach—the world of the soda fountain at Whelan's, where strollers came into an air-conditioned place to shake off the sand of the beach, sip a Coke, buy lotions and plastic sunglasses, and sometimes order a quick meal.

I was taking my breakfast, according to my habit, on a stool at the counter. By this time I was acquainted with Frank, the short-order cook, who had emigrated from Second Avenue in New York twenty years ago for his health and, for sweet health's sake, still managed to cover the leathery pouched skin of age with a fierce Miami tan, despite his long hours in Whelan's service. It relieved the silence to exchange a few morning words with a man who by now knew my face: "Two scrambled light."

"Same as yesterday, Mister."

"Yes, like yesterday." (Triumph in my voice: He remembers me!) "Whole-wheat toast. You got marmalade today?"

"Marmalade." Frank knew my face and my eggs.

Other eaters, like me, were forking up eggs and grits and sipping their Cokes or coffee when the woman entered. She was blotched with sunburn, had a swollen nose, and a mouth open so wide for noise that all her features were distorted. Emitting emergency alarm signals, turning her head and staring, demanding passage, demanding attention, a shouting vehicle, she pushed a stumbling old man along with her. "Ohh," she screamed, "a Bromo! For God's sake a Bromo! My husband is dying, a Bromo, for God's sake!"

The man's face was blue and he seemed barely conscious. He swayed stiffly as she steered him toward a stool near me.

"Oh, a Bromo right now, please!" she wailed.

Frank, behind the counter, looked sideways at her, pretended the impossible—that he did not hear her—and went on making a bacon-lettuce-and-tomato sandwich on whole-wheat toast, light on the mayonnaise.

Two or three of us jumped up to support the old man. His skin had a thick purple glow that said death to all our eyes.

"Oh, have mercy, a Bromo for my poor husband!" the

woman screamed. "He didn't do nothing to you! For God's sake why don't you give it to him?"

Floundering, I watched Frank finish the bee-ell-tee, slide it onto a plate, and hand it to his customer. The hotrodder bent his head to the spilling sandwich and ate as if his life depended on it, thrustingly. In the meantime, the pharmacist, a short man in a white coat, sweating profusely despite the air conditioning, came bustling from his cubicle and said, "Heart attack? You want I should call a doctor, Missus?"

"Ohh, please, dear God, a Bromo!" she shouted.

"I'll call a doctor, he'll be right over."

"Bromo for a dying man! Why don't you give it to him? Mercy, mercy!"

The pharmacist was on the telephone and the howling woman subsided in shrill spasms. Her husband swayed on the stool, his eyes shut, while his wife leaned sobbing against his back to keep him from toppling onto the ground. She refused to let anyone touch him in order to lay him out on the floor—someone's idea—as if this ministry would commit him once and for all to the hands of death. Naturally, my innards shrank from this; the layers of the self closed tight; the flower of feeling was shut, sealed. I wanted to rush in some place, rush away; strike, destroy, *run*; kill Frank, kill the hotrodder, because a man was dying and nobody could do anything. Thus righteousness substitutes for being straight with the world. I was sly and scared. Thus I occupied myself with rage at my friend Frank, who pretended to hear nothing and stubbornly refused to make the glass of Bromo Seltzer.

During the five minutes before the doctor arrived, the scene altered rapidly and tensely. Of course, all the breakfasters but the determined hotrodder stopped their eating. The kid in the leather jacket asked for pretzels with his Coke for sustained strength behind the wheel. The rest of us drifted, lurking behind the sick man on his stool. His wife wept and cursed and heaved out her sobs because no one would supply a Bromo.

Then abruptly the man shook himself and opened his eyes and tried to stand up. He stumbled; his wife pushed him back onto the stool. He shook his head and mumbled. Then rapidly the purple color diminished; his eyes stopped their blind rolling; he began to talk with his wife. He was returning to the living. He and his wife had a whispered consultation. She nodded rapidly at him, like a bird.

Suddenly she alighted and flew out the door. The man, left behind on the stool, said hoarsely, "Lemme have a glass of water, will you, pal?"

Frank gave him the water.

Now the doctor entered, rolling his sleeves down and carrying his black bag open. He had apparently run a block in the tropical morning heat.

"Haha!" said the formerly dying man. Just like that: "Hahaha! Hi, Doc!"

"You're the sick man?" said the doctor. "Let's see now—"

"Hahaha! Don't touch me, Doc," said the old man, leaning away. "Listen, Doc, it's a funny thing. My wife gets herself all excited—aggravated."

"You mean you're all right?" the doctor said.

"Just like a little attack was all I had, hahaha," said the old man.

"You're okay?"

"Look, Doc, I ain't been eating right, you know, enjoying myself, hahaha. A little attack. I get them sometimes. Like a little attack is all."

"Okay," and the doctor firmly, "you don't want me to

look at you? Okay." He nodded briskly to the pharmacist, said, "I've got a patient in my office," and trotted off again into the heat.

The old man smiled and gazed without malice at Frank, who had refused him the Bromo. Instead of leaving a tip he left him one word of explanation before he headed off after his wife. The word was deposited on the counter behind him with an apologetic smile: "Constipation."

Eggs in the plates of all the late breakfasters were left cold and shiny. The hotrodder alone had finished his sandwich, Coke, and pretzels, and left whistling. Angry at last, I discharged an unformulated hostility on Frank: "Why the devil didn't you give the man his Bromo?"

His reply seems an obvious bit of logical disquisition at this remove, but there in the shadow of panic and crisis it struck me with the force of revelation. Rubbing a dirty cloth on the counter—formulating and reformulating a smear of grease before me—he said, "If he was dying of a heart attack, what good would a Bromo do him? And if he was not dying, what good is a Bromo?"

"Yes, but."

"So I have to do my job, but I don't have to listen to nuts."

"But you didn't say anything! That woman was hysterical."

He looked at me with undisguised pity for my ignorance. "That's why I didn't say anything. I been in trouble for saying things before, I learned."

He went back to work; the pharmacist was back in his cubicle, counting pills into a bottle; the doctor had returned to his office. It was eleven o'clock and Frank took down the sign about the breakfast special. A man came in frightened to ask for the special, and Frank pointed to the sign, which was upside down on the counter, and said, "It's five minutes after eleven already. But I'll give it to you." The look of despair faded from the man's face.

In a few days I finished my own job and began the long drive out of the false Florida summer into the northern winter, my wheels passing over all sorts of unfelt beasties, my gullet accepting steaks and chops, my heart leaping with no better welcome to death than before. In Detroit my daughter asked me, "What's God's last name? How big is the whole world? Where do you go when you die?"

The foregoing inconclusive words were written two years ago. Now I have seen fit to return to my cafeteria-and-old-folks slum on lower Collins Avenue, and ostensibly for the same lure of cheap sun, sky, water, beach, boredom. I write, I swim. I stroll on Lincoln Road, I eat steaks and pizza, I sniff the sea with my sunburnt beak, I suck in my belly and run barefoot on the sand, I sleep, I write. In front of one of the new hotels I found a nude in plaster, beckoning, with her hand lifted as if hitching a ride. All aboard, you masturba-tors. Some of the fruit juice and hamburger stands have disappeared; new ones have opened. The Ellis Department Store, Here Since 1919, is closed, looks ransacked, has a box of Fruit of the Loom T-shirts spilled in the window and a U. S. Federal Court bankruptcy notice affixed to its sealed door.

I met a waitress in a restaurant which advertises nine-course dollar dinners. She has a pretty, lively, thirty-five-year-old girl's face, with all the black brightness of eye a man could want; she turns out to be Corsican and we speak French; an artillery sergeant brought her to Florida and apparently tired of her brightness of eye. She has a rattling Corsican accent, likes Edith Piaf records, and gives me extra shrimp bits in my shrimp bits salad. So some things change.

Last time I heard no Edith Piaf and earned no extra forkfuls of shrimp. The sirloin steak she brings me spreads its wings and seems ready to flop off the plate. My gut talks French and I take ease in the flattery of food. I wait and at last she slips into my booth with me and sighs. It is eleven o'clock, time to begin real life. Her history is sad. I feel obliged to offer some recompense for the evil done her by men and luck, and so I listen, wondering how her eyes can remain so bright as the disasters and disillusionments unroll.

When I said good night, she replied with a funny, rapidly fiddling, diddling, twenty-one-fingered gesture at her mouth. I asked what it meant. "Fun and glee," she said, "fun and glee! *Maintenant je suis une vraie Américaine.*" Her eyes burn like stars, but like the stars, she has darkness between them.

A day and a night and another day. The first week passes.

I eat salty bagels in the sun, I listen to the teenage girls after school with their curious mixture of Florida cracker and Bronx accents. I go back into the damp of my room—the peculiar dank assault of cheap tropical bedrooms—and think my novel through once again, examining the pile of manuscript with my intentions in motion like a column of ants working over the struggling body of an insect. And when the life seems to weaken, I leave it and go out onto the beach or into the street.

Madness consists partly in an extreme of isolation? Partly. But the demented tumble down from their associations and memories into other associations and memories; they are sent away into the future with a map of the past which conforms to no agreed past and to no other map—and yet it is their only chart, their history and route, their needs which are unfailingly present. The lonely traveler also brutally inflicts absolute possession of his movements upon the endless day, and the novelty of what he sees joins him in yet another way to his deepest desires and dreads. He returns, he never lets go. There is no escape even in isolation; there is no isolation, merely interrupted and distorted association, until death claims us. Then every man is an island entire of itself.

In love, we seek freedom and purity even more than the comfort of diminished isolation. Those few fortunate ones who have the talent can bear the paradox of love. The rest of us are harassed by our contradictory demands—*join me, make me free.* With age and aging, the model of all voyages (learn and grow, diminish and weary), comes final approach to the ultimate simplicity which love seeks to confound— death. A paradox forever out of balance to answer a grave black simplicity: *we are ill used.* The facts we make for ourselves disappoint the intentions with which we make them. The opposable thumb, which is said to be responsible for civilization and history, gives us no answers here, though with it we can grasp our pens and break insects in our hands. Finally we die, opposable thumbs and all.

In the meantime, I visit my story. We exchange visits. I laugh over it, frown and worry over it, and urge it forward. Then I leave it for the Miami streets. The book follows me; it does not let me visit unaccompanied; it enters me instead and I try to shake it off as an adept at voodoo fights against possession by the importunate god. The opposable thumb is of no use in this contest; both the prize and the weapons have reached beyond tools, even tools of thinking; I am the quadruple god's horse—dream of love, hope of meaning, joy of power, relish in being. Too much burden on one soul. Who asked me to feel sorry or glad for others? They were merely pious who asked me. Why follow their orders? I decide: I *won't.* But I cannot escape my self, which also gives orders.

The flower of feeling opens; the flower shuts; it obeys the freshness of weather. All emotion flowing from health or illness partakes of the pathetic fallacy, identifying moral value with the gifts of nature. My feet want to run; I am wearing Keds, and feel light on the foam rubber soles; but the heat of the sun holds me to earth.

There is a hotel on Washington Boulevard which specializes in "economical, comfortable living for the retired." It is a huge dark building like the Women's House of Detention in Greenwich Village, but without the bars on the rooms, and there are purple lights playing on the palm trees outside, soft music piped throughout the grounds, and the frequent blare of a loudspeaker: "Missus Goldberg to the telephone! Missus Goldberg! *Sadie, answer the phone!*" when the children call from New York. The streets of the neighborhood are filled with chattering of mournful elder statesmen, mostly losers after sixty years of continual negotiation, men with chagrined pouches slipping sideways beneath their eyes, women with hair bursting onto their cheeks and upper lips, as if all at once, near the end, they have decided to make a final try at being better men than their husbands.

To walk through the crowd during the hour following their afternoon naps is to wade in senility. There is a deep-sea lack of light despite all the sun and brisk resort clatter; you gasp for life and run to look in a dusty window. Narcissus wants to be just thirty-five, *"nel mezzo del cammin di nostra vita,"* and not seventy, not seventy! The crowd flutters by. "She thought she could be my daughter-in-law! A girl like that! To be my daughter-in-law! And you know what? Now she is." "I used to be in business. I had a good business. It was a nice store, good location. Furniture. I should have kept my location." "What does the weather report say? Does the weather report ever say anything but the weather?" "Moishe died. He had an attack. Well, we all got to go."

Is it the same voice, the same rhythm? It is the same crowd—grief, isolation, death. There almost always seems to be an ambulance pulling up or pulling away.

It is fine to tell a story, which feels like affirmation, but afterwards, after the morning's writing, then what? Writing is an expression of affirmation, power, longing, but not a proper cause of these emotions in the writer. He is a guide into delight and dread because he can escape victimization (he thinks); he has left a little trail of paper behind him as he threads his way into the maze, and can find his way back (he believes—though the roar of the maze sets up a disarray in anything as fragmentary as his intentions about return). He tracks the minotaur with an open mind. "Maybe I'll like it," he says, "and maybe I won't. At least I'll see." He initiates passion only because he has it—otherwise self-delusion and covetous self-therapy. And so it is not good to be alone for long, entirely alone.

But at least for a time, until they dim out, loneliness sharpens the eyes. I feel like a safecracker; loneliness has also sharpened my fingertips, and my entire body throughout feels the clicking tumblers as I yearn toward the combination. I come to focus, I work. But afterwards, then what? I have retreated from the distractions of Manhattan. There are no telephone calls. No friendship, no duties, no hazards of pique or pleasure. I shall work till the battery runs down, frozen and stilled by this busy emptiness under the sun. I ask myself: Can the silent column of ants reconstruct the living roach at its leisure underground? No, only a tree can make a tree, only a winged roach can make a winged roach. A column of ants works by an invisible will which resides in no one of its jointed parts, but only a swollen green ant can breed an urgent ant.

As I walk on Lincoln Road, the smart shopping area of "the Beach," I ogle the oglers, the sunburned sun-worshipers basted with oil, cream, tonic, and lotion—the touts, boxers, fairies, grandmothers, exiled Cubans, local hotrodders and their gumchewing molls, sportsmen, natty invalids in gabardine, drunks, stockbrokers, antique collectors, Semites and anti-Semites all taking the air together on Lincoln Road. Hill people, swamp people, and ex-pugs sell newspapers flown in from all over—New York, Chicago, Los Angeles ("Smogsville!" cackles a refugee). And New York is harried by flu and Chicago is black with coal and damp. And here we all are on Lincoln Road, with a delicious breeze, courtesy of the steakhouse pumping cool air into the street. So let's buy the hometown paper to see how miserable we might have been, for others are.

On Lincoln Road, fair Lincoln Road in Miami Beach, the Negroes have been freed; freed of existence, that is; only a few black ghosts slip discreetly by. Even if they were not so discreet, they would be invisible, though for a new reason: they are going someplace, namely, to work, or at another hour, home. For them, Lincoln Road is a mere artery for transit, while for the others, Lincoln Road is parlor, sunroom, promontory into health and beauty. For the visitors, Lincoln Road is a slow matter, a recipe for yearned-for slowness, sloth, strolling ease, delicacy of control. The cocky Broadway chapparoonies are wearing their new pleatless "Miami-Tailored Daks." Their bellies do the work of belts, hiding the place where belts would be. Now I'm so slow I don't need a belt, the pants proudly announce; I'm just walkin' along, just struttin' down the avenue, just here and pleasant with myself, and when I take a breath, the expandable elastic waistband expands with me. In the men's room of a bar off Lincoln Road, hung with photographs of wrestlers, there is a curious vending machine which is decorated with a crown and raised scepter and submits a product called DE-LA: "Say Delay, a light lubricating ointment designed to aid in the prevention of premature climax. Odorless. Safe. Stainless. Easy to apply. Directions on package. 50¢ coins only. Machine does not give change."

Machine makes comment, however. Machine is trying to tell us something.

The Negro girl who cleans my room gets yelled at, screamed at, all morning. "Stupid, stupid, stupid! A single room only gets two towels, one face, one bath!" She smiles slyly to herself as if she knows where the manager's DE-LA is hidden. This is the southland, I am reminded, where we have grits for breakfast. But it is not quite dat ole Dixie, boss, which changeth not, nor can age alter it. It is Miami Beach. The Sholem Aleichem Literary Society ("Managed by Tourists—Managed for Tourists") has a For Rent sign on it. "Owner Will Remodel for Any Business."

I decide as I walk: I'll write my book till the battery runs down, though distraction seems necessary; other duties, friends, "real life."

The sirens of the police ambulances work up and down the Beach all day and night, announcing the news as they carry away the attacked, the fallen, the stroked, the perished. A population of the aged sheds its members at the merest trifle of an excuse—a "bottle of cold pop in the sun, a skipped nap, somebody raising his voice suddenly—or no excuse at all. It touches life and someone dies. It treads carelessly and someone dies. The sirens whir and howl and

Negroes courteously open the back door for the corpse. For some reason people smile at the ambulance as they stroll, sucking ice cream. Perhaps they dream of an accident, a distraction: *Siren meets white Thunderbird, boy of forty cut off in his prime, had a girl in there with him, not his wife.* Perhaps thinking: *Not me this time.*

One of those impossible coincidences. Today I met Dr. Meyer leading his blind wife. He was our family doctor in Cleveland, addicted to practical jokes, who always said he wanted to do research, and in fact he had some sort of connection with one of the important drug laboratories. When he retired from practice, he announced to my parents over a bottle of wine that now he would begin his true life's work. I had decided that his practical jokes, bought in Jean's Fun House on East 9th Street—buzzers, false flies, stomach noises, leaky cups—were a symptom of childish anger at adult responsibility. But now that he could retire from practice and try his hand at research. . . . It turned out that his wife had inoperable cataracts; she went blind fast, and he went sour, quiet, mean; and they left Cleveland for Miami Beach, where I saw him leading her, walking with the stiff, frightened step of the unaccustomed blind. He is shrunken; only today do I notice that he is a small man—when I was a boy, he was immense. At present, and forever until the very end, his life's work is to steer his wife to the beach in the morning and sit with her to describe what he sees. He has replaced both practical jokes and dreams of a laboratory with loyalty to his wife, but virtue has made him a furious runt.

Fantasies of thighs, breasts, bellies as I nap on the beach. I awaken, sticky with salt. My nose is peeling. Shall I visit the Corsican waitress again tonight? Shall I ask the Meyers to dinner? But I have made this disappearance into Miami Beach in order to avoid the troubles of others and of myself. I swim again. I doze again. I dream of sex with a woman I overheard describing the proper way to kill a chicken "so it don't suffer. You ask anyone, they'll tell you. And there's nothing like fresh-killed chicken. You can't trust the butchers."

A man in the coffee shop later said to the cashier: "I been sick, that's why you ain't seen me. Doctor said coronary thrombosis. You ever heard of that?"

"Naw. Lots of people got coronaries, but that thrombosis, that's a new thing. The docs keep finding new things so they can charge us."

"Well, I'll tell you, it left me feeling pretty weak."

I went one night to see a road company version of *My Fair Lady* at the Miami Beach Auditorium, which more frequently provides hospitality for wrestling or boxing matches. A maggoty, bored imitation of Rex Harrison, a thick Eliza without any bounce. The audience is quietly taking in the famous sight. They write on their postcards home: Tonight we saw a Broadway show, but the girl was fat.

Crazy Louie on the beach—a frantic grandfather with Latin records, maracas, castanets, silk Cuban shirts, feathers, straw skirt, rubber Halloween masks, a huge earring loosely hooked to his ear by a bent hairpin, thick glasses sliding down his nose, leathery withered legs, dancing and dancing, all sinews and grins and shakes to some inner song while the portable phonograph goes rattle-and-scrape, screech, rattle, and scrape. Amazingly, the crowd which regularly gathers on the sand nearby seems to enjoy his music; some of them shake, too, dreaming of the days when they had lust to squander on their legs. Dr. Meyer's wife smiles as he describes the scene. "Are you smiling, Meyer?" she asks. He says yes, but is lying. Crazy Louie bangs his castanet under her nose and screams *"Olé!"* and she jumps. At last Dr. Meyer smiles.

Then he tells her that sometimes the beginnings of arteriosclerosis can be detected at age twenty-five. "Cuts off the blood supply to the brain. The psychiatrists think they're smart, but they can't do anything about the histological system. The brain dries up like a scab."

"Meyer, you shouldn't use such language."

"You mean histology?"

"I mean scab, Meyer."

Crazy Louie is dancing and cackling, kicking sand. The old ladies in their bathing skirts fan themselves contentedly as he enters his Afro-Cuban apocalypse. On the beach there is a rural, village tolerance of madness. Louie doesn't do any harm. His children sent him down. He is new since my last visit.

And where are my old friends?

The cockroach in the alley is long gone, of course, and its grandchildren unto many generations. But I have found cheap sun again for my sinus, and white ocean breaking against the distractions of Manhattan in winter, spring, summer, fall. I think of a friend, a Jewish chauvinist, arguing with his girl: "When your people were still living in trees and hitting each other with sticks, my people already had sinus trouble."

The Spinoza Forum is gone, replaced by a motel. Dr. Wolfson still goes to the beach every afternoon. But the neighborhood is changed. He has nothing to say to me except that raw beets, honey, and tangerines keep a man virtuous and healthy, no matter what his age.

The woman who knew Thomas Wolfe—did I forget to mention that last time?—and swam as if she wanted to die, and worked as a B-girl . . . gone. She wanted to reconstruct some cabin-in-the-woods dream of perfection, but she could never find the missing pieces. Life is not a jigsaw puzzle; once it has been scrambled, the old picture is gone.

The racing-car driver with whom I chatted a couple of times at breakfast—gone.

The column of ants at the cockroach—gone.

The drummed-up acquaintances—even their names forgotten.

The hotel clerk who wanted to explore in Guatemala— perhaps he is exploring in Guatemala. The new manager of the hotel has never even heard of him.

And the man who died—dead.

I know this for certain, for I have finally discovered an old friend. Frank, the gray bozo behind the counter at Whelan's, is still there. I had taken up new eating habits and did not return to Whelan's during my first week in Miami Beach, but then I did and found him, still building hamburger platters and scrambling eggs. At first he did not remember me. He never knew my name. When I reminded him of the incident about the man who died, and of our long breakfast friendship, a look of irritation captured his face—demands were being made on him—but then his cross mug creased into a smile. He did remember me! He only needed to be reminded!

"You know that old fool," he said. "Later really did die. He's dead. Later died."

There was a new cat in the store. A new special on toothbrushes. A new pharmacist.

I had a hamburger on our old friendship, and Frank put an extra slice of tomato on the side to prove that he remembered me. But why should he? He had been an experience for me—the same now, with balder eyebrows—but what was I to him? For me he existed as an example of something, a moment of frightening history, a troubled memory which I had set down in words. I had needed a friend then, but he did not. I was frightened by death then, and worse, by a way of receiving death, but he was not and perhaps never admits that he might be.

Why does he stay in Miami Beach?

Yes, for a job. Yes, for the sun. But why there?

All right, then why not there?

Why do I go back?

Why did I go back? What happened to those dead and dying ones? They died and were dead; they were swept away. I thought, the first time I went to Miami Beach, that I had made a free choice to be isolated, but I discovered that everyone comes to the state of isolation in time—though not freely. What I did out of apparent health and youth, in the pleasure of work, those others did in sickness and age, in the anxiety of boredom. But eventually work is done, health turns to decay, youth turns to ripeness turns to age; feebleness and dying must precede death except for fighter pilots, who are anachronisms. Miami Beach is an extension, adult education course in how to die, pursued with great seriousness by the enrollees. The old folks work at it with deliberate and modest intensity, in group sessions, complimenting each other on their tans, their sport shirts, their postgraduate skill at finding a proper weather. The young vacationers flush in on packaged tours, immerse themselves in the ceremonial indulgences of resort hotels, eat, swim, and enjoy their honeymoon wrestling, take in Eartha Kitt or Leo de Lion, sigh with boredom and excess, buy bottles of Man Tan at the air terminal ("Arrive With Fresh Sun On Your Cheeks!"), and flee back to real life with a secret conviction that this is leisure? Strictly for the birds, brother.

That first time in Miami Beach, I was a curious observer, obscurely moved, with the face of a man who fearfully unwinds a rope as he visits his dream of the turtle slaughterhouse. The second time (the last time!), two years' change had begun to discover my implication to me; I broke the rope; the model of death is real; the dream of dying is real. The tanned, reduced, heliotropic Doctor Meyer recognized me despite his wife's blindness ("Hannah! Look who's here!"), and when I spoke to her, she gropingly embraced me. This was why I went back—to feel Mrs. Meyer's arms hotly convulsed about my neck, as if I were still a boy in Cleveland, and to know that I was not a young man from Cleveland visiting Miami Beach as he had toured carnivals, the war, the Caribbean, Europe, and taken the boat ride around Manhattan. I was a winter visitor, tired of town, come for the sun, who had been there before.

Am I now satisfied with what I found? Which is: "Later really did die. Later died." Just as in the alley two years ago, in that swept space where there was no longer any roach and no column of ants, history enters upon new epochs which begin to grow familiar to me.

(1962)

THE CELLAR

from *Call It Sleep*

HENRY ROTH

Standing before the kitchen sink and regarding the bright brass faucets that gleamed so far away, each with a bead of water at its nose, slowly swelling, falling, David again became aware that this world had been created without thought of him. He was thirsty, but the iron hip of the sink rested on legs tall almost as his own body, and by no stretch of arm, no leap, could he ever reach the distant tap. Where did the water come from that lurked so secretly in the curve of the brass? Where did it go, gurgling in the drain? What a strange world must be hidden behind the walls of a house! But he was thirsty.

"Mama!" he called, his voice rising above the hiss of sweeping in the frontroom. "Mama, I want a drink."

The unseen broom stopped to listen. "I'll be there in a moment," his mother answered. A chair squealed on its castors; a window chuckled down; his mother's approaching tread.

Standing in the doorway on the top step (two steps led up into the frontroom) his mother smilingly surveyed him. She looked as tall as a tower. The old grey dress she wore rose straight from strong bare ankle to waist, curved round the deep bosom and over the wide shoulders, and set her full throat in a frame of frayed lace. Her smooth, sloping face was flushed now with her work, but faintly so, diffused, the color of a hand beneath wax. She had mild, full lips, brown hair. A vague, fugitive darkness blurred the hollow above her cheekbone, giving to her face and to her large brown eyes, set in their white ovals, a reserved and almost mournful air.

"I want a drink, mama," he repeated.

"I know," she answered, coming down the stairs "I heard you." And casting a quick, sidelong glance at him, she went over to the sink and turned the tap. The water spouted noisily down. She stood there a moment, smiling obscurely, one finger parting the turbulent jet, waiting for the water to cool. Then filling a glass, she handed it down to him.

"When am I going to be big enough?" he asked resentfully as he took the glass in both hands.

"There will come a time," she answered, smiling. She rarely smiled broadly; instead the thin furrow along her upper lip would deepen. "Have little fear."

With eyes still fixed on his mother, he drank the water in breathless, uneven gulps, then returned the glass to her, surprised to see its contents scarcely diminished.

"Why can't I talk with my mouth in the water?"

"No one would hear you. Have you had your fill?"

He nodded, murmuring contentedly.

"And is that all?" she asked. Her voice held a faint challenge.

"Yes," he said hesitantly, meanwhile scanning her face for some clue.

"I thought so," she drew her head back in droll disappointment.

"What?"

"It is summer," she pointed to the window, "the weather grows warm. Whom will you refresh with the icy lips the water lent you?"

"Oh!" he lifted his smiling face.

"You remember nothing," she reproached him, and with a throaty chuckle, lifted him in her arms.

Sinking his fingers in her hair, David kissed her brow. The faint familiar warmth and odor of her skin and hair.

"There!" she laughed, nuzzling his cheek, "but you've waited too long; the sweet chill has dulled. Lips for me," she reminded him, "must always be cool as the water that wet them." She put him down.

"Sometime I'm going to eat some ice," he said warningly, "then you'll like it."

She laughed. And then soberly, "Aren't you ever going down into the street? The morning grows old."

"Aaa!"

"You'd better go. Just for a little while. I'm going to sweep here, you know."

"I want my calendar first," he pouted, invoking his privilege against the evil hour.

"Get it then. But you've got to go down afterwards."

He dragged a chair over beneath the calendar on the wall, clambered up, plucked off the outworn leaf, and fingered the remaining ones to see how far off the next red day was. Red days were Sundays, days his father was home. It always gave David a little qualm of dread to watch them draw near.

"Now you have your leaf," his mother reminded him, "Come." She stretched out her arms.

He held back. "Show me where my birthday is."

"Woe is me!" She exclaimed with an impatient chuckle. "I've shown it to you every day for weeks now."

"Show me again."

She rumpled the pad, lifted a thin plaque of leaves. "July—" she murmured, "July 12th . . . There!" She found it. "July 12th, 1911. You'll be six then."

David regarded the strange figures gravely. "Lots of pages still," he informed her.

"Yes."

"And a black day too."

"On the calendar," she laughed, "only on the calendar. Now do come down!"

Grasping her arm, he jumped down from the chair. "I must hide it now." He explained.

"So you must. I see I'll never finish my work today." Too absorbed in his own affairs to pay much heed to hers, he went over to the pantry beneath the cupboard, opened the door and drew out a shoe-box, his treasure chest.

"See how many I've got already?" he pointed proudly to the fat sheaf of rumpled leaves inside the box.

"Wonderful!" She glanced at the box in perfunctory admiration. "You peel off the year as one might a cabbage. Are you ready for your journey?"

"Yes." He put away the box without a trace of alacrity.

"Where is your sailor blouse?" she murmured looking about. "With the white strings in it? What have I—?" She found it. "There is still a little wind."

David held up his arms for her to slip the blouse over his head.

"Now, my own," she said, kissing his reemerging face. "Go down and play." She led him toward the door and opened it.

"Not too far. And remember if I don't call you, wait until the whistle blows."

He went out into the hallway. Behind him, like an eyelid shutting, the soft closing of the door winked out the light. He assayed the stairs, lapsing below him into darkness, and grasping one by one each slender upright to the banister, went down. David never found himself alone on these stairs, but he wished there were no carpet covering them. How could you hear the sound of your own feet in the dark if a carpet muffled every step you took? And if you couldn't hear the sound of your own feet and couldn't see anything either, how could you be sure you were actually there and not dreaming? A few steps from the bottom landing, he paused and stared rigidly at the cellar door. It bulged with darkness. Would it hold? . . . It held! He jumped from the last steps and raced through the narrow hallway to the light of the street. Flying through the doorway was like butting a wave. A dazzling breaker of sunlight burst over his head, swamped him in reeling blur of brilliance, and then receded . . . A row of frame houses half in thin shade, a pitted gutter, a yawning ashcan, flotsam on the shore, his street.

Blinking and almost shaken, he waited on the low stoop a moment, until his whirling vision steadied. Then for the first time, he noticed that seated on the curbstone near the house was a boy, whom an instant later, he recognized. It was Yussie who had just moved into David's house and who lived on the floor above. Yussie had a very red, fat face. His big sister walked with a limp and wore strange iron slats on one of her legs. What was he doing, David wondered, what did he have in his hands? Stepping down from the stoop, he drew near, and totally disregarded, stood beside him.

Yussie had stripped off the outer shell of an alarm-clock.

Exposed, the brassy, geometric vitals ticked when prodded, whirred and jingled falteringly.

"It still c'n go," Yussie gravely enlightened him. David sat down. Fascinated, he stared at the shining cogs that moved without moving their hearts of light. "So wot makes id?" he asked. In the street David spoke English.

"Kentcha see? Id's coz id's a machine."

"Oh!"

"It wakes op mine fodder in de mawning."

"It wakes op mine fodder too."

"It tells yuh w'en yuh sh'd eat an' w'en yuh have tuh go tuh sleep. It shows yuh w'ea, but I tooked it off."

"I god a calenduh opstai's." David informed him.

"Puh! Who ain' god a calenduh?"

"I save mine. I godda big book outa dem, wit numbuhs on id."

"Who can't do dat?"

"But mine fodder made it," David drove home the one unique point about it all.

"Wot's your fodder?"

"Mine fodder is a printer."

"Mine fodder woiks inna joolery shop. In Brooklyn. Didja ever live in Brooklyn?"

"No." David shook his head.

"We usetuh—right near my fodder's joolery shop on Rainey Avenyuh. W'ea does your fodder woik?"

David tried to think. "I don't know." He finally confessed, hoping that Yussie would not pursue the subject further.

He didn't. Instead "I don' like Brownsville," he said. "I like Brooklyn bedder."

David felt relieved.

"We usetuh find cigahs innuh gudduh," Yussie continued.

"An we usetuh t'row 'em on de ladies, an we usetuh run. Who you like bedder, ladies or gents?"

"Ladies."

"I like mine fodder bedder," said Yussie. "My mudder always holluhs on me." He pried a nail between two wheels. A bright yellow gear suddenly snapped off and fell to the gutter at his feet. He picked it up, blew the dust off, and rose. "Yuh want?"

"Yea," David reached for it.

Yussie was about to drop it into his outstretched palm, but on second thought, drew back. "No. Id's liddle like a penny. Maybe I c'n pud id inna slod machine 'n' gid gum. Hea, yuh c'n take dis one." He fished a larger gear out of his pocket, gave it to David. "Id's a quarter. Yuh wanna come?"

David hesitated. "I godduh waid hea till duh wissle blows."

"W'a wissle?"

"By de fectory. All togedder."

"So?"

"So don I c'n go opstai's."

"So w'y?"

"Cuz dey blow on twelve a'clock an' den dey blow on five a'clock. Den I c'n go op."

Yussie eyed him curiously. "I'm gonna gid gum," he said, shrugging off his perplexity. "In duh slod machine." And he ambled off in the direction of the candy store on the corner.

Holding the little wheel in his hand, David wondered again why it was that every boy on the street knew where his father worked except himself. His father had so many jobs. No sooner did you learn where he was working than be was working somewhere else. And why was he always saying, "They look at me crookedly, with mockery in their eyes! How much can a man endure? May the fire of God consume them!"

A terrifying picture rose in David's mind—the memory of how once at the supper table his mother had dared to say that perhaps the men weren't really looking at him crookedly, perhaps he was only imagining it. His father had snarled then. And with one sudden sweep of his arm had sent food and dishes crashing to the floor. And other pictures came in its train, pictures of the door being kicked open and his father coming in looking pale and savage and sitting down like old men sit down, one trembling hand behind him groping for the chair. He wouldn't speak. His jaws, and even his joints, seemed to have become fused together by a withering rage. David often dreamed of his father's footsteps booming on the stairs, of the glistening doorknob turning, and of himself clutching at knives he couldn't lift from the table.

Brooding, engrossed in his thoughts, engrossed in the rhythmic, accurate teeth of the yellow cog in his hand, the thin bright circles whirling restlessly without motion, David was unaware that a little group of girls had gathered in the gutter some distance away. But when they began to sing, he started and looked up. Their faces were sober, their hands locked in one another; circling slowly in a ring they chanted in a plaintive nasal chorus:

> *"Waltuh, Waltuh, Wiuhlflowuh,*
> *Growin' up so high;*
> *So we are all young ladies,*
> *An' we are ready to die."*

Again and again, they repeated their burden. Their words obscure at first, emerged at last, gathered meaning. The song troubled David strangely. Walter Wildflower was a little boy.

David knew him. He lived in Europe, far away, where David's mother said he was born. He had seen him standing on a hill, far away. Filled with a warm, nostalgic mournfulness, he shut his eyes. Fragments of forgotten rivers floated under the lids, dusty roads, fathomless curve of trees, a branch in a window under flawless light. A world somewhere, somewhere else.

> *"Waltuh, Waltuh, Wiuhlflowuh,*
> *Growin' up so high,"*

His body relaxed, yielding to the rhythm of the song and to the golden June sunlight. He seemed to rise and fall on waves somewhere without him. Within him a voice spoke with no words but with the shift of slow flame. . . .

> *"So we are all young ladies,*
> *An' we are ready to die."*

From the limp, uncurling fingers, the cog rolled to the ground, rang like a coin, fell over on its side. The sudden sound moored him again, fixed him to the quiet, suburban street, the curbstone. The inarticulate flame that had pulsed within him, wavered and went out. He sighed, bent over and picked up the wheel.

When would the whistle blow he wondered. It took long today. . . .

As far back as he could remember, this was the first time that he had ever gone anywhere alone with his father, and already he felt desolated, stirred with dismal forebodings, longing desperately for his mother. His father was so silent and so remote that he felt as though he were alone even at his side.

What if his father should abandon him, leave him in some lonely street. The thought sent shudders of horror through his body. No! No! He couldn't do that!

At last they reached the trolley lines. The sight of people cheered him again, dispelling his fear for a while. They boarded a car, rode what seemed to him a long time and then got off in a crowded street under an elevated. Nervously gripping David's arm, his father guided him across the street. They stopped before the stretched iron wicker of a closed theatre. Colored billboards on either side of them, the odor of stale perfume behind. People hurrying, trains roaring. David gazed about him frightened. To the right of the theatre, in the window of an ice cream parlor, gaudy, colored popcorn danced and drifted, blown by a fan. He looked up apprehensively at his father. He was pale, grim. The fine veins in his nose stood out like a pink cobweb.

"Do you see that door?" He shook him into attention. "In the grey house; See? That man just came out of there."

"Yes, Papa."

"Now you go in there and go up the stairs and you'll see another door. Go right in. And to the first man you see inside, say this: I'm Albert Schearl's son. He wants you to give me the clothes in his locker and the money that's coming to him. Do you understand? When they've given it to you bring it down here. I'll be waiting for you. Now what will you say?" he demanded abruptly.

David began to repeat his instructions in Yiddish.

"Say it in English, you fool!"

He rendered them in English. And when he had satisfied his father that he knew them, he was sent in.

"And don't tell them I'm out here," he was warned as he left. "Remember you came alone!"

Full of misgivings, unnerved at the ordeal of facing strangers alone, strangers of whom his own father seemed apprehensive, he entered the hallway, climbed the stairs. One flight up, he pushed open the door and entered a small room, an office. From somewhere back of this office, machinery clanked and rattled. A bald-headed man smoking a cigar looked up as he came in.

"Well, my boy," he asked smiling, "what do you want?"

For a moment all of his instructions flew out of his head. "My—my fodder sent me hea." He faltered.

"Your father? Who's he?"

"I—I'm Albert Schearl's son," be blurted out. "He sent me I shuh ged his clo's f'om de locker an' his money you owing him."

"Oh, you're Albert Schearl's son," said the man, his expression changing. "And he wants his money, eh?" He nodded with the short vibrating motion of a bell. "You've got some father, my boy. You can tell him that for me. I didn't get a chance. He's crazy. Anybody who—What does he do at home?"

David shook his head guiltily, "Nuttin."

"No?" he chuckled. "Nothin', hey? Well—" he broke off and went over to a small arched window in the rear. "Joe!" he called. "Oh Joe! Come here a minute, will you?"

In a few seconds a gray-haired man in overalls came in.

"Call me, Mr. Lobe?"

"Yea, will you get Schearl's things out of his locker and wrap 'em up for me. His kid's here."

The other man's face broke into a wide, brown-toothed grin. "Is zat his kid?" As if to keep from laughing his tongue worried the quid of tobacco in his cheek.

"Yea."

"He don' look crazy." He burst into a laugh.

"No." Mr. Lobe subdued him with a wave of the hand. "He's a nice kid."

"Your ol' man near brained me wid a hammer," said the man addressing David. "Don' know wot happened, nobody said nuttin." He grinned. "Never saw such a guy, Mr. Lobe. Holy Jesus, he looked like he wuz boinin' up. Didja see de rail he twisted wid his hands? Maybe I oughta to give it to 'im fer a souvenir?"

Mr. Lobe grinned. "Let the kid alone," he said quietly. "Get his stuff."

"O.K." Still chuckling, the gray-haired man went out.

"Sit down, my boy," said Mr. Lobe, pointing to a seat. "We'll have your father's things here in a few minutes."

David sat down. In a few minutes, a girl, bearing a paper in her hand, came into the office.

"Say, Marge," said Mr. Lobe, "find out what Schearl gets, will you."

"Yes, Mr. Lobe." She regarded David, "What's that, his boy?"

"Mmm."

"Looks like him, don't he?"

"Maybe."

"I'd have him arrested," said the girl opening up a large ledger.

"What good would that do?"

"I don't know, it might put some sense into his head."

Mr. Lobe shrugged. "I'm only too glad he didn't kill anybody."

"He ought to be in a padded cell," said the girl scribbling something on a paper.

Mr. Lobe made no response.

"He gets six sixty-two." She put down her pencil. "Shall I get it?"

"Mmm."

The girl went over to a large black safe in a corner, drew out a box, and when she had counted out some money, put it into a small envelope and gave it to Mr. Lobe.

"Come here," he said to David. "What's your name?"

"David."

"David and Goliath," he smiled. "Well, David, have you got a good deep pocket? Let's see." He picked up the tails of David's jacket. "There, that's the one I want." And fingering the small watch-pocket at the waist. "We'll put it in there." He folded the envelope and wedged it in. "Now don't take it out. Don't tell anybody you've got it till you get home, understand? The idea, sending a kid his age on an errand like this."

David, staring ahead of him, under Mr. Lobe's arm, was aware of two faces, peering in at the little window in the back. The eyes of both were fastened on him, regarding him with a curious and amused scrutiny of men beholding for the first time some astonishing freak. They both grinned when the girl, happening to turn in their direction, saw them; one of the men winked and cranked his temple with his hand. As Mr. Lobe turned, both disappeared. A moment later, the gray-haired man returned with a paper-wrapped bundle.

"Here's all I c'n find, Mr. Lobe. His towel, and his shoit an' a jacket."

"All right, Joe," Mr. Lobe took the package from him and turned to David. "Here you are, my boy. Put it under your arm and don't lose it." He tucked it under David's arm. "Not heavy, is it? No? That's good." He opened the door to let David pass. "Good bye." A dry smile whisked over his features. "Pretty tough for you."

Grasping the bundle firmly under his arm, David went slowly down the stairs. So that was how his father quit a

place! He held a hammer in hand, he would have killed somebody. David could almost see him, the hammer raised over
his head, his face contorted in terrific wrath, the rest cringing
away. He shuddered at the image in his mind, stopped
motionless on the stair, terrified at having to confront the
reality. But he must go down; he must meet him; it would be
worse for him if he remained on the stair any longer. He didn't
want to go, but he had to. If only the stairs were twice as high.

He hurried down, came out into the street. His father, his
back pressed close to the iron wicker, was waiting for him,
and when he saw him come out, motioned to him to hurry
and began walking away. David ran after him, caught up to
him finally, and his father, without slackening his pace,
relieved him of the bundle.

"They took long enough," he said, casting a malevolent
glance over his shoulder. It was evident from his face that he
had worked himself into a rage during the interval that David
had left him. "They gave you the money?"

"Yes, Papa."

"How much?"

"Six—six dollars, the girl—"

"Did they say anything to you?" His teeth clenched grimly,
"About me?"

"No, Papa," he answered hurriedly. "Nothing, Papa. They
just gave me the—the money and I went down."

"Where is it?"

"Over here," he pointed to the pocket.

"Well, give it to me!"

With difficulty, David uprooted the envelope from his
pocket. His father snatched it from him, counted the money.

"And so they said nothing, eh?" He seemed to demand a
final confirmation. "None of the men spoke to you, did they?

Only that bald-headed pig with the glasses?" He was watching him narrowly.

"No, Papa. Only that man. He just gave me the money." He knew that while his father's eyes rested on him he must look frank, he must look wide-eyed, simple.

"Very well!" His lips stretched for a brief instant in fleeting satisfaction. "Good!"

They stopped at the corner and waited for the trolley . . .

David never said anything to anyone of what he had discovered, not even to his mother—it was all too terrifying, too unreal to share with someone else. He brooded about it till it entered his sleep, till he no longer could tell where his father was flesh and where dream. Who would believe him if he said, I saw my father lift a hammer; he was standing on a high roof of darkness, and below him were faces uplifted, so many, they stretched like white cobbles to the end of the world; who would believe him? He dared not.

(1934)

THE HISTORY OF THEM ALL

from *Beautiful Losers*

LEONARD COHEN

Catherine Tekakwitha, who are you? Are you (1656–1680)? Is that enough? Are you the Iroquois Virgin? Are you the Lily of the Shores of the Mohawk River? Can I love you in my own way? I am an old scholar, better-looking now than when I was young. That's what sitting on your ass does to your face. I've come after you, Catherine Tekakwitha. I want to know what goes on under that rosy blanket. Do I have any right? I fell in love with a religious picture of you. You were standing among birch trees, my favorite trees. God knows how far up your moccasins were laced. There was a river behind you, no doubt the Mohawk River. Two birds in the left foreground would be delighted if you tickled their white throats or even if you used them as an example of something or other in a parable. Do I have any right to come after you with my dusty mind full of the junk of maybe five thousand books? I hardly even get out to the country very often. Could you teach me about leaves? Do you know anything about narcotic mushrooms? Lady Marilyn just died a few years ago. May I say that some old scholar four hundred years from now, maybe of my own blood, will come after her in the way I come after you? But right now you must know more about heaven. Does it look like one of these little plastic altars that glow in the dark? I swear I won't mind if it does. Are the stars tiny, after all? Can an old scholar find love at last and stop having to pull himself off every night so he can get to sleep? I don't even hate books any more. I've forgotten most of what I've read and, frankly, it never seemed very important to me or to the world. My friend F. used to say in his hopped-up fashion: We've got to learn to stop bravely at the surface. We've got to learn to love appearances. F. died in a padded cell, his brain rotted from too much dirty sex. His face turned black, this I saw with my own eyes, and they say there wasn't much left of his prick. A nurse told me it looked like the inside of a worm. Salut F., old and loud friend! I wonder if your memory will persist. And you, Catherine Tekakwitha, if you must know, I am so human as to suffer from constipation, the rewards of a sedentary life. Is it any wonder I have sent my heart out into the birch trees? Is it any wonder that an old scholar who never made much money wants to climb into your Technicolor postcard?

I am a well-known folklorist, an authority on the A———s, a tribe I have no intention of disgracing by my interest. There are, perhaps, ten full-blooded A———s left, four of them teen-age girls. I will add that F. took full advantage of my anthropological status to fuck all four of them. Old friend, you paid your dues. The A——s seem to have made their appearance in the fifteenth century, or rather, a sizable remnant of the tribe. Their brief history is characterized by incessant defeat. The very name of the tribe, A——, is the word for corpse in the language of all the neighboring tribes. There is no record that this unfortunate people ever won a single battle, while the songs and legends of its enemies are virtually nothing but a sustained howl of triumph. My interest in this pack of failures betrays my character. Borrowing money from me, F. often said: Thanks, you old A——! Catherine Tekakwitha, do you listen?

Catherine Tekakwitha, I have come to rescue you from the Jesuits. Yes, an old scholar dares to think big. I don't know what they are saying about you these days because my Latin is almost defunct. "Que le succès couronne nos espérances, et nous verrons sur les autels, auprès des Martyrs canadiens, une Vierge iroquoise—près des roses du martyre le lis de la virginité." A note by one Ed. L., S.J., written in August 1926. But what does it matter? I don't want to carry my old belligerent life on my journey up the Mohawk River. Pace, Company of Jesus! F. said: A strong man cannot but love the Church. Catherine Tekakwitha, what care we if they cast you in plaster? I am at present studying the plans of a birch-bark canoe. Your brethren have forgotten how to build them. And what if there is a plastic reproduction of your little body on the dashboard of every Montreal taxi? It can't be a bad thing. Love cannot be hoarded. Is there a part of Jesus in every stamped-out crucifix? I think there is. Desire changes the world! What makes the mountainside of maple turn red?

Peace, you manufacturers of religious trinkets! You handle sacred material! Catherine Tekakwitha, do you see how I get carried away? How I want the world to be mystical and good? Are the stars tiny, after all? Who will put us to sleep? Should I save my fingernails? Is matter holy? I want the barber to bury my hair. Catherine Tekakwitha, are you at work on me already?

Marie de l'Incarnation, Marguerite Bourgeoys, Marie-Marguerite d'Youville, maybe you could arouse me if I could move out of myself. I want to get as much as I can. F. said that he'd never once heard of a female saint he wouldn't like to have screwed. What did he mean? F., don't tell me that at last you are becoming profound. F. once said: At sixteen I stopped fucking faces. I had occasioned the remark by expressing disgust at his latest conquest, a young hunchback he had met while touring an orphanage. F. spoke to me that day as if I were truly one of the underprivileged; or perhaps he was not speaking to me at all when he muttered: Who am I to refuse the universe?

The French gave the Iroquois their name. Naming food is one thing, naming a people is another, not that the people in question seem to care today. If they never cared, so much the worse for me: I'm far too willing to shoulder the alleged humiliations of harmless peoples, as evidenced by my life work with the A——s. Why do I feel so lousy when I wake up every morning? Wondering if I'm going to be able to shit or not. Is my body going to work? Will my bowels churn? Has the old machine turned the food brown? Is it surprising that I've tunneled through libraries after news about victims? Fictional victims! All the victims we ourselves do not murder or imprison are fictional victims. I live in a small apartment building. The bottom of the elevator shaft is accessible through the sub-basement. While I sat downtown preparing a paper on lemmings she crawled into the elevator shaft and sat there with her arms around her drawn-up knees (or so the police determined from the mess). I came home every night at twenty to eleven, regular as Kant. She was going to teach me a lesson, my old wife. You and your fictional victims, she used to say. Her life had become gray by imperceptible degrees, for I swear, that very night, probably at the exact moment when she was squeezing into the shaft, I looked up from the lemming research and closed my eyes, remembering her as young and bright, the sun dancing in her hair as she sucked me off in a canoe on Lake Orford. We were the only ones who lived in the sub-basement, we were the only ones who commanded the little elevator into those depths. But she taught no one a lesson, not the kind of lesson she meant. A delivery boy from the Bar-B-Q did the dirty work by misreading the numbers on a warm brown paper bag. Edith! F. spent the night with me. He confessed at 4 a.m. that he'd slept with Edith five or six times in the twenty years he'd known her. Irony! We ordered chicken from the same place and we talked about my poor squashed wife, our fingers greasy, barbecue-sauce drops on the linoleum. Five or six times, a mere friendship. Could I stand on some holy mountain of experience, a long way off, and sweetly nod my Chinese head over their little love? What harm had been done to the stars? You lousy fucker, I said, how many times, five *or* six? Ah, F. smiled, grief makes us precise! So let it be known that the Iroquois, the brethren of Catherine Tekakwitha, were given the name Iroquois by the French. They called themselves Hodenosaunee, which means People of the Long House. They had developed a new dimension to conversation. They ended every speech with the word *hiro,* which means: like I said. Thus each man took full responsibility for intruding into the inarticulate murmur of the spheres. To *hiro* they added the word *koué,* a cry of joy or distress, according to whether it was sung or howled. Thus they essayed to pierce the mysterious curtain which hangs between all talking men: at the end of every utterance a man stepped back, so to speak, and attempted to interpret his words to the listener, attempted to subvert the beguiling intellect with the noise of true emotion. Catherine Tekakwitha, speak to me in *Hiro-Koué.* I have no right to mind what the Jesuits say to the slaves, but on that cool Laurentian night which I work toward, when we are wrapped in our birch-bark rocket, joined in the ancient enduring way, flesh to spirit, and I ask you my old question: are the stars tiny, after all, O Catherine Tekakwitha, answer me in *Hiro-Koué.* That other night F. and I quarreled for hours. We didn't know when morning arrived because the only window of that miserable apartment faced into the ventilation shaft.

—You lousy fucker, how many times, five *or* six?

—Ah, grief makes us precise!

—Five or six, five or six, five or six?

—Listen, my friend, the elevator is working again.

—Listen, F., don't give me any of your mystical shit.

—Seven.

—Seven times with Edith?

—Correct.

—You were trying to protect me with an optional lie?

—Correct.

—And seven itself might just be another option.

—Correct.

—But you were trying to protect me, weren't you? Oh, F., do you think I can learn to perceive the diamonds of good amongst all the shit?

—It is all diamond.

—Damn you, rotten wife-fucker, that answer is no comfort. You ruin everything with your saintly pretensions. This is a bad morning. My wife's in no shape to be buried. They're going to straighten her out in some stinking doll hospital. How am I going to feel in the elevator on my way to the library? Don't give me this all diamond shit, shove it up your occult hole. Help a fellow out. Don't fuck his wife for him.

Thus the conversation ran into the morning we could not perceive. He kept to his diamond line. Catherine Tekakwitha, I wanted to believe him. We talked until we exhausted ourselves, and we pulled each other off, as we did when we were boys in what is now downtown but what was once the woods.

(1966)

NO KADDISH FOR WEINSTEIN

from *Without Feathers*

WOODY ALLEN

Weinstein lay under the covers, staring at the ceiling in a depressed torpor. Outside, sheets of humid air rose from the pavement in stifling waves. The sound of traffic was deafening at this hour, and in addition to all this his bed was on fire. Look at me, he thought. Fifty years old. Half a century. Next year, I will be fifty-one. Then fifty-two. Using this same reasoning, he could figure out his age as much as five years in the future. So little time left, he thought, and so much to accomplish. For one thing, he wanted to learn to drive a car. Adelman, his friend who used to play dreidel with him on Rush Street, had studied driving at the Sorbonne. He could handle a car beautifully and had already driven many places by himself. Weinstein had made a few attempts to steer his father's Chevy but kept winding up on the sidewalk.

He had been a precocious child. An intellectual. At twelve, he had translated the poems of T. S. Eliot into English, after some vandals had broken into the library and translated them into French. And as if his I.Q. did not isolate him enough, he suffered untold injustices and persecutions because of his religion, mostly from his parents. True, the old man was a member of the synagogue, and his mother, too, but they could never accept the fact that their son was Jewish. "How did it happen?" his father asked, bewildered. My face looks Semitic, Weinstein thought every morning as he shaved. He had been mistaken several times for Robert Redford, but on each occasion it was by a blind person. Then there was Feinglass, his other boyhood friend: A Phi Beta Kappa. A labor spy, ratting on the workers. Then a convert to Marxism. A Communist agitator. Betrayed by the Party, he went to Hollywood and became the offscreen voice of a famous cartoon mouse. Ironic.

Weinstein had toyed with the Communists, too. To impress a girl at Rutgers, he had moved to Moscow and joined the Red Army. When he called her for a second date, she was pinned to someone else. Still, his rank of sergeant in the Russian infantry would hurt him later when he needed a security clearance in order to get the free appetizer with his dinner at Longchamps. Also, while at school he had organized some laboratory mice and led them in a strike over work conditions. Actually, it was not so much the politics as the poetry of Marxist theory that got him. He was positive that collectivization could work if everyone would learn the lyrics to "Rag Mop." "The withering away of the state" was a phrase that had stayed with him, ever since his uncle's nose had withered away in Saks Fifth Avenue one day. What, he wondered, can be learned about the true essence of social revolution? Only that it should never be attempted after eating Mexican food.

The Depression shattered Weinstein's Uncle Meyer, who kept his fortune under the mattress. When the market crashed, the government called in all mattresses, and Meyer became a pauper overnight. All that was left for him was to jump out the window, but he lacked the nerve and sat on a window sill of the Flatiron Building from 1930 to 1937.

"These kids with their pot and their sex," Uncle Meyer was fond of saying. "Do they know what it is to sit on a window sill for seven years? There you see life! Of course, everybody looks like ants. But each year Tessie—may she rest in peace—made the Seder right out there on the ledge. The family gathered round for Passover. Oy, nephew! What's the world coming to when they have a bomb that can kill more people than one look at Max Rifkin's daughter?"

Weinstein's so-called friends had all knuckled under to the House Un-American Activities Committee. Blotnick was turned in by his own mother. Sharpstein was turned in by his answering service. Weinstein had been called by the committee and admitted he had given money to the Russian War Relief, and then added, "Oh, yes, I bought Stalin a dining-room set." He refused to name names but said if the committee insisted he would give the heights of the people he had met at meetings. In the end he panicked and instead of taking the Fifth Amendment, took the Third, which enabled him to buy beer in Philadelphia on Sunday.

Weinstein finished shaving and got into the shower. He lathered himself, while steaming water splashed down his bulky back. He thought, Here I am at some fixed point in time and space, taking a shower. I, Isaac Weinstein. One of God's creatures. And then, stepping on the soap, he slid across the floor and rammed his head into the towel rack. It had been a bad week. The previous day, he had got a bad haircut and was still not over the anxiety it caused him. At first the barber had snipped judiciously, but soon Weinstein realized he had gone too far. "Put some back!" he screamed unreasonably.

"I can't," the barber said. "It won't stick."

"Well, then give it to me, Dominic! I want to take it with me!"

"Once it's on the floor of the shop it's mine, Mr. Weinstein."

"Like hell! I want my hair!"

He blustered and raged, and finally felt guilty and left. Goyim, he thought. One way or another, they get you.

Now he emerged from the hotel and walked up Eighth Avenue. Two men were mugging an elderly lady. My God, thought Weinstein, time was when one person could handle that job. Some city. Chaos everyplace. Kant was right: The mind imposes order. It also tells you how much to tip. What a wonderful thing, to be conscious! I wonder what the people in New Jersey do.

He was on his way to see Harriet about the alimony payments. He still loved Harriet, even though while they were married she had systematically attempted to commit adultery with all the *R*'s in the Manhattan telephone directory. He forgave her. But he should have suspected something when his best friend and Harriet took a house in Maine together for three years, without telling him where they were. He didn't *want* to see it—that was it. His sex life with Harriet had stopped early. He slept with her once on the night they first met, once on the evening of the first moon landing, and once to test if his back was all right after a slipped disc. "It's no damn good with you, Harriet," he used to complain. "You're too pure. Every time I have an urge for you I sublimate it by planting a tree in Israel. You remind me of my mother." (Molly Weinstein, may she rest in peace, who slaved for him and made the best stuffed derma in Chicago—a secret recipe until everyone realized she was putting in hashish.)

For lovemaking, Weinstein needed someone quite opposite. Like LuAnne, who made sex an art. The only trouble was
she couldn't count to twenty without taking her shoes off. He
once tried giving her a book on existentialism, but she ate it.
Sexually, Weinstein had always felt inadequate. For one
thing, he felt short. He was five-four in his stocking feet,
although in someone else's stocking feet be could be as tall
as five-six. Dr. Klein, his analyst, got him to see that jumping
in front of a moving train was more hostile than self-destruc-
tive but in either case would ruin the crease in his pants.
Klein was his third analyst. His first was a Jungian, who suggested they try a Ouija board. Before that, he attended
"group," but when it came time for him to speak he got dizzy
and could only recite the names of all the planets. His
problem was women, and he knew it. He was impotent with
any woman who finished college with higher than a B-minus
average. He felt most at home with graduates of typing
school, although if the woman did over sixty words a minute
he panicked and could not perform.

Weinstein rang the bell to Harriet's apartment, and suddenly
she was standing before him. Swelling to maculate giraffe, as
usual, thought Weinstein. It was a private joke that neither of
them understood.

"Hello, Harriet," he said.

"Oh, Ike," she said. "You needn't be so damn self-righteous."

She was right. What a tactless thing to have said. He hated
himself for it.

"How are the kids, Harriet?"

"We never had any kids, Ike."

"That's why I thought four hundred dollars a week was a
lot for child support."

She bit her lip, Weinstein bit his lip. Then he bit her lip. "Harriet" he said, "I . . . I'm broke. Egg futures are down."

"I see. And can't you get help from your *shiksa?*"

"To you, any girl who's not Jewish is a *shiksa.*"

"Can we forget it?" Her voice was choked with recrimination. Weinstein had a sudden urge to kiss her, or if not her, somebody.

"Harriet, where did we go wrong?"

"We never faced reality."

"It wasn't my fault. You said it was north."

"Reality *is* north, Ike."

"No, Harriet. Empty dreams are north. Reality is west. False hopes are east, and I think Louisiana is south."

She still had the power to arouse him. He reached out for her, but she moved away and his hand came to rest in some sour cream.

"Is that why you slept with your analyst?" he finally blurted out. His face was knotted with rage. He felt like fainting but couldn't remember the proper way to fall.

"That was therapy," she said coldly. "According to Freud, sex is the royal road to the unconscious."

"Freud said *dreams* are the road to the unconscious."

"Sex, dreams—you're going to nit-pick?"

"Goodbye, Harriet."

It was no use. *Rien à dire, rien à faire.* Weinstein left and walked over to Union Square. Suddenly hot tears burst forth, as if from a broken dam. Hot, salty tears pent up for ages rushed out in an unabashed wave of emotion. The problem was, they were coming out of his ears. Look at this, he thought; I can't even cry properly. He dabbed his ear with Kleenex and went home.

(1975)

THE MAGIC BARREL

from *The Magic Barrel*

BERNARD MALAMUD

Not long ago there lived in uptown New York, in a small, almost meager room, though crowded with books, Leo Finkle, a rabbinical student in the Yeshivah University. Finkle, after six years of study, was to be ordained in June and had been advised by an acquaintance that he might find it easier to win himself a congregation if he were married. Since he had no present prospects of marriage, after two tormented days of turning it over in his mind, he called in Pinye Salzman, a marriage broker whose two-line advertisement he had read in the *Forward*.

The matchmaker appeared one night out of the dark fourth-floor hallway of the graystone rooming house where Finkle lived, grasping a black, strapped portfolio that had been worn thin with use. Salzman, who had been long in the business, was of slight but dignified build, wearing an old hat, and an overcoat too short and tight for him. He smelled frankly of fish, which he loved to eat, and although he was missing a few teeth, his presence was not displeasing, because of an amiable manner curiously contrasted with mournful eyes. His voice, his lips, his wisp of beard, his bony fingers were animated, but give him a moment of repose and his mild blue eyes revealed a depth of sadness, a characteristic that put Leo a little at ease although the situation, for him, was inherently tense.

He at once informed Salzman why he had asked him to come, explaining that his home was in Cleveland, and that but for his parents, who had married comparatively late in life, he was alone in the world. He had for six years devoted himself almost entirely to his studies, as a result of which, understandably, he had found himself without time for a social life and the company of young women. Therefore he thought it the better part of trial and error—of embarrassing fumbling—to call in an experienced person to advise him on these matters. He remarked in passing that the function of the marriage broker was ancient and honorable, highly approved in the Jewish community, because it made practical the necessary without hindering joy. Moreover, his own parents had been brought together by a matchmaker. They had made, if not a financially profitable marriage—since neither had possessed any worldly goods to speak of—at least a successful one in the sense of their everlasting devotion to each other. Salzman listened in embarrassed surprise, sensing a sort of apology. Later, however, he experienced a glow of pride in his work, an emotion that had left him years ago, and he heartily approved of Finkle.

The two went to their business. Leo had led Salzman to the only clear place in the room, a table near a window that overlooked the lamp-lit city. He seated himself at the matchmaker's side but facing him, attempting by an act of will to suppress the unpleasant tickle in his throat. Salzman eagerly unstrapped his portfolio and removed a loose rubber band from a thin packet of much-handled cards. As he flipped through them, a gesture and sound that physically hurt Leo, the student pretended not to see and gazed steadfastly out the window. Although it was still February, winter was on its last legs, signs of which he had for the first time in years begun to notice. He now observed the round white moon, moving high in the sky through a cloud menagerie, and watched with half-open mouth as it penetrated a huge hen, and dropped out of her like an egg laying itself. Salzman, though pretending through eyeglasses he had just slipped on, to be engaged in scanning the writing on the cards, stole occasional glances at the young man's distinguished face, noting with pleasure the long, severe scholar's nose, brown eyes heavy with learning, sensitive yet ascetic lips, and a certain, almost hollow quality of the dark cheeks. He gazed around at shelves upon shelves of books and let out a soft, contented sigh.

When Leo's eyes fell upon the cards, he counted six spread out in Salzman's hand.

"So few?" he asked in disappointment.

"You wouldn't believe me how much cards I got in my office," Salzman replied. "The drawers are already filled to the top, so I keep them now in a barrel, but is every girl good for a new rabbi?"

Leo blushed at this, regretting all he had revealed of himself in a curriculum vitae he had sent to Salzman. He had thought it best to acquaint him with his strict standards and specifications, but in having done so, felt he had told the marriage broker more than was absolutely necessary.

He hesitantly inquired, "Do you keep photographs of your clients on file?"

"First comes family, amount of dowry, also what kind promises," Salzman replied, unbuttoning his tight coat and settling himself in the chair. "After comes pictures, rabbi."

"Call me Mr. Finkle. I'm not yet a rabbi."

Salzman said he would, but instead called him doctor, which he changed to rabbi when Leo was not listening too attentively.

Salzman adjusted his horn-rimmed spectacles, gently cleared his throat and read in an eager voice the contents of the top card:

"Sophie P. Twenty-four years. Widow one year. No children. Educated high school and two years college. Father promises eight thousand dollars. Has wonderful wholesale business. Also real estate. On the mother's side comes teachers, also one actor. Well known on Second Avenue."

Leo gazed up in surprise. "Did you say a widow?"

"A widow don't mean spoiled, rabbi. She lived with her husband maybe four months. He was a sick boy she made a mistake to marry him."

"Marrying a widow has never entered my mind."

"This is because you have no experience. A widow, especially if she is young and healthy like this girl, is a wonderful person to marry. She will be thankful to you the rest of her life. Believe me, if I was looking now for a bride, I would marry a widow."

Leo reflected, then shook his head.

Salzman hunched his shoulders in an almost imperceptible gesture of disappointment. He placed the card down on the wooden table and began to read another:

"Lily H. High school teacher. Regular. Not a substitute. Has savings and new Dodge car. Lived in Paris one year. Father is successful dentist thirty-five years. Interested in professional man. Well Americanized family. Wonderful opportunity."

"I knew her personally," said Salzman. "I wish you could see this girl. She is a doll. Also very intelligent. All day you could talk to her about books and theyater and what not. She also knows current events."

"I don't believe you mentioned her age?"

"Her age?" Salzman said, raising his brows. "Her age is thirty-two years."

Leo said after a while, "I'm afraid that seems a little too old."

Salzman let out a laugh. "So how old are you, rabbi?"

"Twenty-seven."

"So what is the difference, tell me, between twenty-seven and thirty-two? My own wife is seven years older than me. So what did I suffer?—Nothing. If Rothschild's a daughter wants to marry you, would you say on account her age, no?"

"Yes," Leo said dryly.

Salzman shook off the no in the yes. "Five years don't mean a thing. I give you my word that when you will live with her for one week you will forget her age. What does it mean five years—that she lived more and knows more than somebody who is younger? On this girl, God bless her, years are not wasted. Each one that it comes makes better the bargain."

"What subject does she teach in high school?"

"Languages. If you heard the way she speaks French, you will think it is music. I am in the business twenty-five years, and I recommend her with my whole heart. Believe me, I know what I'm talking, rabbi."

"What's on the next card?" Leo said abruptly.

Salzman reluctantly turned up the third card:

"Ruth K. Nineteen years. Honor student. Father offers

thirteen thousand cash to the right bridegroom. He is a medical doctor. Stomach specialist with marvelous practice.
Brother-in-law owns own garment business. Particular people."

Salzman looked as if he had read his trump card.

"Did you say nineteen?" Leo asked with interest.

"On the dot."

"Is she attractive?" He blushed. "Pretty?"

Salzman kissed his finger tips. "A little doll. On this I give
you my word. Let me call the father tonight and you will see
what means pretty."

But Leo was troubled. "You're sure she's that young?"

"This I am positive. The father will show you the birth
certificate."

"Are you positive there isn't something wrong with her?"
Leo insisted.

"Who says there is wrong?"

"I don't understand why an American girl her age should
go to a marriage broker."

A smile spread over Salzman's face.

"So for the same reason you went, she comes."

Leo flushed. "I am pressed for time."

Salzman, realizing he had been tactless, quickly explained.
"The father came, not her. He wants she should have the
best, so he looks around himself. When we will locate the
right boy he will introduce him and encourage. This makes a
better marriage than if a young girl without experience takes
for herself. I don't have to tell you this."

"But don't you think this young girl believes in love?" Leo
spoke uneasily.

Salzman was about to guffaw but caught himself and said
soberly, "Love comes with the right person, not before."

Leo parted dry lips but did not speak. Noticing that

Salzman had snatched a glance at the next card, he cleverly asked, "How is her health?"

"Perfect," Salzman said, breathing with difficulty. "Of course, she is a little lame on her right foot from an auto accident that it happened to her when she was twelve years, but nobody notices on account she is so brilliant and also beautiful."

Leo got up heavily and went to the window. He felt curiously bitter and upbraided himself for having called in the marriage broker. Finally, he shook his head.

"Why not?" Salzman persisted, the pitch of his voice rising.

"Because I detest stomach specialists."

"So what do you care what is his business? After you marry her do you need him? Who says he must come every Friday night in your house?"

Ashamed of the way the talk was going, Leo dismissed Salzman, who went home with heavy, melancholy eyes.

Though he had felt only relief at the marriage broker's departure, Leo was in low spirits the next day. He explained it as arising from Salzman's failure to produce a suitable bride for him. He did not care for his type of clientele. But when Leo found himself hesitating whether to seek out another matchmaker, one more polished than Pinye, he wondered if it could be—his protestations to the contrary, and although he honored his father and mother—that he did not, in essence, care for the matchmaking institution? This thought he quickly put out of mind yet found himself still upset. All day he ran around in the woods—missed an important appointment, forgot to give out his laundry, walked out of a Broadway cafeteria without paying and had to run back with the ticket in his hand; had even not recognized his landlady in the street when she passed with a friend and courteously called out, "A good evening to you, Doctor Finkle." By nightfall, however, he had regained sufficient calm to sink his nose into a book and there found peace from his thoughts.

Almost at once there came a knock on the door. Before Leo could say enter, Salzman, commercial cupid, was standing in the room. His face was gray and meager, his expression hungry, and he looked as if he would expire on his feet. Yet the marriage broker managed, by some trick of the muscles, to display a broad smile.

"So good evening. I am invited?"

Leo nodded, disturbed to see him again, yet unwilling to ask the man to leave.

Beaming still, Salzman laid his portfolio on the table. "Rabbi, I got for you tonight good news."

"I've asked you not to call me rabbi. I'm still a student."

"Your worries are finished. I have for you a first-class bride."

"Leave me in peace concerning this subject." Leo pretended lack of interest.

"The world will dance at your wedding."

"Please, Mr. Salzman, no more."

"But first must come back my strength," Salzman said weakly. He fumbled with the portfolio straps and took out of the leather case an oily paper bag, from which he extracted a hard, seeded roll and a small, smoked white fish. With a quick motion of his hand he stripped the fish out of its skin and began ravenously to chew. "All day in a rush," he muttered.

Leo watched him eat.

"A sliced tomato you have maybe?" Salzman hesitantly inquired.

"No."

The marriage broker shut his eyes and ate. When he had finished he carefully cleaned up the crumbs and rolled up the remains of the fish, in the paper bag. His spectacled eyes roamed the room until he discovered, amid some piles of books, a one-burner gas stove. Lifting his hat he humbly asked, "A glass tea you got, rabbi?"

Conscience-stricken, Leo rose and brewed the tea. He served it with a chunk of lemon and two cubes of lump sugar, delighting Salzman.

After he had drunk his tea, Salzman's strength and good spirits were restored.

"So tell me, rabbi," he said amiably, "you considered some more the three clients I mentioned yesterday?"

"There was no need to consider."

"Why not?"

"None of them suits me."

"What then suits you?"

Leo let it pass because he could give only a confused answer.

Without waiting for a reply, Salzman asked, "You remember this girl I talked to you—the high school teacher?"

"Age thirty-two?"

But, surprisingly, Salzman's face lit in a smile. "Age twenty-nine."

Leo shot him a look. "Reduced from thirty-two?"

"A mistake," Salzman avowed. "I talked today with the dentist. He took me to his safety deposit box and showed me the birth certificate. She was twenty-nine years last August. They made her a party in the mountains where she went for her vacation. When her father spoke to me the first time I forgot to write the age and I told you thirty-two, but now I remember this was a different client, a widow."

"The same one you told me about? I thought she was twenty-four?"

"A different. Am I responsible that the world is filled with widows?"

"No, but I'm not interested in them, nor for that matter, in school teachers."

Salzman pulled his clasped hands to his breast. Looking at the ceiling he devoutly exclaimed, "Yiddishe kinder, what can I say to somebody that he is not interested in high school teachers? So what then you are interested?"

Leo flushed but controlled himself.

"In what else will you be interested," Salzman went on, "if you not interested in this fine girl that she speaks four languages and has personally in the bank ten thousand dollars? Also her father guarantees further twelve thousand. Also she has a new car, wonderful clothes, talks on all subjects, and she will give you a first-class home and children. How near do we come in our life to paradise?"

"If she's so wonderful, why wasn't she married ten years ago?"

"Why?" said Salzman with a heavy laugh. "—Why? Because she is *partikiler*. This is why. She wants the *best*."

Leo was silent, amused at how he had entangled himself. But Salzman had aroused his interest in Lily H., and he began seriously to consider calling on her. When the marriage broker observed how intently Leo's mind was at work on the facts he had supplied, he felt certain they would soon come to an agreement.

Late Saturday afternoon, conscious of Salzman, Leo Finkle walked with Lily Hirschorn along Riverside Drive. He walked briskly and erectly, wearing with distinction the black fedora he had that morning taken with trepidation out of the dusty hat box on his closet shelf, and the heavy black Saturday coat he had thoroughly whisked clean. Leo also owned a walking stick, a present from a distant relative, but quickly put temptation aside and did not use it. Lily, petite and not unpretty, had on something signifying the approach of spring. She was au courant, animatedly, with all sorts of subjects, and he weighed her words and found her surprisingly sound—score another for Salzman, whom he uneasily sensed to be somewhere around, hiding perhaps high in a tree along the street, flashing the lady signals with a pocket mirror; or perhaps a cloven-hoofed Pan, piping nuptial ditties as he danced his invisible way before them, strewing wild buds on the walk and purple grapes in their path, symbolizing fruit of a union, though there was of course still none.

Lily startled Leo by remarking, "I was thinking of Mr. Salzman, a curious figure, wouldn't you say?"

Not certain what to answer, he nodded.

She bravely went on, blushing, "I for one am grateful for his introducing us. Aren't you?"

He courteously replied, "I am."

"I mean," she said with a little laugh—and it was all in good taste, or at least gave the effect of being not in bad— "do you mind that we came together so?"

He was not displeased with her honesty, recognizing that she meant to set the relationship aright, and understanding that it took a certain amount of experience in life, and courage, to want to do it quite that way. One had to have some sort of past to make that kind of beginning.

He said that he did not mind. Salzman's function was traditional and honorable—valuable for what it might achieve, which, he pointed out, was frequently nothing.

Lily agreed with a sigh. They walked on for a while and she said after a long silence, again with a nervous laugh, "Would you mind if I asked you something a little bit personal? Frankly, I find the subject fascinating." Although Leo shrugged, she went on half embarrassedly, "How was it that you came to your calling? I mean was it a sudden passionate inspiration?"

Leo, after a time, slowly replied, "I was always interested in the Law."

"You saw revealed in it the presence of the Highest?"

He nodded and changed the subject. "I understand that you spent a little time in Paris, Miss Hirschorn?"

"Oh, did Mr. Salzman tell you, Rabbi Finkle?" Leo winced but she went on, "It was ages ago and almost forgotten. I remember I had to return for my sister's wedding."

And Lily would not be put off. "When," she asked in a trembly voice, "did you become enamored of God?"

He stared at her. Then it came to him that she was talking not about Leo Finkle, but of a total stranger, some mystical figure, perhaps even passionate prophet that Salzman had dreamed up for her—no relation to the living or dead. Leo trembled with rage and weakness. The trickster had obviously sold her a bill of goods, just as he had him, who'd expected to become acquainted with a young lady of twenty-nine, only to behold, the moment he laid eyes upon her strained and anxious face, a woman past thirty-five and aging rapidly. Only his self control had kept him this long in her presence.

"I am not," he said gravely, "a talented religious person," and in seeking words to go on, found himself possessed by shame and fear. "I think," he said in a strained manner, "that I came to God not because I loved Him, but because I did not."

This confession he spoke harshly because its unexpectedness shook him.

Lily wilted. Leo saw a profusion of loaves of bread go flying like ducks high over his head, not unlike the winged loaves by which he had counted himself to sleep last night. Mercifully, then, it snowed, which he would not put past Salzman's machinations.

He was infuriated with the marriage broker and swore he would throw him out of the room the minute he reappeared. But Salzman did not come that night, and when Leo's anger had subsided, an unaccountable despair grew in its place. At first he thought this was caused by his disappointment in Lily, but before long it became evident that he had involved himself with Salzman without a true knowledge of his own intent. He gradually realized—with an emptiness that seized him with six hands—that he had called in the broker to find him a bride because he was incapable of doing it himself. This terrifying insight he had derived as a result of his meeting and conversation with Lily Hirschorn. Her probing questions had somehow irritated him into revealing—to himself more than her—the true nature of his relationship to God, and from that it had come upon him, with shocking force, that apart from his parents, he had never loved anyone. Or perhaps it went the other way, that he did not love God so well as he might, because he had not loved man. It seemed to Leo that his whole life stood starkly revealed and he saw himself for the first time as he truly was—unloved and loveless. This bitter but somehow not fully unexpected revelation brought him to a point of panic, controlled only by extraordinary effort. He covered his face with his hands and cried.

The week that followed was the worst of his life. He did not eat and lost weight. His beard darkened and grew ragged. He stopped attending seminars and almost never opened a book. He seriously considered leaving the Yeshivah, although he was deeply troubled at the thought of the loss of all his years of study—saw them like pages torn from a book, strewn over the city—and at the devastating effect of this decision upon his parents. But he had lived without knowledge of himself, and never in the Five Books and all the Commentaries—mea culpa—had the truth been revealed to him. He did not know where to turn, and in all this desolating loneliness there was no *to whom,* although he often thought of Lily but not once could bring himself to go downstairs and make the call. He became touchy and irritable, especially with his landlady, who asked him all manner of personal questions; on the other hand, sensing his own disagreeableness, he waylaid her on the stairs and apologized abjectly, until mortified, she ran from him. Out of this, however, he drew the consolation that he was a Jew and that a Jew suffered. But gradually, as the long and terrible week drew to a close, he regained his composure and some idea of purpose in life: to go on as planned. Although he was imperfect, the ideal was not. As for his quest of a bride, the thought of continuing afflicted him with anxiety and heartburn, yet perhaps with this new knowledge of himself he would be more successful than in the past. Perhaps love would now come to him and a bride to that love. And for this sanctified seeking who needed a Salzman?

The marriage broker, a skeleton with haunted eyes, returned that very night. He looked, withal, the picture of frustrated expectancy—as if he had steadfastly waited the week at Miss Lily Hirschorn's side for a telephone call that never came.

Casually coughing, Salzman came immediately to the point: "So how did you like her?"

Leo's anger rose and he could not refrain from chiding the matchmaker: "Why did you lie to me, Salzman?"

Salzman's pale face went dead white, the world had snowed on him.

"Did you not state that she was twenty-nine?" Leo insisted.

"I give you my word—"

"She was thirty-five, if a day. *At least* thirty-five."

"Of this don't be too sure. Her father told me—"

"Never mind. The worst of it was that you lied to her."

"How did I lie to her, tell me?"

"You told her things about me that weren't true. You made me out to be more, consequently less than I am. She had in mind a totally different person, a sort of semi-mystical Wonder Rabbi."

"All I said, you was a religious man."

"I can imagine."

Salzman sighed. "This is my weakness that I have," he confessed. "My wife says to me I shouldn't be a salesman, but when I have two fine people that they would be wonderful to be married, I am so happy that I talk too much." He smiled wanly. "This is why Salzman is a poor man."

Leo's anger left him. "Well, Salzman, I'm afraid that's all."

The marriage broker fastened hungry eyes on him.

"You don't want any more a bride?"

"I do," said Leo, "but I have decided to seek her in a different way. I am no longer interested in an arranged marriage. To be frank, I now admit the necessity of premarital love. That is, I want to be in love with the one I marry."

"Love?" said Salzman, astounded. After a moment he

remarked, "For us, our love is our life, not for the ladies. In the ghetto they—"

"I know, I know," said Leo. "I've thought of it often. Love, I have said to myself, should be a by-product of living and worship rather than its own end. Yet for myself I find it necessary to establish the level of my need and fulfill it."

Salzman shrugged but answered, "Listen, rabbi, if you want love, this I can find for you also. I have such beautiful clients that you will love them the minute your eyes will see them."

Leo smiled unhappily, "I'm afraid you don't understand."

But Salzman hastily unstrapped his portfolio and withdrew a manila packet from it.

"Pictures," he said, quickly laying the envelope on the table.

Leo called after him to take the pictures away, but as if on the wings of the wind, Salzman had disappeared.

March came. Leo had returned to his regular routine. Although he felt not quite himself yet—lacked energy—he was making plans for a more active social life. Of course it would cost something, but he was an expert in cutting corners; and when there were no corners left he would make circles rounder. All the while Salzman's pictures had lain on the table, gathering dust. Occasionally as Leo sat studying, or enjoying a cup of tea, his eyes fell on the manila envelope, but he never opened it.

The days went by and no social life to speak of developed with a member of the opposite sex—it was difficult, given the circumstances of his situation. One morning Leo toiled up the stairs to his room and stared out the window at the city. Although the day was bright his view of it was dark. For some time he watched the people in the street below hurrying along and then turned with a heavy heart to his little room. On the table was the packet. With a sudden relentless gesture he tore it open. For a half-hour he stood by the table in a state of excitement, examining the photographs of the ladies Salzman had included. Finally, with a deep sigh he put them down. There were six, of varying degrees of attractiveness, but look at them long enough and they all became Lily Hirschorn: all past their prime, all starved behind bright smiles, not a true personality in the lot. Life, despite their frantic yoohooings, had passed them by; they were pictures in a brief case that stank of fish. After a while, however, as Leo attempted to return the photographs into the envelope, he found in it another, a snapshot of the type taken by a machine for a quarter. He gazed at it a moment and let out a cry.

Her face deeply moved him. Why, he could at first not say. It gave him the impression of youth—spring flowers, yet age—a sense of having been used to the bone, wasted; this came from the eyes, which were hauntingly familiar, yet absolutely strange. He had a vivid impression that he had met her before, but try as he might he could not place her although he could almost recall her name, as if he had read it in her own handwriting. No, this couldn't be; he would have remembered her. It was not, he affirmed, that she had an extraordinary beauty—no, though her face was attractive enough; it was that *something* about her moved him. Feature for feature, even some of the ladies of the photographs could do better; but she leaped forth to his heart—had *lived,* or wanted to—more than just wanted, perhaps regretted how she had lived—had somehow deeply suffered: it could be seen in the depths of those reluctant eyes, and from the way the light enclosed and shone from her, and within her, opening realms of possibility: this was her own. Her he desired. His head ached and eyes narrowed with the intensity of his gazing, then as if an obscure fog had blown up in the mind, he experienced fear of her and was aware that he had received an impression, somehow, of evil. He shuddered, saying softly, it is thus with us all. Leo brewed some tea in a small pot and sat sipping it without sugar, to calm himself. But before he had finished drinking, again with excitement he examined the face and found it good: good for Leo Finkle. Only such a one could understand him and help him seek whatever he was seeking. She might, perhaps, love him. How she had happened to be among the discards in Salzman's barrel he could never guess, but he knew he must urgently go find her.

Leo rushed downstairs, grabbed up the Bronx telephone book, and searched for Salzman's home address. He was not listed, nor was his office. Neither was he in the Manhattan book. But Leo remembered having written down the address on a slip of paper after he had read Salzman's advertisement in the "personals" column of the *Forward*. He ran up to his room and tore through his papers, without luck. It was exasperating. Just when he needed the matchmaker he was nowhere to be found. Fortunately Leo remembered to look in his wallet. There on a card he found his name written and a Bronx address. No phone number was listed, the reason— Leo now recalled—he had originally communicated with Salzman by letter. He got on his coat, put a hat on over his skull cap and hurried to the subway station. All the way to the far end of the Bronx he sat on the edge of his seat. He was more than once tempted to take out the picture and see if the girl's face was as he remembered it, but he refrained, allowing the snapshot to remain in his inside coat pocket, content to have her so close. When the train pulled into the station he was waiting at the door and bolted out. He quickly located the street Salzman had advertised.

The building he sought was less than a block from the subway, but it was not an office building, nor even a loft, nor a store in which one could rent office space. It was a very old tenement house. Leo found Salzman's name in pencil on a soiled tag under the bell and climbed three dark flights to his apartment. When he knocked, the door was opened by a thin, asthmatic, gray-haired woman, in felt slippers.

"Yes?" she said, expecting nothing. She listened without listening. He could have sworn he had seen her, too, before but knew it was an illusion.

"Salzman—does he live here? Pinye Salzman," he said, "the matchmaker?"

She stared at him a long minute. "Of course."

He felt embarrassed. "Is he in?"

"No," Her mouth, though left open, offered nothing more.

"The matter is urgent. Can you tell me where his office is?"

"In the air." She pointed upward.

"You mean he has no office?" Leo asked.

"In his socks."

He peered into the apartment. It was sunless and dingy, one large room divided by a half-open curtain, beyond which he could see a sagging metal bed. The near side of a room was crowded with rickety chairs, old bureaus, a three-legged table, racks of cooking utensils, and all the apparatus of a kitchen. But there was no sign of Salzman or his magic barrel, probably also a figment of the imagination. An odor of frying fish made Leo weak to the knees.

"Where is he?" he insisted. "I've got to see your husband."

At length she answered, "So who knows where he is?

Every time he thinks a new thought he runs to a different place. Go home, he will find you."

"Tell him Leo Finkle."

She gave no sign she had heard.

He walked downstairs, depressed.

But Salzman, breathless, stood waiting at his door.

Leo was astounded and overjoyed. "How did you get here before me?"

"I rushed."

"Come inside."

They entered. Leo fixed tea, and a sardine sandwich for Salzman. As they were drinking he reached behind him for the packet of pictures and handed them to the marriage broker.

Salzman put down his glass and said expectantly, "You found somebody you like?"

"Not among these."

The marriage broker turned away.

"Here is the one I want." Leo held forth the snapshot.

Salzman slipped on his glasses and took the picture into his trembling hand. He turned ghastly and let out a groan.

"What's the matter?" cried Leo.

"Excuse me. Was an accident this picture. She isn't for you."

Salzman frantically shoved the manila packet into his portfolio. He thrust the snapshot into his pocket and fled down the stairs.

Leo, after momentary paralysis, gave chase and cornered the marriage broker in the vestibule. The landlady made hysterical outcries but neither of them listened.

"Give me back the picture, Salzman."

"No." The pain in his eyes was terrible.

"Tell me who she is then."

"This I can't tell you. Excuse me."

He made to depart, but Leo, forgetting himself, seized the matchmaker by his tight coat and shook him frenziedly.

"Please," sighed Salzman. *"Please."*

Leo ashamedly let him go. "Tell me who she is," he begged. "It's very important for me to know."

"She is not for you. She is a wild one—wild, without shame. This is not a bride for a rabbi."

"What do you mean wild?"

"Like an animal. Like a dog. For her to be poor was a sin. This is why to me she is dead now."

"In God's name, what do you mean?"

"Her I can't introduce to you," Salzman cried.

"Why are you so excited?"

"Why, he asks," Salzman said, bursting into tears. "This is my baby, my Stella, she should burn in hell."

Leo hurried up to bed and hid under the covers. Under the covers he thought his life through. Although he soon fell asleep he could not sleep her out of his mind. He woke, beating his breast. Though he prayed to be rid of her, his prayers went unanswered. Through days of torment he endlessly struggled not to love her; fearing success, he escaped it. He then concluded to convert her to goodness, himself to God. The idea alternately nauseated and exalted him.

He perhaps did not know that he had come to a final decision until he encountered Salzman in a Broadway cafeteria. He was sitting alone at a rear table, sucking the bony remains of a fish. The marriage broker appeared haggard, and transparent to the point of vanishing.

Salzman looked up at first without recognizing him. Leo had grown a pointed beard and his eyes were weighted with wisdom.

"Salzman," he said, "love has at last come to my heart."

"Who can love from a picture?" mocked the marriage broker.

"It is not impossible."

"If you can love her, then you can love anybody. Let me show you some new clients that they just sent me their photographs. One is a little doll."

"Just her I want," Leo murmured.

"Don't be a fool, doctor. Don't bother with her."

"Put me in touch with her, Salzman," Leo said humbly. "Perhaps I can be of service."

Salzman had stopped eating and Leo understood with emotion that it was now arranged.

Leaving the cafeteria, he was, however, afflicted by a tormenting suspicion that Salzman had planned it all to happen this way.

Leo was informed by letter that she would meet him on a certain corner, and she was there one spring night, waiting under a street lamp. He appeared, carrying a small bouquet of violets and rosebuds. Stella stood by the lamp post, smoking. She wore white with red shoes, which fitted his expectations, although in a troubled moment he had imagined the dress red, and only the shoes white. She wafted uneasily and shyly. From afar he saw that her eyes—clearly her father's—were filled with desperate innocence. He pictured, in her, his own redemption. Violins and lit candles revolved in the sky. Leo ran forward with flowers outthrust.

Around the corner, Salzman, leaning against a wall, chanted prayers for the dead.

(1958)

I STAND HERE IRONING
from *Tell Me a Riddle*

TILLIE OLSEN

I stand here ironing, and what you asked me moves tormented back and forth with the iron.

"I wish you would manage the time to come in and talk with me about your daughter. I'm sure you can help me understand her. She's a youngster who needs help and whom I'm deeply interested in helping."

"Who needs help." . . . Even if I came, what good would it do? You think because I am her mother I have a key, or that in some way you could use me as a key? She has lived for nineteen years. There is all that life that has happened outside of me, beyond me.

And when is there time to remember, to sift, to weigh, to estimate, to total? I will start and there will be an interruption and I will have to gather it all together again. Or I will become engulfed with all I did or did not do, with what should have been and what cannot be helped.

She was a beautiful baby. The first and only one of our five that was beautiful at birth. You do not guess how new and uneasy her tenancy in her now-loveliness. You did not know her all those years she was thought homely, or see her poring over her baby pictures, making me tell her over and over how beautiful she had been—and would be, I would tell her—and was now, to the seeing eye. But the seeing eyes were few or nonexistent. Including mine.

I nursed her. They feel that's important nowadays. I nursed all the children, but with her, with all the fierce rigidity of first motherhood, I did like the books then said. Though her cries battered me to trembling and my breasts ached with swollenness, I waited till the clock decreed.

Why do I put that first? I do not even know if it matters, or if it explains anything.

She was a beautiful baby. She blew shining bubbles of sound. She loved motion, loved light, loved color and music and textures. She would lie on the floor in her blue overalls patting the surface so hard in ecstasy her hands and feet would blur. She was a miracle to me, but when she was eight months old I had to leave her daytimes with the woman downstairs to whom she was no miracle at all, for I worked or looked for work and for Emily's father, who "could no longer endure" (he wrote in his good-bye note) "sharing want with us."

I was nineteen. It was the pre-relief, pre-WPA world of the depression. I would start running as soon as I got off the streetcar, running up the stairs, the place smelling sour, and awake or asleep to startle awake, when she saw me she would break into a clogged weeping that could not be comforted, a weeping I can hear yet.

After a while I found a job hashing at night so I could be with her days, and it was better. But it came to where I had to bring her to his family and leave her.

It took a long time to raise the money for her fare back. Then she got chicken pox and I had to wait longer. When she finally came, I hardly knew her, walking quick and nervous like her father, looking like her father, thin, and dressed in a shoddy red that yellowed her skin and glared at the pock-marks. All the baby loveliness gone.

She was two. Old enough for nursery school they said, and I did not know then what I know now—the fatigue of the long day, and the lacerations of group life in the kinds of nurseries that are only parking places for children.

Except that it would have made no difference if I had known. It was the only place there was. It was the only way we could be together, the only way I could hold a job.

And even without knowing, I knew. I knew the teacher that was evil because all these years it has curdled into my memory, the little boy hunched in the corner, her rasp, "why aren't you outside, because Alvin hits you? that's no reason, go out, scaredy." I knew Emily hated it even if she did not clutch and implore "don't go Mommy" like the other children, mornings.

She always had a reason why we should stay home. Momma, you look sick. Momma, I feel sick. Momma, the teachers aren't there today, they're sick. Momma, we can't go, there was a fire there last night. Momma, it's a holiday today, no school, they told me.

But never a direct protest, never rebellion. I think of our others in their three-, four-year-oldness—the explosions, the tempers, the denunciations, the demands—and I feel suddenly ill. I put the iron down. What in me demanded that goodness in her? And what was the cost, the cost to her of such goodness?

The old man living in the back once said in his gentle way:

"You should smile at Emily more when you look at her." What *was* in my face when I looked at her? I loved her. There were all the acts of love.

It was only with the others I remembered what he said, and it was the face of joy, and not of care or tightness or worry I turned to them—too late for Emily. She does not smile easily, let alone almost always as her brothers and sisters do. Her face is closed and sombre, but when she wants, how fluid. You must have seen it in her pantomimes, you spoke of her rare gift for comedy on the stage that rouses a laughter out of the audience so dear they applaud and applaud and do not want to let her go.

Where does it come from, that comedy? There was none of it in her when she came back to me that second time, after I had had to send her away again. She had a new daddy now to learn to love, and I think perhaps it was a better time.

Except when we left her alone nights, telling ourselves she was old enough.

"Can't you go some other time, Mommy, like tomorrow?" she would ask. "Will it be just a little while you'll be gone? Do you promise?"

The time we came back, the front door open, the clock on the floor in the hall. She rigid awake. "It wasn't just a little while. I didn't cry. Three times I called you, just three times, and then I ran downstairs to open the door so you could come faster. The clock talked loud. I threw it away, it scared me what it talked."

She said the clock talked loud again that night I went to the hospital to have Susan. She was delirious with the fever that comes before red measles, but she was fully conscious all the week I was gone and the week after we were home when she could not come near the new baby or me.

She did not get well. She stayed skeleton thin, not wanting to eat, and night after night she had nightmares. She would call for me, and I would rouse from exhaustion to sleepily call back: "You're all right, darling, go to sleep, it's just a dream," and if she still called, in a sterner voice, "now go to sleep, Emily, there's nothing to hurt you." Twice, only twice, when I had to get up for Susan anyhow, I went in to sit with her.

Now when it is too late (as if she would let me hold and comfort her like I do the others) I get up and go to her at once at her moan or restless stirring. "Are you awake, Emily? Can I get you something?" And the answer is always the same: "No, I'm all right, go back to sleep, Mother."

They persuaded me at the clinic to send her away to a convalescent home in the country where "she can have the kind of food and care you can't manage for her, and you'll be free to concentrate on the new baby." They still send children to that place. I see pictures on the society page of sleek young women planning affairs to raise money for it, or dancing at the affairs, or decorating Easter eggs or filling Christmas stockings for the children.

They never have a picture of the children so I do not know if the girls still wear those gigantic red bows and the ravaged looks on the every other Sunday when parents can come to visit "unless otherwise notified"—as we were notified the first six weeks.

Oh it is a handsome place, green lawns and tall trees and fluted flower beds. High up on the balconies of each cottage the children stand, the girls in their red bows and white dresses, the boys in white suits and giant red ties. The parents stand below shrieking up to be heard and the children shriek down to be heard, and between them the invisible wall "Not To Be Contaminated by Parental Germs or Physical Affection."

There was a tiny girl who always stood hand in hand with Emily. Her parents never came. One visit she was gone. "They moved her to Rose Cottage" Emily shouted in explanation. "They don't like you to love anybody here."

She wrote once a week, the labored writing of a seven-year-old. "I am fine. How is the baby. If I write my leter nicly I will have a star. Love." There never was a star. We wrote every other day, letters she could never hold or keep but only hear read—once. "We simply do not have room for children to keep any personal possessions," they patiently explained when we pieced one Sunday's shrieking together to plead how much it would mean to Emily, who loved so to keep things, to be allowed to keep her letters and cards.

Each visit she looked frailer. "She isn't eating," they told us.

(They had runny eggs for breakfast or mush with lumps, Emily said later, I'd hold it in my mouth and not swallow. Nothing ever tasted good, just when they had chicken.)

It took us eight months to get her released home, and only the fact that she gained back so little of her seven lost pounds convinced the social worker.

I used to try to hold and love her after she came back, but her body would stay stiff, and after a while she'd push away. She ate little. Food sickened her, and I think much of life too. Oh she had physical lightness and brightness, twinkling by on skates, bouncing like a ball up and down up and down over the jump rope, skimming over the hill; but these were momentary.

She fretted about her appearance, thin and dark and foreign-looking at a time when every little girl was supposed to look or thought she should look a chubby blonde replica of Shirley Temple. The doorbell sometimes rang for her, but no one seemed to come and play in the house or be a best friend. Maybe because we moved so much.

There was a boy she loved painfully through two school semesters. Months later she told me how she had taken pennies from my purse to buy him candy. "Licorice was his favorite and I brought him some every day, but he still liked Jennifer better'n me. Why, Mommy?" The kind of question for which there is no answer.

School was a worry to her. She was not glib or quick in a world where glibness and quickness were easily confused with ability to learn. To her overworked and exasperated teachers she was an overconscientious "slow learner" who kept trying to catch up and was absent entirely too often.

I let her be absent, though sometimes the illness was imaginary. How different from my now-strictness about attendance with the others. I wasn't working. We had a new baby, I was home anyhow. Sometimes, after Susan grew old enough, I would keep her home from school, too, to have them all together.

Mostly Emily had asthma, and her breathing, harsh and labored, would fill the house with a curiously tranquil sound. I would bring the two old dresser mirrors and her boxes of collections to her bed. She would select beads and single earrings, bottle tops and shells, dried flowers and pebbles, old postcards and scraps, all sorts of oddments; then she and Susan would play Kingdom, setting up landscapes and furniture, peopling them with action.

Those were the only times of peaceful companionship between her and Susan. I have edged away from it, that poisonous feeling between them, that terrible balancing of hurts and needs I had to do between the two, and did so badly, those earlier years.

Oh there are conflicts between the others too, each one

human, needing, demanding, hurting, taking—but only between Emily and Susan, no, Emily toward Susan that corroding resentment. It seems so obvious on the surface, yet it is not obvious. Susan, the second child, Susan, golden- and curly-haired and chubby, quick and articulate and assured, everything in appearance and manner Emily was not; Susan, not able to resist Emily's precious things, losing or sometimes clumsily breaking them; Susan telling jokes and riddles to company for applause while Emily sat silent (to say to me later: that was *my* riddle, Mother, I told it to Susan); Susan, who for all the five years' difference in age was just a year behind Emily in developing physically.

I am glad for that slow physical development that widened the difference between her and her contemporaries, though she suffered over it. She was too vulnerable for that terrible world of youthful competition, of preening and parading, of constant measuring of yourself against every other, of envy, "If I had that copper hair," "If I had that skin. . . ." She tormented herself enough about not looking like the others, there was enough of the unsureness, the having to be conscious of words before you speak, the constant caring—what are they thinking of me? without having it all magnified by the merciless physical drives.

Ronnie is calling. He is wet and I change him. It is rare there is such a cry now. That time of motherhood is almost behind me when the ear is not one's own but must always be racked and listening for the child cry, the child call. We sit for a while and I hold him, looking out over the city spread in charcoal with its soft aisles of light. *"Shoogily,"* he breathes and curls closer. I carry him back to bed, asleep. *Shoogily.* A funny word, a family word, inherited from Emily, invented by her to say: *comfort.*

In this and other ways she leaves her seal, I say aloud. And startle at my saying it. What do I mean? What did I start to gather together, to try and make coherent? I was at the terrible, growing years. War years. I do not remember them well. I was working, there were four smaller ones now, there was not time for her. She had to help be a mother, and housekeeper, and shopper. She had to set her seal. Mornings of crisis and near hysteria trying to get lunches packed, hair combed, coats and shoes found, everyone to school or Child Care on time, the baby ready for transportation. And always the paper scribbled on by a smaller one, the book looked at by Susan then mislaid, the homework not done. Running out to that huge school where she was one, she was lost, she was a drop; suffering over the unpreparedness, stammering and unsure in her classes.

There was so little time left at night after the kids were bedded down. She would struggle over books, always eating (it was in those years she developed her enormous appetite that is legendary in our family) and I would be ironing, or preparing food for the next day, or writing V-mail to Bill, or tending the baby. Sometimes, to make me laugh, or out of her despair, she would imitate happenings or types at school.

I think I said once: "Why don't you do something like this in the school amateur show?" One morning she phoned me at work, hardly understandable through the weeping: "Mother, I did it. I won, I won; they gave me first prize; they clapped and clapped and wouldn't let me go."

Now suddenly she was Somebody, and as imprisoned in her difference as she had been in anonymity.

She began to be asked to perform at other high schools, even in colleges, then at city and statewide affairs. The first one we went to, I only recognized her that first moment when thin, shy, she almost drowned herself into the curtains. Then: Was this Emily? The control, the command, the convulsing and deadly clowning, the spell, then the roaring, stamping audience, unwilling to let this rare and precious laughter out of their lives.

Afterwards: You ought to do something about her with a gift like that—but without money or knowing how, what does one do? We have left it all to her, and the gift has as often eddied inside, clogged and clotted, as been used and growing.

She is coming. She runs up the stairs two at a time with her light graceful step, and I know she is happy tonight. Whatever it was that occasioned your call did not happen today.

"Aren't you ever going to finish the ironing, Mother? Whistler painted his mother in a rocker. I'd have to paint mine standing over an ironing board." This is one of her communicative nights and she tells me everything and nothing as she fixes herself a plate of food out of the icebox.

She is so lovely. Why did you want me to come in at all? Why were you concerned? She will find her way.

She starts up the stairs to bed. "Don't get me up with the rest in the morning." "But I thought you were having midterms." "Oh, those," she comes back in, kisses me, and says quite lightly, "in a couple of years when we'll all be atom-dead they won't matter a bit."

She has said it before. She *believes* it. But because I have been dredging the past, and all that compounds a human being is so heavy and meaningful in me, I cannot endure it tonight.

I will never total it all. I will never come in to say: She was a child seldom smiled at. Her father left me before she was a year old. I had to work her first six years when there was work, or I sent her home and to his relatives. There were those years she had care she hated. She was dark and thin and foreign-looking in a world where the prestige went to blondeness and curly hair and dimples, she was slow where glibness was prized. She was a child of anxious, not proud, love. We were poor and could not afford for her the soil of easy growth. I was a young mother, I was a distracted mother. There were other children pushing up, demanding. Her younger sister seemed all that she was not. There were years she did not want me to touch her. She kept too much in herself, her life was such she had to keep too much in herself. My wisdom came too late. She has much to her and probably little will come of it. She is a child of her age, of depression, of war, of fear.

Let her be. So all that is in her will not bloom—but in how many does it? There is still enough left to live by. Only help her to know—help make it so there is cause for her to know—that she is more than this dress on the ironing board, helpless before the iron.

(1961)

KADDISH PARTS 1, 3, AND 4

from *Kaddish*

ALLEN GINSBERG

For Naomi Ginsberg 1894–1956

I

Strange now to think of you, gone without corsets & eyes, while I walk on the sunny pavement of Greenwich Village.

downtown Manhattan, clear winter noon, and I've been up all night, talking, talking, reading the Kaddish aloud listening to Ray Charles blues shout blind on the phonograph

the rhythm the rhythm—and your memory in my head three years after—And read Adonais' last triumphant stanzas aloud—wept, realizing how we suffer—

And how Death is that remedy all singers dream of, sing, remember, prophesy as in the Hebrew Anthem, or the Buddhist Book of Answers—and my own imagination of a withered leaf—at dawn—

Dreaming back thru life, Your time—and mine accelerating toward Apocalypse,

the final moment—the flower burning in the Day—and what
    comes after,
looking back on the mind itself that saw an American city
a flash away, and the great dream of Me or China, or you and
    a phantom Russia, or a crumpled bed that never
    existed—
like a poem in the dark—escaped back to Oblivion—
No more to say, and nothing to weep for but the Beings in the
    Dream, trapped in its disappearance,
sighing, screaming with it, buying and selling pieces of
    phantom, worshipping each other,
worshipping the God included in it all—longing or
    inevitability?—while it lasts, a Vision—anything more?
It leaps about me, as I go out and walk the street, look back
    over my shoulder, Seventh Avenue, the battlements of
    window office buildings shouldering each other high,
    under a cloud, tall as the sky an instant—and the sky
    above—an old blue place.
or down the Avenue to the South, to—as I walk toward the
    Lower East Side—where you walked 50 years ago, little,
    girl—from Russia, eating the first poisonous tomatoes of
    America—frightened on the dock—
then struggling in the crowds of Orchard Street toward
    what?—toward Newark—
toward candy store, first home-made sodas of the century,
    handchurned ice cream in backroom on musty brown-
    floor boards—
Toward education marriage nervous breakdown, operation,
    teaching school, and learning to be mad, in a dream—
    what is this life?
Toward the Key in the window—and the great Key lays its
    head of light on top of Manhattan, and over the floor, and

lays down on the sidewalk—in a single vast beam, moving,
as I walk down First toward the Yiddish Theater—and
the place of poverty

you knew, and I know, but without caring now—Strange to
have moved thru Paterson, and the West, and Europe
and here again,

with the cries of Spaniards now in the doorstoops doors and
dark boys on the street, fire escapes old as you

—Tho you're not old now, that's left here with me—

Myself, anyhow, maybe as old as the universe—and I guess
that dies with us—enough to cancel all that comes—
What came is gone forever every time—

That's good! That leaves it open for no regret—no fear radia-
tors, lacklove, torture even toothache in the end—

Though while it comes it is a lion that eats the soul—and the
lamb, the soul, in us, alas, offering itself in sacrifice to
change's fierce hunger—hair and teeth—and the roar of
bonepain, skull bare, break rib, rot-skin, braintricked
Implacability.

Ai! ai! we do worse! We are in a fix! And you're out, Death let
you out, Death had the Mercy, you're done with your
century, done with God, done with the path thru it—
Done with yourself at last—Pure—Back to the Babe
dark before your Father, before us all—before the
world—

There, rest. No more suffering for you. I know where you've
gone, it's good.

No more flowers in the summer fields of New York, no joy
now, no more fear of Louis,

and no more of his sweetness and glasses, his high school
decades, debts, loves, frightened telephone calls, con-
ception beds, relatives, hands—

No more of sister Elanor,—she gone before you—we kept it
    secret—you killed her—or she killed herself to bear with
    you—an arthritic heart—But Death's killed you both—
    No matter—

Nor your memory of your mother, 1915 tears in silent movies
    weeks and weeks—forgetting, agrieve watching Marie
    Dressler address humanity, Chaplin dance in youth,

or Boris Godinov, Chaliapin's at the Met, halling his voice of
    a weeping Czar—by standing room with Elanor & Max—
    watching also the Capitalists take seats in Orchestra,
    white furs, diamonds,

with the YPSL's hitch-hiking thru Pennsylvania, in black
    baggy gym skirts pants, photograph of 4 girls holding
    each other round the waste, and laughing eye, too coy,
    virginal solitude of 1920

all girls grown old, or dead, now, and that long hair in the
    grave—lucky to have husbands later—

You made it—I came too—Eugene my brother before (still
    grieving now and will gream on to his last stiff hand, as
    he goes thru his cancer—or kill—later perhaps—soon
    he will think—)

And it's the last moment I remember, which I see them all,
    thru myself, now—tho not you

I didn't foresee what you felt—what more hideous gape of
    bad mouth came first—to you—and were you prepared?

To go where? In that Dark—that—in that God? a radiance? A
    Lord in the Void? Like an eye in the black cloud in a
    dream? Adonoi at last, with you?

Beyond my remembrance! Incapable to guess! Not merely
    the yellow skull in the grave, or a box of worm dust, and
    a stained ribbon—Deathshead with Halo? can you
    believe it?

Is it only the sun that shines once for the mind, only the flash
of existence, than none ever was?

Nothing beyond what we have—what you had—that so
pitiful—yet Triumph,

to have been here, and changed, like a tree, broken, or
flower—fed to the ground—but mad, with its petals, colored, thinking Great Universe, shaken, cut in the head,
leaf stript, hid in an egg crate hospital, cloth wrapped,
sore—freaked in the moon brain, Naughtless.

No flower like that flower, which knew itself in the garden,
and fought the knife—lost

Cut down by an idiot Snowman's icy—even in the Spring—
strange ghost thought—some Death—Sharp icicle in his
hand—crowned with old roses—a dog for his eyes—
cock of a sweatshop—heart of electric irons.

All the accumulations of life, that wear us out—clocks,
bodies, consciousness, shoe, breasts—begotten sons—
your Communism—'Paranoia' into hospitals.

You once kicked Elanor in the leg, she died of heart failure
later. You of stroke. Asleep? within a year, the two of
you, sisters in death. Is Elanor happy?

Max grieves alive in an office on Lower Broadway, lone large
mustache over midnight Accountings, not sure. His life
passes—as he sees—and what does he doubt now? Still
dream of making money, or that might have made
money, hired nurse, had children, found even your
Immortality, Naomi?

I'll see him soon. Now I've got to cut through—to talk to
you—as I didn't when you had a mouth.

Forever. And we're bound for that, Forever—like Emily Dick-
inson's horses—headed to the End.

They know the way—These Steeds—run faster than we

think—it's our own life they cross—and take with
them.

Magnificent, mourned no more, marred of heart, mind
behind, married dreamed, mortal changed—Ass and face
done with murder.
In the world, given, flower maddened, made no Utopia,
shut under pine, aimed in Earth, balmed in Lone, Jehovah,
accept.
Nameless, One Faced, Forever beyond me, beginning-
less, endless, Father in death. Tho I am not there for this
Prophecy, I am unmarried, I'm hymnless, I'm Heavenless,
headless in blisshood I would still adore
Thee, Heaven, after Death, only One blessed in Nothing-
ness, not light or darkness, Dayless Eternity—
Take this, this Psalm, from me, burst from my hand in a
day, some of my Time, now given to Nothing—to praise
Thee—But Death
This is the end, the redemption from Wilderness, way
for the Wonderer, House sought for All, black handkerchief
washed clean by weeping—page beyond Psalm—Last
change of mine and Naomi—to God's perfect Darkness—
Death, stay thy phantoms!

III

Only to have not forgotten the beginning in which she drank
    cheap sodas in the morgues of Newark,
only to have seen her weeping on grey tables in long wards
    of her universe
only to have known the weird ideas of Hitler at the door, the
    wires in her head, the three big sticks

rammed down her back, the voices in the ceiling shrieking
    out her ugly early lays for 30 years,
only to have seen the time-jumps, memory lapse, the crash
    of wars, the roar and silence of a vast electric shock,
only to have seen her painting crude pictures of Elevateds
    running over the rooftops of the Bronx
her brothers dead in Riverside or Russia, her lone in Long
    Island writing a last letter—and her image in the sun-
    light at the window
'The key is in the sunlight at the window in the bars the key
    is in the sunlight,'
only to have come to that dark night on iron bed by stroke
    when the sun gone down on Long Island
and the vast Atlantic roars outside the great call of Being to
    its own
to come back out of the Nightmare—divided creation—with
    her head lain on a pillow of the hospital to die
—in one last glimpse—all Earth one everlasting Light in the
    familiar blackout—no tears for this vision—
But that the key should be left behind—at the window—the
    key in the sunlight—to the living—that can take
that slice of light in hand—and turn the door—and look
    back see
Creation glistening backwards to the same grave, size of
    universe,
size of the tick of the hospital's clock on the archway over
    the white door—

IV

O mother
what have I left out

O mother
what have I forgotten
O mother
farewell
with a long black shoe
farewell
with Communist Party and a broken stocking
farewell
with six dark hairs on the wen of your breast
farewell
with your old dress and a long black beard around the vagina
farewell
with your sagging belly
with your fear of Hitler
with your mouth of bad short stories
with your fingers of rotten mandolines
with your arms of fat Paterson porches
with your belly of strikes and smokestacks
with your chin of Trotsky and the Spanish War
with your voice singing for the decaying overbroken workers
with your nose of bad lay with your nose of the smell of the
        pickles of Newark
with your eyes
with your eyes of Russia
with your eyes of no money
with your eyes of false China
with your eyes of Aunt Elanor
with your eyes of starving India
with your eyes pissing in the park
with your eyes of America taking a fall
with your eyes of your failure at the piano
with your eyes of your relatives in California

with your eyes of Ma Rainey dying in an ambulance
with your eyes of Czechoslovakia attacked by robots
with your eyes going to painting class at night in the Bronx
with your eyes of the killer Grandma you see on the horizon
  from the Fire-Escape
with your eyes running naked out of the apartment
  screaming into the hall
with your eyes being led away by policemen to an ambulance
with your eyes strapped down on the operating table
with your eyes with the pancreas removed
with your eyes of appendix operation
with your eyes of abortion
with your eyes of ovaries removed
with your eyes of shock
with your eyes of lobotomy
with your eyes of divorce
with your eyes of stroke
with your eyes alone
with your eyes
with your eyes
with your Death full of Flowers

(1961)

THE LITTLE GOAT

from *Haunch Paunch and Jowl*

SAMUEL ORNITZ

FIRST PERIOD

I begin my history. I want to tell everything. Everything: so that even if I tell pathological lies the truth will shine out like grains of gold in the upturned muck. . . . I grope for first definite memories.

Early childhood is a mist world: fantastic and fearful, glamorous and grotesque. One is not really born into life until one breaks through this fine-webbed cocoon of vagueness. . . . I am nine; that stands out fully and firmly blocked. . . . Ramshackle New York during the sprawling awkward age of its growth. . . . A keen December evening. Gas lamps burning orange beacons upon the blue sea of a wintry night. I am returning from *cheder* (Hebrew School).

I close the door behind me. The kerosene lamp with its sooty chimney and ragged wick smokes more than ever. It stands high on a shelf and its uncertain light makes a foggy etching of our kitchen . . . blurred charcoal figures of mother and father

and Uncle Philip seated close by the cook-stove drinking tea
. . . and of the furnishings, exaggerated silhouettes.

Throwing my books on a chair I snatch up the huge slab
of bread and the apple mother laid out for me and without a
word start for the street. I am in a hurry to join the Ludlow
Street Gang. Just yesterday I was admitted to its glorious
ranks as the fourteenth leader. I was not Leader the Fourteenth, but of the whole gang fourteenth in prowess and
importance. However, I had only thirteen superiors. Being
the lowest step in the ladder I was most frequently trod
upon; but it was sweet suffering, the travail of a hero. . . .
When I became a Ludlow Streeter I swept away the last rag
of swaddling clothes and life became real. . . . So I hurry
away, silently, detachedly, as a man of importance. . . . But
Uncle Philip's voice halts me. Meanwhile, I am busy
munching the apple. Here is Uncle Philip lecturing like a
Rabbi on a fast day. He intimidates: not he, but his way of
speaking Yiddish. It is not just Yiddish—guttural, jargonish,
haphazard; but an arresting, rhythmical, logical language. . . .
Yiddish, the lingo of greenhorns, was held in contempt by
the Ludlow Streeters who felt mightily their Americanism.
Yet even the gang fought shy of making fun of the green Uncle
Philip for he had a way of accompanying his Yiddish with
gestures that left smarting memories.

"*Nu, yeshiva bochar* (seminary student), what says one?
So, like a wanton puff,—in and out. A grab and gone. *Fertig!*
(Done). And now what of your social duties, your filial
respects! What are you aiming to be? A man for men? Or a
drayman, companion of horses? Really, what says one?"

"*Tahke,* what says one?" interrupts kindly, chiding
mamma.

My mouth is chockful of bread and apple and I nearly

choke with indignation when she calls me by my hateful love name—*"Ziegelle"* (little goat).

Papa looks on in his brooding way, hunched in his chair, as always too tired and spent to talk. His eyes light gratefully on the young and vigorous Philip, family mentor, whom he idealizes and loves so much . . . just as though he were not his brother-in-law. Philip, he says, is his star of hope showing the way out of the wilderness—the sweatshop.

"Remember," quoth Philip in his best manner of Talmudical harangue, "gone are the diaper days. This day you are nine." . . . Follows a solemn pause. . . . "Tomorrow begins your tenth year——"

"The tenth year. Long years to you, *Ziegelle.*"

Ziegelle! ziegelle! Eternally, the little goat. The curse of my life. The Ludlow Streeters know me by no other name. They greet me with "maa, maa" and tug my chin as though pulling a beard. . . . A love name indeed! Other children did not have to put up with an insulting diminutive, *à la Russe*. They were called, say *poppale* (little father) or *zadelle* (little grandfather), or *hertzalle* (little heart), but I, only I was marked for scorn as the little goat. Wherefore?

Philip rose and placed his glass on the table. We did not boast saucers at that time. With a gallant bow he took mother's glass. Father continues to gnaw a lump of sugar and draw tea from his glass with a complacent hiss. . . . As Philip moves between the lamp and the table shadows dance on the wall, shadows that take the shape of goats cavorting at my discomfiture. And I want to throw things at them.

"Meyer," says Philip, raising an impressive finger, "remember that learning without breeding is like a *kugel* (pudding) without *gribbenes* (rendered chicken fat). It is food without flavor: so with a man, a fellow without favor."

"Gee," I plead in English, "I ain't got time for everything."

A quick reproving gesture menaces me to silence.

"Speak to me *momme loschen* (mother tongue) not that nasty gibberish of the streets."

Again he humiliates me—he—the greenhorn. He knows I am not speaking genteel American.

I make a plea . . . in Yiddish . . . and because my phrasing is facile, mother smiles proudly and even Uncle Philip's stern demeanor softens.

"All day I have been in English school, and then in *cheder* all evening, and I want to play with the boys a little bit. And it was hard in *cheder* today, for I had to read a page of *Targum* and *Rashi* without even one mistake.

Mother beams. . . . "*Nicht schlecht* (not bad), *nu* what say you, Philip? And only nine."

"But your studies are not done," says Philip. "A lesson in manners is never out of place. Remember, Meyer, no matter how wealthy, no matter how learned, you will be as nothing if not a gentleman." The last word he enunciates sharply in English.

"What is that—that a gentleman?" I ask.

"A gentleman. Ah! A gentleman—hem—is a person whom you cannot exactly describe—hum—but whom you know to be a gentleman the second you set eyes on him." . . . He looks at me steadily, expectantly, but my face is blank with ignorance.

"Then, Uncle Philip, I won't know what it is a—gentleman—till I see one."

"Not until then, Meyer."

"All right," I offer conciliatingly, "I will be on the watch out for one." . . . But Philip seems disappointed.

"So, Meyer," he muses, "so, you can read the old French-Hebrew text of *Rashi* and *Aramic Targum,* the dialect that Christ spoke, but you know not a gentleman—so."

"Christ spoke it," I whisper in a cautious echo, reluctant to utter the forbidden name.

Mother flutters in alarm. Father stirs uneasily.

"Brother," she says, "mention not the unspeakable one."

"Bah, unmentionable, why, why keep the boy ignorant—"

"I am not ignorant, Uncle Philip, although you can't expect me to know a gentleman when I never even saw one."

"And then," demands Philip with apparent displeasure, "am I not a gentleman?"

"No, you are my Uncle Philip."

"So it is," mutters Philip, "because I am your uncle."

He takes a small notebook from his pocket and holding it up says, "Observe, Meyer, this booklet, it is entirely given over to your affairs." He turns to the first leaf and reads, "Notes upon the education of my nephew, Meyer Hirsch." Then, using his knee as a rest, writes and reads aloud at the same time. "Item one: Family Pride."

The gang is at the corner huddled about a wood fire in a grocer's milk can with large holes cut out for vents. It is a compact circle seated shoulder to shoulder on assorted boxes. I long, passionately, to be part of it and hear the grave and grim pow-wow of the chieftains, and share the pungent promise of potatoes baking in the embers. . . . I hover, hopefully, and scrape my feet, and place a suppliant hand on the shoulder of the humblest of the gathering, the thirteenth leader, but he puts it off with a quick shrug . . . a terrible feeling of being left out in the cold . . . and I become angry, and a daring idea is born. . . . I pull Hymie, the twelfth leader, from his place. . . . Words are not needed; the challenge speaks volumes. . . . A scrap! Partisan cries—"Give it to him, Hymie"; "Use your left"; "Come on, nannie-goat, butt him in the *kischkes* (guts)." . . . The surprise attack gives me an edge on him, and soon Hymie is persuaded to relinquish his place at the fire and the twelfth leadership. And the thirteenth leader by inaction and silence abdicates his right. Thus I dispose of two enemies by first vanquishing the stronger. . . . My first victory . . . my first seat at the fire . . . and I tingle with joy. . . . And then came the potatoes. What if they were charred. A feast of feasts. . . . I thrill to the talk of war, war on the nearest clan, the Essex Street Guerrillas. . . . Says Boolkie, in manner and tone cryptic, as fitting a first leader, "Don't take none of their guff. "We'll give them what for any time they wants it." . . . The fire is now a mellow glow of embers. . . . A sudden alarm! A lookout shrilly warns: "A *shammos!* A *shammos!*" (Synagogue beadle. In the secret lingo of the gang *shammos* was the warning that a policeman was coming). Whereupon, the indomitable clan of Ludlow Streeters scatters in all directions.

I fly to the cellar of our house, where works and lives Berel, a fixer of harness. Berel smiles at my headlong, breathless entry. He sits before his bench mending reins. Lutz, the *shicker goy* (drunken Gentile), seated on a box, is laboriously sewing up a rent in his pants. He is the local *Shabbos* (Sabbath) fire lighter and lodges with Berel. These two and Yoshke the *Golitzianer* (Galician), a peddler, sleep in this small cellar workroom. Yoshke is already asleep on a couch with a sagging belly. Lutz beds on the floor and Berel boasts a cot.

I like Berel. He doesn't talk to me: he talks with me. He is a teller of tales, tales of the forests and fields of his sunny and verdant Bessarabia. And he is a wit, but always kindly. For instance, as now, he never neglects to greet me as a grown-up, not ironically, but caressingly, "What make you, (How are you) *Reb* (Mr.) Meyer?"

"Ollaright, a pretty thanks to you for asking, *Reb* Berel."

"Is it from a bear you are running, or has your shadow tripped you in the dark alley?"

"Oh, no, I have not a fear of such things. I just escaped from a policeman." I confide proudly.

He whistles and smacks his lips in awesome tribute to my daredeviltry. "Sit you down here, sit on this saddle, my adventurous friend, you must be tired."

I watch Berel sewing thongs of leather. . . . "Those reins you are fixing, I guess must be for a little pony."

"No, Meyer, they are for a goat."

A goat, . . . the very mention of my bearded nemesis is enough to spoil this glorious night.

"I guess you know all about horses, don't you, Berel?"

"Yes, something."

"Do you know all about goats, too?"

"Yes, when I was a boy I used to take care of herds of goats."

"Then tell me, Berel, be so good, what's the matter nobody likes a goat and everybody makes fun of them."

"First place, nothing bothers a goat and that makes people angry. A goat manages to get along where any other creature would perish. Stubble, twigs, anything is food and nourishment for him. He is a sidestepper, can walk a narrow ledge or a fence, if need be. He is for himself; unfeeling, and befriends no one. An unlikable, ugly thing with a most unreasonable smell. And I have noticed that a goat is the only thing ridicule can't kill."

Surely a pleasing portrait of my namesake, and it made me despondent. . . . Lutz, done with his stitching, stares vacantly at the lamp. Berel is busy with an awl. Suddenly, Yoshke shrieks in his sleep, one word piteous, imploring, *"Mommale"* (little mother).

Berel putters away and Lutz stares, unblinkingly, and the silence is of a tomb.

"Mommale, mommale," hums Berel under his breath, *"scheine mommale,"* in the minor tones of a *Yom Kippur* chant. (Little mother, little mother, lovely little mother).

I watch Yoshke in shocked surprise: here is a bearded man crying in his sleep for his mother.

"Poor Yoshke," says Berel with a sigh. "Yoshke was hurt today, Yoshke who is as gentle as a lamb. . . . A policeman felled him to the ground."

"A policeman! Yes? What for?"

"Yoshke had no more than taken his place with his pushcart on Hester Street when the policeman came around to collect the graft, a quarter a day from each peddler. Yoshke begged the policeman to wait a little while until he could get money from customers, explaining that he had spent his last cent on a stock of potatoes. The policeman's answer was to club him to the gutter."

Yoshke stirred fitfully.

"He's got no one, Yoshke, and he's as gentle as a lamb, and I'm thinking it's not a world for lambs." . . .

And he smiled at me, sadly, sagely, "I think, Meyer, I think a goat has a got a better chance in this world."

(1923)

LETTER FROM MOGILEV

from *The Dark Lady from Belorusse*

JEROME CHARYN

We would walk the streets, a prodigy in short pants and his mother, so defiantly beautiful that all transactions stopped, and we'd enter a slow-motion world where women, men, children, dogs, cats, and firemen in their trucks would look at her with such longing in their eyes, that I felt like some usurper who was carrying her off to another hill. I was only five in '42, a nervous boy who couldn't spell his own name. My mother wore her silver fox coat, designed and cut for her by my father, Sam, who was a foreman in a Manhattan fur shop. The coat was contraband, and should have gone to the Navy. My father's shop had a contract with the War Department to supply the Navy with fur-lined vests so its admirals and ordinary sailors wouldn't freeze to death aboard some battleship.

It was a darkly romantic time. The Bronx sat near the Atlantic Ocean without a proper seawall, and there was talk of attack squads arriving in little rubber boats off some tricky submarine, getting into the sewer system, and gobbling up my native ground. But I never saw a Nazi on our walks. And what power would any of them have had against the shimmering outline of my mother in her silver fox coat? She was born in 1911, like Ginger Rogers and Jean Harlow, but she didn't have their platinum look: she was the dark lady from Belorusse.

We weren't on a pleasure stroll. It was our daily trip to the post office, where my mother was expecting a letter from Mogilev, in White Russia, where her brother lived, a schoolteacher who'd raised her after their own mother had died. I'm not sure why this letter couldn't have been delivered to the mailbox in our building. Had the Germans seized Mogilev, and my uncle could only write via some secret system in the Soviet underground?

The postmaster would always come out from behind his window when my mother appeared. He was a cranky little man who wore slippers and liked to shout at his clerks. But he was kind to the dark lady's little boy. He would take me through his side of the wall and show me the "graveyard," a gigantic sack where all the dead letters lay, sad undeliverable things, with postmarks from all over the planet. I would sift through the pile, look at the pictures on the stamps, smell the glue, while the postmaster squeezed my mother's hand. But not even this wizard of the mail could produce a letter from Mogilev.

She would tremble on the journey home as we climbed hill after hill. She walked like a drunken lady. It was from my mother that I learned how memory could kill. She could survive as long as she had word from Mogilev. But there was no word in the middle of a war, only mountains of dead-letter boxes between Belorusse and the Bronx.

She started smoking cigarettes. And I had to smother a fallen match and slap at the little fires that seemed to collect in her wake. I would dust the walls with a dry mop and attend to my mother's goose, opening the oven door to stab at the bird with a fork, until it was the way my father liked it, dark and crisp and unchewable.

I would put his whisky on the table, pour him a shot, and jabber endlessly, ask him whatever nonsense came into my head, to camouflage my mother's silences. But as soon as he left the house, she would pretend that her brother was calling from Mogilev (we didn't even have a telephone), and she'd laugh and cry in a Russian that was so melodious, I would get confused until I believed that *all* language was born on a phantom phone.

Her English had no music; it was halting and cruel, like a twisted tongue. But I was a clever little bastard. I would clutch at her phrases like building blocks and sing my own backward sentence-songs. "In the sea, mama, drowns many broken ships." I'd never been to the sea. But I could imagine the great Atlantic where those German subs prowled like crocodiles. My mother had promised to take me across the bridge into Manhattan and watch the ocean liners that lay hobbled in the Hudson and couldn't get into the war. But there was always that letter from Mogilev on her mind, and she didn't seem able to plot the simple logic of our trip.

And so we were marooned in the Bronx. My mother got more morose. She would stand in front of the mirror for an hour with a pot of rouge and a canister of lipstick and paint her face. Then she'd start to cry and ruin all the work she did, enormous teardrops eating into the paint with their own salty acid. I'd follow her into the street and head for the post office, people staring at this flaw in the dark lady, the tracks in her face. It couldn't have made her less appealing, because the postmaster was twice as attentive.

"Some coffee, Mrs. Charyn?" he said, and coffee was hard to find. He'd have pieces of candy for me, and cups of cocoa, which marked my own lips. But my mother was deeply discouraged. The pain had eaten into her ritual.

"No letter Mogilev?"

"It will come, Mrs. Charyn. Russian letters are notorious. They ride very slow, but they never fail."

He'd dance around her in his slippers, scowl at his clerks, pirouette with his coffeepot, but my mother hardly noticed. She hadn't risked disappointment day after day to become part of his coffee club. He couldn't have charmed her with all the candy in the world.

And I was lost at sea. I had to pilot my mother from place to place, undress her, cook my father's goose. But I was getting lucky. I didn't have to go to school. Kindergarten had been canceled in the Bronx. There was a terrible shortage of teachers, and someone must have figured that five-year-olds like me could sit at home with wooden blocks and a pound of clay. I didn't have time for clay. I had to groom my mother, coax her into shape, fool my father into believing she was perfectly fine. I fed him Scotch and gin. He was wall-eyed when he left the dinner table. He would ask my mother questions, and I would answer, once, twice, until I got slapped.

"Mind your business, Baby."

Baby, that's what he would call his own kid to make him suffer. I couldn't read or write, but I could listen to the radio. I heard the battle reports, how the British commandos were making amphibious landings in the middle of the desert, and knocking the hell out of Hitler's Africa Corps. I asked my father to call me Soldier or Little Sergeant, but he never did.

Dad was the sergeant, not me. Cutting fur-lined vests for a lot of admirals had kept him out of the war, but he still had his own uniform: a white helmet that looked like a shallow pot and a white armband with a complicated insignia (a blue circle with a triangle of red and white stripes sitting inside). My father was an air-raid warden with the rank of sergeant. He would patrol the streets after dark with a silver whistle around his neck and make sure that every single window in his assigned radius of blocks had a blackout curtain. If a light blazed from a window, he'd warn you with his whistle and shout, "Lights out, smarty." And if that didn't work, he could call the cops or summon you before the Civilian Defense Board. He was an impeccable warden, my dad, heartless within his own small hegemony, willing to risk the wrath of friends, neighbors, anyone who misbehaved. He'd herd you into a cellar if he ever caught you in the street during an air-raid drill. Some people wouldn't listen to Sergeant Sam, some rebelled, beat him into the ground until other wardens arrived, or a cop rescued him. Even in '42, his first year as a warden, he had a medal from Mayor LaGuardia, chief of Civilian Defense. I caught LaGuardia on the radio. "We have our soldiers in Brooklyn and the Bronx, brave men who go forth without a gun, who guard the home front against saboteurs and unpatriotic people. What would I do without my wardens?"

And if dad came home with a bruised eye and a broken whistle, his armband torn, a big dent in his white hat, it was the Baby who had to search for Mercurochrome, while my mother sat forlorn in the living room, dreaming of Russian mail. He was much more solicitous in moments of sorrow, almost endearing with dirt on his face. He'd clutch my hand, look at FDR's picture on the wall, while I swabbed his eye with a cotton stick.

"Baby, shouldn't we write to the President?"

"He's busy, dad, he's drowning in mail. A warden can't complain. How would it look if you snitch? You'll give the Bronx a bad name."

Of course I couldn't speak in full flowing sentences. My melody went something like this: "Drownin', dad, the prez. Eatin' vanilla envelopes. And you better be quiet. The Bronx will kill a tattytale."

Dad got my drift.

"Who's a tattytale?"

But he wouldn't have slapped me with Franklin Delano Roosevelt on the wall. Even in her distraction, my mother blessed FDR whenever she lit a candle. The blood that flowed in him was our blood too.

Anyway, dad couldn't have written to Roosevelt. He was as unlettered as I was, as feeble with the pen. He could barely scratch a few words in his Civilian Defense reports. And so he suffered quietly, licked his wounds, and we went to church on the high holidays, with his face still black and blue. I had to dress my mother, make sure her mascara didn't run. We didn't belong to that temple on the Grand Concourse, Adath Israel, with its white stone pillars and big brass door. Adath Israel was where all the millionaire doctors and lawyers went. The services were held in English. The assistant rabbi at Adath Israel was also a painter and a poet. He gave classes at night for kids in the neighborhood. We called him Len. He was in love with the dark lady. That's why he encouraged me, let me into his class. He wanted us to join the temple, but my father wouldn't go near any place that didn't have a cantor. That was the disadvantage of English. A cantor would have had nothing to sing.

We went to the old synagogue at the bottom of the hill. It was made of crumbling brick; portions of the steeple would rain down from the roof. There had been three fires at the synagogue since the war began, and the "incendiary bomb," as we called it, was always about to close. But we had Gilbert Rogovin, who'd been a choirboy here and had studied at the cantors' college in Cincinnati, Ohio. Our cantor could have made a fortune singing holy songs on Fifth Avenue, but he always returned to the Bronx. He was a bigwig at the Cincinnati Opera House. He played Spanish barbers and mad Moroccan kings when he wasn't with us.

He was married to the diva Marilyn Kraus, and he would always bring her to our crumbling synagogue. She was a Herculean beauty, six feet tall, with the hands of a football player and a full, floating figure. When she trod up to the balcony, where all the women sat, the stairs shivered under her feet. The balcony was full of opera fans who worshiped Marilyn, called her Desdemona, and I wondered if this Desdemona was another dark lady from Belorusse.

I had the privilege of sitting with my mother and all the other women, because I was only five. Desdemona hunkered down next to us on our narrow bench, her enormous hands cradled in her lap, like a despotic queen of the balcony. She waved to the cantor, who wore a white robe and was about to wave back when he discovered the woman near his wife. The breath seemed to go out of his body. He was just like those firemen who had seen my mother for the first time. Lost in her world of letter boxes, she didn't even smile at him. The cantor was all alone; he couldn't pierce the devotion in her dark eyes. He stood among his choirboys, started to sing. But he wasn't like a postmaster dancing in slippers. He was the custodian of songs. He brought my mother out of her dream with his opening syllables. A woman swooned. I had to run and find her smelling salts . . .

He leaned against the gate with a cigarette in his mouth. A cantor wasn't allowed to smoke on the high holidays. But Rogovin could do no wrong. Desdemona wasn't with him. She must have gone back to their suite at the Concourse Plaza. My mother and I had ventured out of the synagogue with Sergeant Sam, who'd become a local hero because of his little calvaries as an air-raid warden. He was like a special policeman with a wounded face. The cantor saluted him. "Sergeant, I'd like to borrow your boy."

None of us had ever been that close to the cantor, who had little white hairs in his nose. He wore a strange perfume, smelled like a certain red flower at the Bronx Zoo.

"It's an honor," my father said. "But how can I help you? The boy is five. He doesn't have working papers. He can't spell."

"It's a sad story. My old mother has been pestering me to have a child. I had to invent one."

"You lied to her, Cantor?"

"It's scandalous. But mom's half blind, lives at a nursing home in the Bronx. Have to make mom happy before she dies."

Rogovin sobbed into his handkerchief. I'd never seen a cantor cry. His tears were the size of my mother's crystal earrings. Dad took pity on him.

"Cantor, please . . . we'll lend you the boy." He turned to my mother in bewildered fury. "Do something. We can't let the cantor choke on his tears."

I'm not sure if my mother was dreaming of Mogilev at that moment. But she came out of her trance long enough to slap Rogovin in the face. Dad was even more perplexed. The wives of air-raid wardens weren't supposed to perform criminal acts, and assaulting cantors in a public place was worse than criminal; it was a sin against God, because God favored a cantor above all other beings. God loved a good song.

My mother slapped him again. Rogovin wasn't surprised. I saw him smile under the hand he used to cover his mouth.

My father made a fist. "I'll kill you," he said to the dark lady.

"Sergeant," the cantor said, "you shouldn't provoke Madame. She'll just go on hitting me."

"I don't understand," dad said.

"Its simple. My missus was in the balcony with Madame. They got to talking about me . . ."

"Balconies. Missus. I don't understand."

I was just as baffled. I hadn't been able to hear Desdemona whisper a word.

"Foolish," my mother said to dad. "Is no nursing home, is no blind ladies. His mother eats, drinks like a horse."

"I don't understand."

My mother seized Rogovin's thumb and placed it near her breast. "Is clear now? The cantor is lust and lecher."

Rogovin bowed to me, kissed my hand like some kind of Continental, and ran to his hotel.

My father had been so diligent in producing fur-lined vests, his boss was sending him to Florida for a week. Most wartime vacations had to be canceled, because the Army and Navy were running munitions and men on the railroads. But dad had a special pass, signed by Secretary of the Navy Frank Knox. I didn't learn about Florida until a little later— Miami Beach was a furrier's paradise, where manufacturers and their prize workers would have a yearly fling with local prostitutes and dark ladies from Havana and New Orleans. And when I grew aware of the word *prostitute,* around the age of six or seven, I understood the arguments my mother had with Sergeant Sam about his sojourns at the Flagler Hotel.

She would hurl a shoe at his head, empty the perfume bottles he'd brought back from Florida, set fire to the photographs he'd hidden in some secret pocket of his valise. He'd always return terrifically tanned, looking like Clark Gable with a guilty grin.

But Gable could have been a ghost in '42. My mother didn't even watch him pack. He left in a hurry, without his air-raid warden's hat, gave me five single-dollar bills to spend in his absence, a small fortune from one of the Navy's favorite sons. I was glad to see him go. I wouldn't have to groom my mother, make her presentable to dad, hide her sorrow from him, cook his goose, load him down with whisky so he wouldn't discover her long silences.

The day he was gone her suitor arrived. I don't know what else to call him. He advertised himself as my uncle, but he didn't have our famous cheekbones and Tatar eyes. He couldn't have belonged to that tribe of Mongolian Jews who terrorized the Caucasus until they were conquered by Tamerlane the Great. Chick Eisenstadt was a big ruddy fellow who'd once worked with my mother in a Manhattan dress shop. She'd been a seamstress before she got married. The whole shop had been in love with her, according to Chick, but he was the one who linked his own history with hers long after the dress shop disappeared. He'd floundered until the war. Chick was the only one of my "relatives" who'd ever been to Sing Sing. It was convenient to have a convict in the family. He could tell you stories of the biggest outlaws. And he knew my father's timetable. He would appear whenever Sergeant Sam wasn't around.

He took us for a ride in his Cadillac. Chick wasn't supposed to have a car. Gasoline had been rationed, and there was a ban on nonessential driving. But Chick was a black marketeer who gave generals and war administrators silk stockings for their wives. He had a card that authorized him to chauffeur "essential people," like doctors and tycoons from war plants. Cops would peek into the Cadillac, glance at my mother, smile, call me "Roosevelt's little pioneer."

We crossed into Manhattan with Chick, who took me to the ocean liners that lay tilted in the harbor, like sleeping beauties with smokestacks, and I was seized with an anxiety I'd never had before. An ocean liner was larger than my imagination. It was like the imprint of a world I couldn't fathom from the Bronx. The one bridge I had was Chick.

He never bribed me, never offered expensive gifts that would have made me despise my own dad. But he took us to the only White Russian restaurant on the Grand Concourse, Bitter Eagles, where his cronies would ogle us; he'd sweat in the middle of a meal, sitting with his secret family. Sing Sing had ruined his health. He had a chronic cough, and his hands still shook from the beatings his fellow prisoners had delivered to him. Chick was thirty-five, three years older than my mother, but his hair had gone white in Sing Sing, and he looked like a wartorn cavalier.

He stared at my mother, helpless before her plate of pirogi, and said, "Faigele, what's wrong?" My mother's name was Fannie, but her admirers and friends called her Faigele, which was supposed to mean little bird in my Tatar dictionary.

"Mogilev," my mother said. One word. And Chick could intuit the entire tale.

"Your brother, the schoolteacher. His letters are no longer coming. And you're worried to death."

"The Nazis are sitting in Mogilev," I said. "Chickie, I heard it on the radio."

Chick watched my mother's grief. "Radios can lie. It's called propaganda."

"The Germans are paying the radio to tell lies?"

"I didn't say Germans. It could be the White House. And the President doesn't have to pay. Don't you get it? The President talks about a defeat that never took place. Hitler relaxes and starts to get sloppy. And we turn the tables on him."

I wouldn't argue with Chick. A black marketeer ought to know. But I didn't believe that Roosevelt would ever lie about Mogilev.

"Faigele, if there's a letter, I'll find it."

We went to the post office after lunch. The postmaster stood in his slippers, eying my mother and her black marketeer, who eyed him back.

"Mister, could one of your own men have been tampering with the mail?"

"Impossible," the postmaster said as Chick stuffed his pockets with silk stockings.

"Come on, I'll help you look for the letter. It has to be here."

They searched the back room, inspected every pouch, but there were no letters from Mogilev. "I'm sorry, Mrs. Charyn," the postmaster said. "Russian mail has been trickling in, but not a scratch from Belorusse."

Faigele took to her bed. "My two bitter eagles," she mumbled, blinking at me and Chick. It was a complete collapse. Chick's own doctor came, examined her, said he couldn't cure heartbreak and withered emotions. He recommended a rest home in the Catskills where he sent all his worst cases.

"Doc," Chick said, "she's not a case. She's a glorious woman, Faigele. She's expecting a letter from Mogilev."

"You're the wizard. You can produce silk stockings. Why not one lousy letter? But what's it all about? Did she leave a boyfriend behind?"

"A brother," Chickie said.

The doctor rolled his eyes. "Isn't it unnatural to miss a brother so much?"

Chick grabbed him by the collar, and I didn't know it then, but it was a very brave act. This doctor was Meyer Lansky's personal physician. He'd poisoned people for the mob. He was the highest-paid internist in the Bronx.

I brought Chick and him a glass of my father's best schnapps. And then Chick explained to him the story of Faigele and Mordecai, who'd come from a family of small landowners in the Tatar town of Grodno, where Meyer Lansky was born. Mordecai was the oldest at ten, with a couple of kid sisters—Anna, five, and Faigele, two—when their mother died (their dad had run to America and made his own life). A ten-year-old boy couldn't hold on to the family fortune. He had to lease himself, become a little slave to protect his sisters. He was sold into the tzar's army at fifteen, escaped, "kidnapped" Anna and Faigele, hid out with them in the marshes, landed in Mogilev in the middle of the Russian Revolution without papers or a crust of bread. The boy was sixteen and he learned to steal. In a time of shadowlands, he became a shadow until he could reinvent himself as a schoolteacher. He had forged documents from a commissar of education who'd been killed. He had pupils in his first classes who were older than himself. He had to bribe an inspector from Minsk: it was like the tzar's government without a tzar, but the Cossacks had been told by some Soviet prince to love all the Tatar Jews. Mordecai saved his money and was able to send Anna out of Belorusse in 1923. But Faigele wouldn't go. He pleaded with her. The inspectors would catch him soon—an illiterate teacher. He couldn't breathe until his little sister was safe.

"But I am safe," she said, "here with you."

He'd start to cry, this gaunt man who was always on the verge of getting TB. She left for America in 1927. He promised to join her in six months but never did.

She became a Manhattan refugee, lived with her father and a stepmother who begrudged every bit of food she swallowed. She went to night school, worked in a dress shop, dreaming of Mordecai. She had to get out of her father's house. Enter Sam, the furrier who never lost a day's work during the Depression.

Faigele married him, but nothing could sustain her—not children, not God, not romance—nothing except those letters that would arrive religiously from Mogilev.

The doctor licked his schnapps. "Chickie, a glorious woman, righto, but where do you fit in? You're not the husband, you're not the brother, you're not the father of this little boy."

"None your stinking business," said Chick, already drunk. "I fill the empty spaces. I'm satisfied."

"If you want to revive her, friend, you'll just have to forge that letter . . . pretend you're with the tzar's police."

"I don't have to pretend. But how will I get Russian stamps?"

The doctor tapped my skull. "Baby, where's your mother's stash of mail?"

I steered them right to the little wooden chest my mother had brought from Belorusse; the letters were inside. Chick was mainly interested in the stamps and the quality of paper and Mordecai's penmanship, but the doctor began to read the letters in whatever Russian he still had at his command (he was born in Kiev).

"The man's a poet, Chick."

He recited from the letters, but Chick cut him off. "Keep it to yourself, doc."

"Are you insane? Poetry belongs to the world."

"But the letters belong to Faigele."

Every stamp had a different face. I saw the brown eagle of Belorusse; Tatar princes and kings; Stalin, the little father of his people, looking like a walrus. The doctor pulled a pair of scissors out of his medical bag. He wanted to cut off a few of the stamps; Chick told him to put the scissors back. He wouldn't mutilate my mother's property.

"I give up," the doctor said, while Chick and I went down to the stationery store, where I helped him pick out a blue envelope and a pad that could have passed for Russian paper. Then we walked to Bitter Eagles, found a man who was willing to trade Russian stamps in his family album for the promise of butter, eggs, and Colombian coffee.

Chick went to work practicing Mordecai's pen strokes. Time seemed to clot around him and the letter he was going to write. The doctor abandoned wife, children, mistresses, all his other patients, including Meyer Lansky, to mastermind a letter from Mogilev made in the Bronx. I brewed cups of black tea and fed them coffee cake from Bitter Eagles.

It took Chick an hour to do "Dear Faigele" in Mordecai's Russian hand and get the first paragraph going. They had to tiptoe around the war because Chick wouldn't load the letter with lurid details. "I am only starving a little bit," he wrote in schoolteacher Russian and signed Mordecai's name. He addressed the envelope, I glued on the stamps, and we all fell asleep in the living room on different chairs.

A knocking sound came right through my dreams. I got up, stumbled to the door. The postmaster stood in his slippers with a letter in his hand. He was very excited. "Gentlemen, it arrived, right out of the blue." Chick offered him some of our fabulous coffee cake, speckled with dark chocolate. "Delicious," he said. No one thanked him for the letter, which had come in a crumpled white envelope, all the stamps missing. The postmaster left. Chick tore up *our* letter and we went in to wake up my mother and give her the other letter from Mogilev.

She danced out of bed like a mermaid with a nightgown on (I'd never seen a mermaid, so I had to imagine one). She savored the letter, but she wouldn't read it until she prepared our tea. The doctor was startled by her metamorphosis. Faigele's coloring had come back. She disappeared into the bedroom and closed the door.

"The angels would be envious of such a creature," the doctor said.

We waited like orphans until my mother came out. She wouldn't share Mordecai's language with us. "Is still schoolteacher," she said, summarizing the plot. "But without school. Was bombed."

The doctor returned to his practice. Chickie had to go out of town. My father got back from Miami with his movie-star tan, but Faigele was the one who had all the flush. He put on his air-raid helmet and patrolled the streets. I imagined him in the blackout, looking for renegade cubes of light. Poor Sergeant Sam, who could never really capture the dark lady, or her radiance.

(1997)

THE AMERICAN SUN & WIND
MOVING PICTURE COMPANY

from *News from the New American Diaspora and
Other Tales of Exile*

JAY NEUGEBOREN

In the forest, high above the lake, I imagined that I was, far below, trapped beneath the black ice. I gathered sticks for kindling, pressed them close to my chest, then brought the bundle, like a gift, to the edge of the woods. I saw that Mr. Lesko and his horse were already out on the ice, clouds of steam pouring from the horse's nostrils.

Beside the small fire, my uncle Max was unwrapping the camera from its blanket—lifting it tenderly, as if it were an infant—then setting it upon the tripod: a sign that we would soon begin. I closed my eyes and prayed that I wasn't too late—that I had not stayed in the forest too long, and that there was still time for me to help make up our new story.

I could make a story out of anything—a nail, a glass, a shoe, a tree, a mirror, a button, a window, a wall—and for every story I made up and gave away, I also made one up I told no one about—one I stored inside me, in the rooms where I kept my most precious memories and pictures.

Below me, Mr. Lesko was hitching his horse to the ice plow, and when he urged his horse forward, I climbed into his head and saw that he was hoping the horse would resist him so that he might use his whip. The sleighs—pungs, we called them—were on land, next to the icehouse, and while I was gone Mr. Lesko and his son had cut a runway into the lake's shallow end, for floating the cakes of ice to shore.

I closed my eyes, made a picture of the lake, and labeled the picture as if I were back at our studio, printing out an opening title for one of the moving pictures my family made:

FORT LEE, NEW JERSEY, NOVEMBER 12, 1915

I opened my eyes and saw that my uncle Max was fishing inside his suitcase for his lenses and film. My mother was lifting dresses and hats from the clothing bag my father held open for her. My uncle Karl was talking with Mr. Lesko, showing him where he wanted the ice cut.

I made my way down the hill and started across the lake to where the fire was burning below the camera. I had helped build it there—lit the first match to the greasy newspapers so that, the heat rising steadily, the oil in the camera would remain soft and the gears would not freeze.

I looked into the black ice—the first ice of winter—veined like marble, clear like glass. In the space between land and snow, I knew, small animals and insects lived all winter long. I wondered if there were a space like that between water and ice, where I might lie down.

In ancient times, Max taught me, men would build memory palaces inside their minds, and in each of the palace's rooms they would keep furniture, and on the furniture they would place objects. They invented systems and conjured up images by which they could name the rooms, and recall which rooms contained which objects and how the rooms led to and from one another. Sometimes they did this to remember the objects themselves, and sometimes the objects were there to remind them of other objects, or of lists or texts they wanted to set to heart—of the words to the Psalms, or the names of the saints, or where all the stars in the universe were located.

In our own times, Max said, people still organized their memories in similar ways, but now instead of being kings, priests, or philosophers living in temples and palaces, they were magicians, memory artists, and idiot savants working in vaudeville, at county fairs, or in circuses.

My father's three suitcases, like steps leading to an invisible stage, sat side by side on the ice, next to the sleds on which we transported our equipment, and inside the suitcases were his accordion, his violin, and his clarinet. When Karl wanted actors and actresses to show more feeling, he had my father play for them. My father played his violin during love scenes. He played his accordion during barroom scenes and cowboy movies. He played his clarinet, his flute, or small pump organ for night scenes, or when people were dying.

I deposited my bundle of sticks next to the fire. Max tapped the side of the camera. Is this one reel? he asked.

No, I said. It's not real until you open the shutter, turn the handle, and let the light inside.

Stop with the nonsense, Karl said. Two reels, he said.

This one's a two-reeler we gotta finish by the end of the week.

Max winked at me. But if it's *too* real, I asked, how will we be able to bear it?

And we don't need your crappy routines either, you two, Karl snapped. If I want your opinion, I'll give it to you.

Leave the boy alone, my father said. He's a good boy, even if he looks like a girl.

Mr. Lesko's son was on the ice now too, but I could not tell which was the father and which the son. They both wore beaver coats, the fur turned to the inside, and black leather hats with earflaps. One of them walked on the far side of the horse, pushing an ice marker back and forth along the surface of the lake, making a checkerboard of squares.

Max's warm breath was on my face. Joey? he asked.

I closed my eyes. I see a woman drowning, I said.

Karl came closer. And—? he asked. Okay. So she's drowning. So what else—?

I see her drowning, I said, and she's caught inside a hole in the ice, trying to climb out, to save herself.

And then—? Karl asked.

There's a man, and he has a whip in his hand. I looked up at the hill where I had been a short while before, and I pointed. And there's a frightened child up there, alone in the forest.

Why? Max asked.

Because the woman had to marry the man after she gave birth to the child. But the man beat the child, and one day, when it was old enough, it ran away.

I like it, Karl said. This we can sell—whips, and a mother and child we can weep for, and then a chase.

Whipping and weeping, my father said brightly. We all looked at him. He shrugged. Whoopee, he added, softly.

My mother put her arm around his neck. Shh, she said. She looked toward me. What else, sweetheart?

Well, there's another man, I think, and he looks exactly like the man with the whip, except that his eyes are different. This man is the man she truly loves, and he's running through the forest as fast as he can.

The horse! Karl said. Come on with the horse before I freeze my nuts off.

But why a horse? Max asked.

Why a horse! Karl exclaimed. Because we've *got* a horse—that's why!

Sure, my father said. Do the best with what you've got and leave the rest to God. That's what I always say.

My philosopher, my mother said, then kissed my father, laughed, reached inside her coat, pulled out a pistol, and fired it at the sky.

Come on and get me, you dirty varmints! she cried out.

I hugged her hard. *I've got you!* I shouted.

My little baby Joey, she whispered. My angel boy. Don't ever let them hurt you. Promise me, all right?

I promise, I said.

My mother was the most beautiful woman in the world when she got like this—going from hot to cold, from anger to love to sadness and back again. She held me at a distance. Such a sweet nose, she said. She tugged once on each of my ears, then lifted my cap and roughed my hair. What a waste, what a waste. Maybe your father's right—that you should have been a girl.

My father took me from her, lifted me high in the air. Get a load of those tiny ears, he said. And those gorgeous curls.

Shh, Max said. He's a boy, not a girl. Leave him be.

Hurry! Karl said. We gotta hurry. Look! Karl pointed to the far end of the lake, where, behind the northern range of low, rolling hills, a wide, black wall of clouds rose up like a mountain. The clouds moved toward us as if the ocean were behind them, pushing them through the sky.

The Leskos pulled chisels from their overcoats, knelt down, and started hammering and chopping along the lines they had made with their ice marker. Karl slapped at his shoulders and walked in circles around the fire, first one way, and then the other.

This is why I'm moving to California, he said. All right? In California we can make movies every day of the year without freezing our tushes off. In California, Edison and his thugs won't burn down our studio and break our cameras. Everyone else is out there already. Griffith's making features he's gonna charge two bucks a seat for—two bucks, for crying out loud!—and I'm still pissing my life away with these two-reelers.

Max cupped his palm over my eyes. Joey? he asked.

I see a horse falling through the ice, I said. The woman and the child are holding on to the horse and the two men who look the same are trying to pull them from the ice. And there's blood. I see lots of blood, and it's turning the water black.

Terrific, Karl said. Love, danger, violence, rescue—we stick to the basics. That's terrific, Joey. Really terrific. So okay. So one of you geniuses tell me—where do we start?

Inside the icehouse, my mother said.

Why the icehouse? Karl asked.

So we can get warm, my mother said. Then she started running across the ice in long strides, gliding and making believe her boots were ice skates. She jumped over the open runway, stopped, put more bullets into the chamber of her pistol, spun the chamber, clicked it closed. She was having one of her wild days, when you never knew what she would do next. She turned toward us and shouted, as if she were leading a cavalry charge: Ready or not, here we come—The American Sun and Wind Moving Picture Company!

Then she fired her gun into the air, three times, and the

explosions blasted through my skull like the sound the lake would make if it were splitting open. I heard a man scream. The Leskos were trying to control their horse, which was hammering the air with its hooves. The screaming came from the hilltop where I had been standing a few minutes before. A man stood there now, his hands clasped above his heart.

Holy mackerel! my mother said. I finally did it.

Max! Karl yelled. Start shooting—we'll figure out the story later. Hurry, Max. Camera! Camera!

Max did what Karl told him to, while the man on the hill, hands pressed to his heart, twirled in a circle, tumbled down the slope, rolling this way and that so that I was afraid his skull would smash against boulders and tree trunks.

It's Izzie! my father shouted, clapping his hands. I watched Izzie carom off a rock, sail onto the ice, and spin around, facedown. He lay there for a few seconds, as if dead, and I ran toward him.

When I was no more than ten feet away, he stood up, grinned, doffed his cap, and bowed.

Hurray for Izzie! I yelled.

Izzie was my mother's cousin, our stunt man when he was sober, and often when he was not. He could walk on the ledges of high buildings, stand on the wings of flying airplanes, jump out of burning windows, and ride wild horses. He could duel with swords, drive cars like a maniac, and fight with his fists like Battling Levinsky.

How's my favorite little guy? he asked, and before I could answer, he hoisted me into the air and was racing across the ice with me. I stretched my legs and arms way out, as if I were an airplane. We zoomed in for a landing, and he set me down beside the fire and started in kissing my mother.

My father grabbed Izzie and began waltzing him around in

circles while he sang the words to "The Beautiful Blue Danube."

Karl was screaming through his megaphone that time was money, that we were robbing him blind, that by the time we finished shooting in the icehouse and got back out here, we'd have lost our light.

Easy does it, cousin, Izzie said, his arm around Karl's shoulder. Like I always say, the main thing in life is to have a good time and not to get hurt. Everything else is extra.

Not to get hurt? Karl shot back. Ha! I think maybe what we got here is a major case of the pot calling the kettle black.

I never risk injury, Izzie said, and he repeated words he always gave to people when they told him he took chances: Everything I do in this life is figured out exactly.

The Leskos put away their chisels. One of them took a pair of ice tongs from the leather harness on the side of the horse, opened the tongs wide, hooked them into the cake of ice. But even before they lifted out the first cake, I realized that only some of the blood in the lake was coming from where the horse was scraping its neck and legs raw against the sharp edges of ice.

Izzie rubbed his hands together. So what are we waiting for? Let's put this show on the road.

But what if it rains or it snows? my father asked. We have to think about that also. What if there's a storm? What do we do then?

We shoot our moving picture, Karl said, whether it rains, whether it snows, whether it storms, or whether it stinks.

My father lifted his accordion, shrugged the straps into place over his shoulders, began playing "My Bonnie Lies over the Ocean." My mother reached into the small telescope bag in which she kept her makeup, took out her mirror and her lipstick, passed the gold tube back and forth through the flames to thaw it, then lifted the lid and twisted the tube of red wax upward. She stacked my father's suitcases to eye level, set her mirror on top, and began doing her lips.

I saw fountains of blood explode from the bottom of the lake. The wind was roaring through the water like thunder, tearing holes in whatever was in its way—rocks, animals, trees, children—and I closed my eyes again, the way I did when I wanted a scene to change, and I saw that below the ice, water, and mud, an entire lost world existed—cities, buildings, castles, people—and that it was from this world that the blood was rising.

Here, sweetheart, my mother said. It's time. She handed me the mirror and the lipstick, so that, for our story, I could begin to make myself into her daughter.

I looked at my image in the mirror—stared through the dark holes in the middle of my eyes and imagined that on the wall at the back of my skull, my face, like the pictures inside Max's camera, was upside down.

So tell me, Joey, Izzie asked. Would you like to be our director? He handed me Karl's megaphone. Taped to the wide end of the funnel was a circle of cardboard, and in the middle of the cardboard my uncle had cut out a rectangle, so his megaphone could double as a viewfinder. I looked through his viewfinder at my mother, squinting until the only thing I could see were her lips. They were wine red and moist, and someday soon they would fill entire screens— forty feet wide and thirty feet high in the theaters in New York City.

The boy wants to be a director, Izzie said.

Fine with me, Karl said. I had enough already for a lifetime. Take over. He got my blessing.

Good. So here comes everything you need to know, Izzie said. Are you ready?

Ready, I said.

Okay. Then repeat after me—Camera.

Camera!

Action.

Action!

Cut.

Cut!

Now you know everything Karl knows, he said, and he kissed me hard on the mouth. Now you're a director.

The Leskos were floating cakes of ice along the runway, toward shore. I held a strip of black velvet up, next to the camera. When my mother turned and looked at it, her pupils dilated, and her pale blue eyes went dark.

Cut! Karl said, and Max stopped shooting. My mother looked away. I put the strip of velvet in my pocket, and while Max counted, I back-cranked the camera for him, eight turns. Then he tilted the camera down, its lens pointed at the open water, and he cranked the handle forward, so that before one scene ended the next would begin. That way my mother's eyes would seem to dissolve in the dark water of the lake. You would see her face, aflame with fear, and then you would see her eyes grow dark with despair, after which the scene would melt, and you would move right through her eyes until you were staring into water as deep and black as the night.

One of the Leskos hooked a cake of ice with a pike pole, dragged the cake onto a plank. When the Leskos had six cakes of ice lined up, they jammed them together, shoved a slab of wood into them at one end—there were two metal spikes in the wood—attached the slab of wood to the horse by rope, and made the horse pull the blocks of ice along the plank, to shore.

By this time the Leskos had carved out a section of the lake that was as large and square as the diamond of a baseball field. Max raised his camera slowly, set it in position, and photographed the northern crescent of the lake where Mr. Lesko was walking behind his horse, plowing the ice. Mr. Lesko played my mother's cruel husband. Mr. Lesko's son played The Gentle Stranger. He wore a ragged brown wool coat Izzie had given him, and he worked without a hat, so that the winter light, playing through his curls from behind, made him appear very gentle.

I was wearing a wig made of real hair—long auburn tresses—and under my black coat, on top my regular clothes, I now had on a white blouse and a blue pinafore.

Action! Karl shouted through his megaphone.

Mr. Lesko stopped plowing, took out his whip, raised it above his shoulder.

Camera! Karl shouted.

Max began cranking, and Mr. Lesko started whipping his horse.

No! I screamed. And I shot out from where I stood, streaked across the ice, grabbed at his arm. He threw me off easily.

Cut! Karl shouted.

Wonderful, Joey! he called. That was wonderful! I didn't expect you to do that.

I had not expected to do it either, but I didn't say so. Izzie took the whip from Mr. Lesko's hand, raised it high in the air, as if he were going to strike him, but instead he pivoted and lashed out at the horse. The whip cracked, making a sound like a bullet firing, but the lash never touched the horse's flank.

This is your last warning, Izzie said. If you whip the horse again, I'll whip you. Is that clear? And you *never* touch the boy.

Mr. Lesko said nothing.

Izzie scares me with his anger, my mother said. He never used to be so angry.

He needs a drink, my father said. He always gets this way when he needs a drink. I watched Izzie squat down and dip his hand in the water, to test its coldness. I watched Mr. Lesko coil his whip. I watched my father take out a small pair of scissors with which he snipped the fingers from a pair of wool gloves, so that, the pink tips of his fingers exposed, he could continue to play his instruments in the cold.

Behind the clouds, the light in the sky was starting to fade, and I imagined sitting with my mother on a ledge of ice, above the open channel, after everyone else was gone. I imagined us slipping quietly over the edge, descending noiselessly through water, and passing through the lake's sandy bottom. I had given them one story and now I was making up another, one I could keep inside me forever—about how my mother and I made our way into the lost world below the lake, where we found out the source of all the howling and blood.

Max photographed Mr. Lesko's eyes, and then he photographed the horse's eyes. Next he photographed Mr. Lesko's son, who was using tongs to lift blocks of ice from the plank onto the sleigh. When Mr. Lesko's son looked at his father, his eyes became soft, like the eyes of a wounded animal.

Brilliant! Karl said, peering through his viewfinder. You're a genius, Joey, to have thought of making the husband and the lover the same man.

Their faces are the same, but their eyes are opposite, Max said.

Yes, Karl said. You can make miracles with eyes, Max—I gotta hand you that. In life, you see, eyes are just little things in a face, with skin that goes up and down over them, but in moving pictures, the eyes—oh the eyes are everything.

Max unscrewed the camera and wrapped it in a blanket. I helped load the sleds with our equipment, and then we walked back across the ice, up onto land, through the snow, to the icehouse.

Our story that day was simple, and we made it up as we went along the way we always did.

My mother was living a harsh and lonely life, married to Mr. Lesko and caring for me, her beloved daughter. In early scenes, which we would shoot back at our studio the next day and then patch in later, you would see the two of us slaving away for Mr. Lesko in his kitchen, and submitting to his tyranny, until the day upon which The Gentle Stranger wandered into our world.

The Gentle Stranger owned a book of poems, and in the evenings, when our chores were done, he read to us from Tennyson, Swinburne, and Shelley. Karl liked to put sections of poems into the titles because if the pictures didn't tell people what to feel, he said, the words would.

Max disagreed. He believed our stories should be told in pictures only, so that anyone in the world, in any time and place, could understand them. Because all the stories I made up came to me in a series of pictures that marched across the screen inside my head—pictures that seemed less real the instant I even *tried* to find words to describe them—I agreed with Max.

We think in pictures, Max always said. Not words.

Even though I agreed with him, whenever I found pictures and people in my head I wanted to save, I gave them names, the way I named The Gentle Stranger, and I invented titles to put on the doors and windows of their rooms, so that someday, if I wanted to, I would be able to find them again.

The Gentle Stranger Finds a New Home
With the Mother and Her Love Child

In exchange for food and lodging, The Gentle Stranger worked for Mr. Lesko, cutting wood and harvesting ice. Mr. Lesko let him use the icehouse for a home, and he slept there at night, wrapped in old blankets, between walls of ice and sawdust.

Then one night, after Mr. Lesko got drunk and fell asleep, we stole away to the icehouse, and my mother told The Gentle Stranger our story: how she had been sent to work for Mr. Lesko as a housekeeper, and how Mr. Lesko had forced himself upon her, after which, in her shame, she had had no choice but to become his wife.

Perhaps it was God's will, my mother said, drawing me close to her. For had I not submitted to Mr. Lesko, my most precious jewel would not be here.

That was when The Gentle Stranger declared his love for my mother. He went down on his knees and clasped my mother's hands. I have never loved another as I love you, he said. You have rescued me from the dead. Without you I cannot live.

My mother's true heart showed in her eyes, but she pulled her hands free and turned away.

I am a married woman, she said.

I looked at The Gentle Stranger and I looked at my mother. I took his hand and I took hers—the hand on which she wore her wedding band—and I joined their hands together.

Then we argued.

Karl said that next my mother and The Gentle Stranger should plan to murder Mr. Lesko—to arrange for an accident, where he drowned in the lake.

My father said that the three of us should just run away together and start a new life. Let love reign triumphant! he said.

Oh Simon, my mother said, and she rested her head on my father's shoulder. You're the dearest man in the world, aren't you?

I like happy endings that make me cry, my father said.

Izzie said the problem was that we didn't know who The Gentle Stranger was and why he was there and why he was saved from the dead. If they killed Mr. Lesko, they'd get caught and go to jail and I'd be an orphan. Why, he asked, should people pay good money to see lives that were more miserable than their own?

Izzie's right, my father said.

I said that maybe The Gentle Stranger had originally come to the lake intending to commit suicide. When he looked into the water, however, he had seen, not his own reflection, but that of my mother, and seeing her eyes, he had decided to live.

Max beamed, said we could start with the scene in the ice-house—of them holding hands—and then go to a dreamlike flashback, by using a piece of fine gauze over the lens, of The Gentle Stranger staring at my mother's image in the water— her fingers clasped together in prayer, her hands themselves seeming to dissolve, only to reappear and rise up, as if dis-embodied, from the depths of the lake.

In addition to which, Izzie said, who would ever believe a square hole in an ice-covered lake was natural? Everyone would think we were tricking them with miniatures and false shots we'd cooked up in the studio.

Karl said the story was getting too complicated and too expensive. He asked my opinion, and I suggested we combine the two stories: The Gentle Stranger and my mother could still plot to murder Mr. Lesko—but because they were incapable of such an act, they could also change their minds at the last minute.

And then, Karl said, just when they change their minds—I got it, I got it!—there can be a terrible accident that kills Mr. Lesko anyway.

Except that, because they planned the murder, I said, nobody will believe it was an accident, and they'll be made to suffer forever for what they did *not* do.

Because we were going to shoot indoors, Max changed to the longest of his three lenses and set the aperture wide open. To make use of the available light, we kept the door of the icehouse open and set up a clothesline between two trees, a stiff white bedsheet hanging from it to reflect light into the house. Later, Karl said, we would tint this part of the film blue, to transform it into night.

Max could mix wonderful colors—gold for dawn, yellow for candlelight, red for war scenes, peach-glow for sunsets—and sometimes, late at night in the old trolley barn we had converted into our studio and home, he would let me bathe the strips of film in dyes and choose the colors we would use, not just to indicate the time of day, as now, or, by adding color to the usual black-and-white stock, to emphasize what was happening—the way we did for battles and weddings—but to create the atmosphere that helped you understand the *feelings* in the scenes: pale blues for sadness, glowing ambers for peacefulness, crimsons for passion, ruby reds for lust, forest greens for happiness.

But the colors for feelings—unlike the colors for night,

war, dawn, fire, sunsets, and candlelight—were never fixed. Sometimes forest green could show how happy our people were, while at other times it could reveal their fear. Sometimes bathing a scene in indigo could let you sense the joy the characters were experiencing, and sometimes it helped you to feel that the actors and actresses were merely, like the color itself, blue.

As soon as Karl had arranged the scene the way he wanted, in the icehouse, my mother wrapped me in a cloak, and gave me a basket of food, a letter placed at the bottom of the basket, to take to The Gentle Stranger, who was hiding in the forest, waiting for us.

But if you meet in the forest, how would the accident take place on the lake? Karl asked. I told you before—we got a lake, we use a lake.

Okay, Izzie said. This is how it works. We cut through the rope so when he's chasing them through the forest with his horse and sleigh, the rope snaps, the sleigh throws him off flying, and he goes tumbling down the hill into the water.

But we have to figure out how it becomes an accident instead of murder, Karl said.

Maybe it's the opposite of the Red Sea, my father said. Maybe the lake closes shut with ice, and then it opens again and he falls in, splash!

Good, Simon, Izzie said. Terrific. So we chop out a chunk of ice and tow it in, and then we tow it back out. You can show me floating in the lake, face down, in Mr. Lesko's coat and his hat, like I'm drowned, and then the child pokes me with the pike pole, and turns me over and I'll give you a look from under water that will make people freeze in their seats.

Izzie began smearing his arms and legs with grease, for when he would be drowning in the lake, and while he did I remembered the first picture I had seen inside my head, with which I had begun our story, of a woman drowning, only I didn't undertand how that was to come true anymore, since we had changed things and decided that Mr. Lesko would be the one to drown.

As soon as Mr. Lesko found my mother's letter and read it, he took out his whip. My mother crawled backward across the snow, to the icehouse, her forearm across her eyes. Mr. Lesko's arm came flashing down and I leapt in front of my mother, covering her body with my own. The whip's lash cut into my cheek, and the burning sensation—warm and liquid—felt wonderful.

I had not known that this would happen.

Before my mother could tend to me, Izzie had lifted Mr. Lesko from the ground and was pounding him against the side of the icehouse. Mr. Lesko's son lifted a pike pole and tried to stab Izzie, but Izzie saw him coming and stepped aside.

The pike pole rammed into Mr. Lesko's side.

Keep shooting, Karl said. Keep shooting. We'll cut it all up later.

They're cut up now, my father said. He put down his accordion and packed handfuls of snow onto the side of my face. Izzie reached inside his coat, pulled out a leather-covered flask, and took a long drink. He shouldn't drink while he works, my father said.

Don't drink while you work, my mother said.

If I need a wife, I'll buy one, Izzie snapped.

Falling into the lake will sober him up, my father said. Everything Izzie does is figured out exactly.

We moved to the top of the hill and Max set up his camera

there, first to show us racing through the forest to warn The Gentle Stranger that Mr. Lesko was coming to do him harm—and then to show Mr. Lesko charging through the forest with his horse and sleigh.

We photographed my mother sawing through the horse's reins with a kitchen knife. We photographed us changing our mind, and trying to tie the reins back together, but before we could, Mr. Lesko, believing we were trying to escape, beat us away with his whip.

So we fled into the forest, past Max's camera, and it felt wonderful to run across the frozen ground, holding tight to my mother's hand, my curled tresses flying out behind me, the frigid air kissing my cheek and sealing the blood there. Izzie put on Mr. Lesko's coat and hat and shoved Mr. Lesko from the sleigh. Mr. Lesko tried to stop him—to tell him he had not finished tying the reins back together—but Izzie knocked him to the ground.

Izzie rode away, then turned back. Max photographed me and my mother slipping down the hill, hand in hand, to the lake. The Gentle Stranger stood in the middle of the lake, waiting for us, but where our camera had been, jagged slabs of ice now floated like small islands. Our plan was to jump from island to island, toward the south end of the lake, where there was a waterfall.

Max could photograph us from the other side of the waterfall and, even though we would be nowhere near the fall, he could foreshorten the distance and make it appear we were in danger of plunging over, to our death.

Max photographed Izzie, diguised as Mr. Lesko, speeding across the snow in his horse and sleigh. Then he moved his camera back onto the ice and photographed me and my mother running along the shore until we found a place from which to step out onto the ice. The fire on the lake was gone and Max said we had to hurry, for the cold air could cause flashes of static electricty inside the camera.

My mother and I set out across the lake, and we called to The Gentle Stranger.

Izzie started down the hill. I saw that the real Mr. Lesko was smiling, and I called out to Izzie to be careful. The reins! I called. The reins!

It doesn't matter, my father said. You heard Karl. Whether it rains or it snows or it stinks, we shoot.

But it was too late. The reins snapped. The horse buckled, as if its forelegs had been chopped off. It tumbled downhill, crashed into a tree, and kept rolling. The sleigh skidded on a single runner in an opposite direction. Izzie leapt out, but he had not planned to do so at that spot, and though he avoided crashing into a tree, he landed hard, shoulder first, against a boulder, and spun upside down, in a somersault, clutching at his shoulder.

Wonderful! Karl called out through his megaphone.

My father pulled at the rope that was hooked into the slab of ice we were riding on, so that at the exact moment when the horse reached the shore, the ice moved, and the horse fell directly into water, its head cracking against the ice's edge.

I heard a sound come from its neck, like that of a tree snapping in high wind.

In the open water, the blood pooled.

Izzie rolled into the water behind the horse.

Mr. Lesko stopped smiling. He held to his side, where Izzie had rammed the pike pole, as if it were only now that he felt the pain. His horse thrashed at the water, trying to climb out, and the more wildly it thrashed, the more the blood in the water foamed.

My mother watched Izzie lift his hand, grasp at air, then sink beneath the water's bubbling skin. Her eyes rolled up in their sockets. She fainted, and lay across our island of ice, one leg caught under her, her hair trailing in the water.

The Gentle Stranger came toward us, leaping from island to island, as if to rescue me and my mother, but when he got to us, he plunged straight into the water and grabbed for the horse's reins.

From the shore, Mr. Lesko walked into the lake.

Where's Izzie? my father asked. He cupped his hands around his mouth, and called out: Izzie—! Oh Izzie! Where *are* you?

The horse floated up and rolled onto its side.

Then Izzie rose to the surface. Shit, he said. It's colder than a pair of witch's tits down there.

Suddenly, the horse rose up from the water, above Izzie, as if it were about to fly.

The horse! I cried. The horse!

Izzie turned, but too late, and the horse dropped down upon him with its full weight. Izzie disappeared beneath the horse and the water. The horse had one hoof on our island of ice, but the hoof slipped and the horse fell backward, its neck catching on a point of the ice, the ice tearing out a long gash and stripping the skin away. As if sprung from a trap, a splintered bone shot through the exposed flesh.

Mr. Lesko waded through the water as if he were walking through brambles.

We have to save them, Max said.

Keep shooting, Karl said. Don't stop.

But they could die, Max said. This is really happening.

Luck! Karl said. Sometimes, after you give up all hope, and when you least expect it, you get lucky. Go figure.

Izzie appeared behind us, climbed onto our island. I think the horse is dead, he said.

See? Karl said. When it comes to stunts, Izzie never takes chances. Keep shooting, Max. Only leave Mr. Lesko out of the frame. We can't have two husbands show up in the same scene.

My mother opened her eyes. You're alive, she said to me. You're alive!

My mother stood. And you too, she said to Izzie, but when she moved to embrace him, Mr. Lesko, struggling in water where he could no longer stand, snatched at her ankle.

My mother tumbled over the island's edge, into the water.

Wonderful! Karl said.

That wasn't supposed to happen, my father said.

Yes it was, Karl said. Don't you remember what Joey said about seeing a woman drowning, about the woman and the child holding to the horse, about the horse in the water?

Ah! my father said. You're right again.

So I dove into the water to rescue my mother. I saw her dark hair floating through the blood, and I reached out, closed my hands around the hair, but at that instant the horse rolled up between us, as if it were a huge barrel, and I found myself holding to the horse's blood-drenched mane.

Mr. Lesko's son was on the shore now, tying a rope to the reins, and pulling. I turned and saw pink water drip from the corner of my mother's mouth. Her eyelids moved up, globes of milk-white gelatin, like those we set before the projector's lens, rolling where her blue eyes had been.

I felt as if my chest were being crushed between walls of thick limestone. Mr. Lesko and his son pulled steadily on the rope, to haul their horse from the water.

My mother's mouth was open, and her lips were white. In

the camera, I thought, black was white and white was black. In my mother's telescope bag there would still be a perfect, red impression of her mouth, on tissue, where she had blotted it.

The storm is here, my father said, pointing to the sky.

We have to help them, Max said. They'll get frostbite. They'll lose their toes, their fingers.

Keep shooting, Karl said. It's even better than what the boy saw. It's real!

Then nobody will believe it, my father said.

Max left the camera, grabbed blankets from the ground—the blankets in which he kept his spools of film and extra lenses—and he rushed toward us.

Make a fire, he said to my father. Make a fire. Quickly.

Karl took Max's place and cranked the camera's handle.

If we don't use it now, we'll use it later, he said. Nothing is wasted. Nothing is lost.

I climbed out of the water. My teeth were clicking like dice. Max wrapped me in a blanket, and began rubbing my cheeks with his hands.

You have the heart of a murderer, Max said to Karl.

Don't make me laugh, Karl said. Did I cut the reins? Did I shove them in the water? Did I kill the horse?

Izzie emerged from the water, my mother in his arms. He set her down on the snow, covered her with blankets, put a flask of whiskey to her lips.

Listen, my brave brother, Karl said to Max. Did *you* leap into the water to save them?

The horse lay on its side, blood spilling from its mouth as if a long strip of red film were unfurling from its innards.

Mr. Lesko pried open the horse's teeth and blood shot out onto his face as if pumped from a fire hose.

The horse twitched, pawed the air with its hooves.

Suddenly my mother stood up, as if she were neither wet, nor cold, nor frightened. She reached under her coat and took out her pistol.

She went to the horse, put the muzzle of the pistol to its forehead, and fired twice.

Mr. Lesko and his son went down on their knees. They each made the sign of the cross. Above us, the dark clouds were lower than the hills, separating and spreading now as if, like thin, soiled cloth, the sky itself were rotting.

Mr. Lesko bent his head, pressed it against the horse's neck, and wept.

Cut! Karl said. Cut! We got it.

(2005)

ESCAPE FROM CIVILIZATION
from *The Collected Stories*

ISAAC BASHEVIS SINGER
TRANSLATED BY ISAAC BASHEVIS SINGER
AND RUTH SCHACHNER FINKEL

I began to plan my escape from civilization not long after learning the meaning of the word. But the village of Bilgoray, where I lived until I was eighteen, didn't have enough civilization to run away from. Later, when I went to Warsaw, all I could do was run back to Bilgoray. The idea took on substance only after I arrived in New York. It was here that I started to suffer from some kind of allergy—rose fever, hay fever, dust, who knows? I took pills by the bottleful, but they didn't do much good. The heat that early spring was as intense as in August. The furnished room where I lived on the West Side was stifling. I am not one to consult with doctors, but I paid a visit to Dr. Gnizdatka, whom I knew from Warsaw and who faithfully read anything that I managed to get published in the Yiddish press.

Dr. Gnizdatka inserted a speculum into my nostrils and a tongue depressor into my mouth and said, *"Paskudno."* ("Bad.")

"What should I do?"

"Move somewhere near the ocean."

"Where is the ocean?"

"Go to Sea Gate."

The moment Dr. Gnizdatka spoke the name, I realized that the time had finally come to escape from civilization, and that Sea Gate could serve the same purpose as Haiti or Madagascar. The following morning, I went to the bank and withdrew my savings of seventy-eight dollars, checked out of my room, packed all my belongings into a large cardboard suitcase, and walked to the subway. In a cafeteria on East Broadway, someone had told me that it was easy to get a furnished room in Sea Gate. I carried a few books to be my spiritual mainstay while away from civilization: the Bible, Spinoza's *Ethics,* Schopenhauer's *The World as Will and Idea,* as well as a textbook with mathematical formulas. I was then an ardent Spinozist and, according to Spinoza, one can reach immortality only if one meditates upon adequate ideas, which means mathematics.

Because of the heat in New York city, I expected Coney Island to be crowded and the beach lined with bathers. But at Stillwell Avenue, where I got off the train, it was winter. How surprising that in the hour it took me to get from Manhattan to the Island the weather had changed. The sky was overcast, a cold wind blew, and a needle-like rain had begun to fall. The Surf Avenue trolley was empty. At the entrance to Sea Gate there was actually a gate to keep the area private. Two policemen stationed there stopped me and asked who I was and what business I had in Sea Gate. I almost said, "I am running away from civilization," but I answered, "I came to rent a room."

"And you brought your baggage along?"

These interrogations in a country that is supposed to be free insulted me, and I asked, "Is that forbidden?"

One policeman whispered something to the other, and both of them laughed. I received permission to cross the frontier.

The rain intensified. I would have liked to ask someone where I could get a room, but there was no one to ask. Sea Gate looked desolate, still deeply sunk in its winter sleep. For courage I reminded myself of Sven Hedin, Nansen, Captain Scott, Amundsen, and other explorers who left the comforts of the cities to discover the mysteries of the world. The rain pounded on my cardboard suitcase like hail. Perhaps it *was* hailing. The wind tore the hat off my head, and it rolled and flew about like an imp. Suddenly through the downpour I saw a woman beckoning to me from the porch of a house. Her mouth moved, but the wind carried her voice away. She signaled me to come over and find protection from the wild elements. I found myself facing a fancy house with a gabled roof, columns, an ornate door. I walked onto the porch, dropped my suitcase (books and manuscripts can be as heavy as stones), wiped my face with a handkerchief, and was able to see the woman more clearly: a brunette who seemed to be in her thirties, with an olive complexion, black eyes, and classic features. There was something European about her. Her eyebrows were thick. There was no sign of cosmetics on her face. She wore a coat and a beret that reminded me of Poland. She spoke to me in English, but when I answered her and she heard my accent she shifted to Yiddish.

"Who are you looking for? I saw you walking in the rain with that heavy suitcase, and I thought I might . . ."

I told her I had come to rent a room and she smiled, not without irony.

"Is this the way you look for a room? Carrying your luggage? Please come inside. I have a house full of rooms that are to let."

She led me into a parlor, the like of which I had seen only in the movies—Oriental rugs, gold-framed pictures, and an elaborate staircase with carvings and a red velvet bannister. Had I entered an ancient palace? The woman was saying, "Isn't that odd? I've just opened the house this minute. It's been closed for the winter. The weather turned warm and I decided perhaps it's time. As a rule, the season here begins in late May or early June."

"Why is the house closed in the winter?" I asked.

"There's no steam. It's an old building—seventy or eighty years old. It can be heated, but the system is complicated. The heat comes through here." She indicated a brass grate in the floor.

I now realized it was much colder inside than outside. There was a staleness in the air characteristic of places that have been without sun for a long time. We stood silent for a moment. Then she asked, "Are you wanting to move in immediately? The electricity isn't turned on yet and the telephone hasn't been connected. Usually boarders come to make arrangements, pay a deposit, and move in when the weather has become really warm."

"I gave up my room in the city."

The woman looked at me inquisitively and after some hesitation said, "I could swear I've seen your picture in the newspaper."

"Yes, they printed my photograph last week."

"Are you Warshawsky?"

"That's me."

"God in Heaven!"

• • •

Darkness had fallen and Esther Royskes lit a candle in a copper candlestick. We were sitting in the kitchen eating supper, like man and wife. She had already told me her whole story: the trouble her ex-husband, a Communist poet, gave her; how she finally divorced him; and how he ran away with his lover to California and left Esther to take care of their two little girls. Two years ago, she had rented this house with the hope that she could earn a living from it, but it did not bring her enough income. People waited until after the Fourth of July and tried to get bargains. Last year, a number of her rooms remained empty.

I put my hand into my pocket, took out the seventy-eight dollars, and offered to give her a down payment, but she protested. "No, you are not going to do that!"

"Why not?"

"First, you have to see what you are taking. It is damp and dark here. You may, God forbid, get a cold. And where will you eat? I would gladly cook for you, but since you tell me you plan to become a vegetarian it may be difficult."

"I will eat in Coney Island."

"You will ruin your stomach. All you get there is hot dogs. A man who packs his valise and comes to Sea Gate without any forethought is not practical. It's a miracle that brought you to me."

"Yes, it is a miracle."

Her black eyes gazed at me half mockingly, and I knew that this was the beginning of a serious relationship. She seemed to be aware of it, too. She spoke to me of things that are usually not told to a stranger. The shadows cast on her face by the candlelight reminded me of a charcoal sketch on a canvas. She said, "Last week I was lying in bed reading your story in the paper. The girls were asleep, but I love to read at night. Who writes about ghosts nowadays, I wondered, and in a Yiddish newspaper to boot! You may not believe me but I thought that I would like to meet you. Isn't that strange?"

"Yes, strange."

"I want to tell you that there is a romantic story connected with this house. A millionaire built it for his mistress. Then Sea Gate was still a place for the rich and American aristocrats. After his death, his mistress remained here until she died. The furnishings are hers—even the library. She seemed not to have left any will, and the bank sold everything intact. For years it remained unoccupied."

"Was she beautiful?"

"Come, I will show you her portrait."

Esther picked up the candlestick. We had to pass through a number of dark rooms to get from the kitchen to the parlor. I stumbled on the thresholds and bumped into rocking chairs. I tripped over a bulge in a rug. Esther took me by the wrist. I felt the warmth of her hand. She asked me, "Are you cold?"

"No. A little."

In the flickering light of the candle, we stood and gazed at the portrait of the mistress. Her hair was arranged in a high pompadour; her low-cut dress exposed her long neck and the upper part of her breasts. Her eyes seemed alive in the semidarkness. Esther said, "Everything passes. I still find pressed flowers and leaves in her books, but there's nothing left of her."

"I'm sure her spirit roams these rooms at night."

The candlestick in Esther's hand trembled and the walls, the pictures, and the furniture shook like stage props in a theater. "Don't say that. I will be afraid to sleep!"

We looked at each other like two mind readers. I remember

what I thought then: A situation that a novelist would have to build up slowly, gradually, through a number of chapters, over months or perhaps years, fate has arranged in minutes, in a few strokes. Everything was ready—the characters, the circumstances, the motivations. Well, but in a true drama one can never foresee what will happen the next instant.

The rain had stopped and we were back in the kitchen, drinking tea. I thought it was late, but when I looked at my wristwatch it showed twenty-five past eight. Esther glanced at her watch, too. We sat there for a while, silent. I could see that she was pondering something that required an immediate decision, and I knew what it was. I could almost hear a voice in her mind—perhaps it was the genius of the female species—saying, "It shouldn't come to him so easily. What does a man think when he's able to get a woman so quickly?"

Esther nodded. "The rain has stopped."

"Yes."

"Listen to me," she said. "You can have the best room in this house, and we will not haggle about money. I will be honored and happy to have you here. But it's too early for you to move in. I intended to spend the night here, but now I am going to lock up the house and go home to my children."

"Why don't you want to stay over? Because of me?" I asked, ashamed of my own words.

Esther looked at me questioningly. "Let it be so."

Then she said something that, according to the rules of female diplomacy, she should not have said: "Everything must ripen."

"Very well."

"Where will you sleep now that you've given up your room?"

"I will manage somehow."

"When do you intend to move in?"

"As quickly as possible."

"Will May 15th be too long for you to wait?"

"No, not too long."

"In that case, everything is decided."

And she looked at me with an expression of resentment. Perhaps she expected me to implore her and try to persuade her. But imploring and persuading have never been a part of my male strategy. In the few hours I spent with Esther I had become somewhat surer of myself. I figured that she was about ten years my senior. I had girded myself with the patience necessary to one prepared to give up civilization and its vanities.

Neither of us had removed our coats—it was too cold—so we didn't have to put them on. I took my suitcase, Esther her overnight bag. She blew out the candle. She said, "If you hadn't mentioned her spirit, I might have stayed."

"I'm sure her spirit is a good one."

"Even good spirits sometimes cause mischief."

We left the house and Esther locked the door. The sky was now clear—light as from an invisible moon. Stars twinkled. The revolving beam from a nearby tower fell on one side of Esther's face. I didn't know why, but I imagined that it was the first night of Passover. I became aware that the house stood apart from other houses and was encircled by lawns. The ocean was only a block away. Because of the howling wind I couldn't hear its sounds earlier, but the winds had subsided and now I heard the waters churning, foaming, like a cosmic stew in a cosmic caldron. In the distance, a tugboat was towing three dark barges. I could barely believe that just an hour away from Manhattan one could reach such quiet.

Esther spoke haltingly. "You wanted to give me an advance before, but I refused to take it. If you are serious about the room, I will accept one, just to make sure that . . ."

"Will twenty dollars be enough?"

"Yes, enough. I ask for it only so that you won't change your mind," she said, and laughed self-consciously.

In the night light, I counted out twenty dollars. We walked together to the gate. I recognized one of the policemen who had been on duty when I arrived. He looked at us and our suitcases knowingly, as if, like a wizard, he had guessed our secrets. He smiled and winked, and I heard him say, "Are you two going back to civilization?"

(1972)

AUTHOR BIOGRAPHIES

WOODY ALLEN was born in Brooklyn in 1935. He is one of the most celebrated film directors of the past fifty years. He is also a talented writer of fiction, and one can imagine the stories he *might* have written had he not moved so rapidly from film to film. There is a sneaking resemblance between Allen's comic Jewish heroes (invariably played by himself) and the Portnoy of Philip Roth. "The Whores of Mensa" and "No Kaddish for Weintstein" are comic masterpieces that reveal Allen's biting humor and remarkable ear for the delicious lunacies of everyday speech.

SAUL BELLOW (1915–2005) was born in Lachine, Quebec, a suburb of Montreal, and was raised in Chicago. He is one of the most important American writers, and his accolades are too many to list. In 1976 he was awarded the Nobel Prize for Literature, for *Humboldt's Gift* (1975). Of his novel *The Adventures of Augie March,* the author Martin Amis said, "*Augie March* is the Great American Novel. Search no further."

JEROME CHARYN was born in the Bronx in 1937. He has made New York his own perverse paradise, where anything can happen and often does. He has written ten novels about a murderously romantic detective, Isaac Sidel, who becomes the police chief and mayor of New York and will soon be vice president of the United States. Charyn's most recent novel, *The Green Lantern,* was a finalist for the PEN/Faulkner Award in Fiction. Distinguished Professor of Film Studies at the American University of Paris, he is currently completing a book on Quentin Tarantino.

LEONARD COHEN was born in Montreal in 1934. We honor him as a songwriter, poet, and singer, but *Beautiful Losers* (1966) is one of the most deeply lyrical books ever written—a sexy, savage song, a story about pornographic scholars, sweet revolutionaries, and a strange Indian princess. It's a pity that Cohen stopped writing novels, although his songs are like little time bombs in narrative form.

STANLEY ELKIN (1939–1995) was born in the Bronx. His family moved to Chicago when he was three. His father was a traveling salesman, and the child's very life became a kind of "road novel" that the adult writer would use in his fiction—which is always about a strange, mad, magical quest that explodes in funny, terrifying language. In 1973 Elkin was diagnosed with multiple sclerosis, and the damage of this degenerative, incurable disease would invade his fiction and make it darker and even funnier (as in *The Magic Kingdom*). "The Guest," about the vagaries of a mediocre jazz musician, is one of the most poignant stories ever written about loneliness.

ALLEN GINSBERG (1926–1997) was born in Newark, New Jersey, like Philip Roth. His father was a high school teacher and also a poet. Ginsberg's long, elegiac poem, *Howl,* published in 1956, would become a battle cry for the whole Beat Generation and would make Ginsburg the most celebrated poet in America.

HERBERT GOLD was born in Cleveland in 1924 and was educated at Columbia College and the Sorbonne. His *The Man Who Was Not With It* is a kind of eloquent song to the underside of American life and was one of Vladimir Nabokov's favorite novels. *Fathers* is a loving testimony of Gold's own particular roots. He is a writer who has kept his sanity in an increasingly macabre world.

BERNARD MALAMUD (1914–1986) was born and raised in Brooklyn. No other writer has dealt with Jewish immigrant life—its smells, its sounds, its pathos—with the same imaginative poetry as Malamud. His first collection of stories, *The Magic Barrel* (1958), won the National Book Award. Its title story, about a rabbinical student longing for love, is one of the authentic masterpieces of American fiction—funny, poignant, with a flair and a flavor all its own.

LEONARD MICHAELS (1933–2003) is the author of *Going Places, I Would Have Saved Them If I Could, Shuffle,* and, most recently, *Time Out of Mind.* During his career he received awards from the Guggenheim Foundation, the American Academy and Institute of Arts and Letters, and the National Endowment for the Arts.

JAY NEUGEBOREN is the author of fourteen books, including the nationally acclaimed memoir, *Imagining Robert: My Brother, Madness, and Survival*, two collections of award-winning stories (*Corky's Brother* and *Don't Worry About the Kids*) and two prize-winning novels, *The Stolen Jew* and *Before My Life Began*.

TILLIE OLSEN'S birth was never recorded, but she claims to have been born somewhere in Nebraska in 1912 or 1913. She was the daughter of immigrants who fled to the United States from Czarist Russia after the failed revolution of 1905. She never finished high school, since she had to start working long before she was eighteen. She was like a cannibal when it came to books, devouring whatever she could. In 1961 she published "Tell Me a Riddle," which won the O. Henry Award as best short story of the year; it is one of the most poignant and poetic pieces of writing about the disintegration of Jewish family life.

SAMUEL ORNITZ (1890–1957) was born on Manhattan's Lower East Side, the son of a prosperous dry-goods merchant. Ornitz is forgotten as a writer and is remembered, when he is remembered, primarily as one of the "Hollywood Ten"— screenwriters and directors such as Albert Maltz and Edward Dmytryk who defied the House Un-American Activities Committee in 1947. But in 1923, Ornitz published a very strange book. *Haunch Paunch and Jowl,* supposedly an exposé by a corrupt Jewish judge, was actually a work of autobiographical fiction. No other book in American literature reveals a time and place—the Lower East Side at the beginning of the twentieth century—with so much sadness and poetry. Ornitz writes about the underside of the Jewish immigrant's drive for success, the pain and madness of those who "made it" and those who didn't.

CYNTHIA OZICK was born in Manhattan in 1928 and moved to the Bronx with her Russian immigrant parents, the owners of a drugstore. She attended Hunter College High School, a haven for eccentric, brilliant young women such as herself. She has written marvelous, sinewy stories and several novels and is also a formidable critic. Her book of essays, *Art and Ardor* (1983), is a powerful and lyrical defense of the art of writing. "A writer is dreamed and transfigured into being by spells, wishes, goldfish, silhouettes of trees, boxes of fairy tales dropped in the mud . . ." (from "A Drugstore in Winter"). "Levitation," about a party of Jewish intellectuals on Manhattan's Upper West Side, reveals Ozick's fierce intelligence and the dreamlike spells of a genuine writer of prose.

GRACE PALEY was born in the Bronx in 1922. Her first collection of stories, *The Little Disturbances of Man,* was published in 1959 and would reveal her as a remarkable writer with an inimitable voice—sexy, chaotic, full of muscular warmth. "Goodbye and Good Luck," about a vivacious ticket seller at a Yiddish theater who falls in love with Volodya Vlashkin, "the Valentino of Second Avenue," rattles us with "deep feelings, a wild imagination, and a style whose toughness and bumpiness arise not out of exasperation with the language, but the daring and heart of a genuine writer of prose," as Philip Roth has said.

Born on the Lower East Side to immigrant parents from Galicia, HENRY ROTH (1906–1995) would publish *Call It Sleep* in 1934. The novel was praised and quickly forgotten. Roth was resurrected in the 1960s, when *Call It Sleep* was reissued, but he did not publish another book until near the end of his life. No matter: *Call It Sleep* is one of the masterpieces of American fiction—a modernist work with a syntax all its own and a heartbreaking music, as it mingles Yiddish, ghetto English, and all the melodies of James Joyce.

PHILIP ROTH was born in Newark, New Jersey, in 1933 and mythologized that city in *American Pastoral* (1997), which won the Pulitzer Prize. *Portnoy's Complaint* (1969) is the funniest and zaniest novel ever written about Jews in America; it reads like one long, heartbreaking riff.

DELMORE SCHWARTZ (1913–1966) was born into a middle-class Jewish family from Brooklyn. Poet, essayist, raconteur, and writer of short stories, he was plagued by mental illness and died alone in a hotel on Times Square. "In Dreams Begin Responsibilities" is one of the most haunting stories ever written by an American—with all the dreamlike power of a poem in prose.

ISAAC BASHEVIS SINGER (1904–1991) was born in Poland to a family of rabbis. He arrived in America in 1935, overshadowed by his older brother, I. J. Singer, who already had an international reputation, while Isaac was barely known. But Isaac survived and would triumph as a writer after years of obscurity. He has one of the strangest *and* strongest oeuvres in all of literature: an entire new body of work was "discovered" after his death, including two of his very best novels, *Scum* and *Shadows on the Hudson*. Singer is like a melodious dybbuk that looms larger and larger with each passing year.

ANZIA YEZIERSKA (1885–1970) was born in a mud hut in the village of Pinsk to Jewish parents living in poverty near the border between Russia and Poland. At fifteen she emigrated with her family to New York City, where she worked in a sweatshop while she studied English at night school. After three years she was granted a scholarship at Columbia University to train as a domestic-science teacher. In 1910 she was briefly married to an attorney, and then she married a teacher. Yezierska gave birth to a daughter, but she found life as a wife and mother so oppressive that she gave up her child to her husband's care. For the rest of her life she devoted herself to her career as a writer.

PERMISSIONS

We gratefully acknowledge everyone who gave permission for material to appear in this book. We have made every effort to contact copyright holders. If an error or omission is brought to our attention, we will be pleased to correct the situation in future editions of this book. For further information, please contact the publisher.

Introduction, "Inside the Hornet's Head" by Jerome Charyn, first appeared in *Midstream,* September/October 2003.